CAMBRIDGE LIBRARY COLLECTION

Books of enduring scholarly value

Printing and Publishing History

The interface between authors and their readers is a fascinating subject in its own right, revealing a great deal about social attitudes, technological progress, aesthetic values, fashionable interests, political positions, economic constraints, and individual personalities. This part of the Cambridge Library Collection reissues classic studies in the area of printing and publishing history that shed light on developments in typography and book design, printing and binding, the rise and fall of publishing houses and periodicals, and the roles of authors and illustrators. It documents the ebb and flow of the book trade supplying a wide range of customers with products from almanacs to novels, bibles to erotica, and poetry to statistics.

Samuel Pepys and the World He Lived In

Henry Benjamin Wheatley (1838–1917) was an eminent bibliographer, author and editor who served as assistant secretary to the Royal Society of Arts between 1879 and his retirement in 1908. He also had a particular interest in the life of Samuel Pepys (1633–1703), founding the Samuel Pepys Club in 1903 and producing the most reliable edition of Pepys' diary until the Latham edition (1970–83). This volume, first published in 1880, contains a detailed biography of Pepys. Using contemporary sources, Wheatley discusses Pepys' achievements during the period his diary was kept, his progression in the Navy Board and his resignation in 1689. Wheatley also provides fascinating descriptions of Restoration society, manners and customs, exploring the historical context of Samuel Pepys' life through discussions of various incidents taken from his diary. This volume remains a standard reference for the historical context of Pepys' diary and life.

T0381922

Cambridge University Press has long been a pioneer in the reissuing of out-of-print titles from its own backlist, producing digital reprints of books that are still sought after by scholars and students but could not be reprinted economically using traditional technology. The Cambridge Library Collection extends this activity to a wider range of books which are still of importance to researchers and professionals, either for the source material they contain, or as landmarks in the history of their academic discipline.

Drawing from the world-renowned collections in the Cambridge University Library, and guided by the advice of experts in each subject area, Cambridge University Press is using state-of-the-art scanning machines in its own Printing House to capture the content of each book selected for inclusion. The files are processed to give a consistently clear, crisp image, and the books finished to the high quality standard for which the Press is recognised around the world. The latest print-on-demand technology ensures that the books will remain available indefinitely, and that orders for single or multiple copies can quickly be supplied.

The Cambridge Library Collection will bring back to life books of enduring scholarly value (including out-of-copyright works originally issued by other publishers) across a wide range of disciplines in the humanities and social sciences and in science and technology.

Samuel Pepys and the World He Lived In

HENRY BENJAMIN WHEATLEY

CAMBRIDGE
UNIVERSITY PRESS

CAMBRIDGE UNIVERSITY PRESS

Cambridge, New York, Melbourne, Madrid, Cape Town, Singapore,
São Paolo, Delhi, Dubai, Tokyo, Mexico City

Published in the United States of America by Cambridge University Press, New York

www.cambridge.org
Information on this title: www.cambridge.org/9781108021524

© in this compilation Cambridge University Press 2010

This edition first published 1880
This digitally printed version 2010

ISBN 978-1-108-02152-4 Paperback

SAMUEL PEPYS AND THE WORLD
HE LIVED IN.

Samuel Pepys

AND THE

WORLD HE LIVED IN.

BY

HENRY B. WHEATLEY, F.S.A.

"His Diary is like a good sirloin, which requires only
to be basted with its own drippings."—*Athenæum*, 1848,
page 551.

Second Edition.

LONDON:

BICKERS AND SON, I, LEICESTER SQUARE

1880.

CHISWICK PRESS: CHARLES WHITTINGHAM AND CO. TOOKS COURT,
CHANCERY LANE.

PREFACE.

HIS little book does not need any
long Preface, as the title sufficiently
explains the object aimed at. Although the various subjects re-
ferred to in the " Diary " are annotated in the
different editions, there is in none of these any
complete analysis of the entire work or of the
incidents of Pepys's life.

I have endeavoured in the following pages to
draw together some of the most interesting incidents of the " Diary " relating both to Pepys's
life and to the manners of his time, and also to
illustrate them from other sources. I have used
the best edition of the " Diary," by the Rev.
Mynors Bright ; but in order that this book may
form a companion to all editions I have referred

to the date of the entries rather than to the volume and page. It must therefore be understood that the passages referred to when not met with in the other editions will be found among the hitherto unpublished matter of that of Mr. Bright. It has been my endeavour to illustrate the contents of this entertaining work more completely than has previously been attempted, and several of the circumstances of Pepys's life are here brought prominently forward for the first time. I may add that the whole of the present volume was printed off before the appearance of the excellent article in the July number of the "Edinburgh Review" (1880), as otherwise it might be supposed that certain points had been suggested by that article. I have, however, availed myself of its pages to make a correction of a small matter in the Index.

Mr. T. C. Noble has kindly sent me, since the completion of this book, a copy of Pepys's original marriage certificate from the Registers of St. Margaret's Church, Westminster, and I therefore insert it here to complete the account in Chapter I. "Samuell Peps of this parish Gent & Elizabeth De S^{nt} Michell of Martins in the ffeilds Spinster. Published October 19th, 22nd, 29th [1655] and were married by Richard Sherwyn Esqr one of the Justices of the Peace of the Cittie and Lyberties of Westm^r December 1st. (Signed) Ri. Sherwyn."

The pronunciation of Pepys's name has long been a disputed point, but although the most usual form at the present day is *Peps*, there can be little doubt that in his own time the name was pronounced as if written *Peeps*. The reasons for this opinion are : (1) that the name was sometimes so spelt phonetically by some of his contemporaries, as in the Coffee-house paper quoted in the " Diary " (ed. Mynors Bright, vol. vi. p. 292) : " On Tuesday last Mr. Peeps went to Windsor," &c. ; (2) that this pronunciation is still the received one at Magdalene College, Cambridge; and (3) that the present bearers of the name so pronounce it.

In conclusion, it is my pleasing duty to express here my best thanks to those friends who have kindly assisted me in my work. Chief among these are Professor Newton, F.R.S., who, as Fellow of Magdalene College, facilitated my inquiries respecting the Pepysian Library, Mr. Pattrick, Senior Fellow and President of the College, Mr. Pepys Cockerell, Mr. George Scharf, F.S.A., Mr. Richard B. Prosser, of the Patent Office, who communicated the docu-

ments relating to Mrs. Pepys's father, and Colonel
Pasley, whose List of the Secretaries of the Admiralty, &c., in the Appendix will be found of
great value, not merely in illustrating Pepys's
life, but as a real addition to our information
respecting the history of the Navy.

H. B. W.

5, Minford Gardens, W.,
September, 1880.

P.S. Since the first publication of this book I
have received an interesting letter from Mr.
Walter Courtenay Pepys, a member of the Cot-
tenham branch of the Pepys family, who, while
agreeing with the statement above as to the
Diarist's pronunciation, reminds me that his
branch have pronounced the name as " Pep-pis "
for at least one hundred years. In favour of
this pronunciation Mr. Pepys adds that the
French branch, which is now settled at La
Rochelle, but came from Languedoc and originally from Italy (where the name exists as
" Peppi "), now spell the name "Pepy."

CONTENTS.

b

SAMUEL PEPYS AND THE
WORLD HE LIVED IN.

CHAPTER I.

PEPYS BEFORE THE DIARY.

" He was a *pollard* man, without the *top* (*i. e.* the reason
as the source of ideas, or immediate yet not sensuous truths,
having their evidence in themselves ; or the imagination or
idealizing power, by symbols mediating between the reason
and the understanding), but on this account more broadly
and luxuriantly branching out from the upper trunk."—
COLERIDGE'S MS. note in his copy of the " Diary " (*Notes
and Queries*, 1st S. vol. vi. p. 215).

AMUEL PEPYS was the first of
a well-established stock to make
a name in the outer world, but
since his time the family can boast
of having had amongst its mem-
bers a Court physician, a bishop, and a lord
chancellor.

The earliest recorded Pepys was named
Thomas, and appears, on the authority of the
Court Rolls of the manor of Pelhams, in Cotten-

ham, to have been bailiff of the Abbot of Crowland's lands in Cambridgeshire, in the early part of the reign of Henry VI.[1] From that time the family flourished, and there seems to be some reason for believing that certain members enriched themselves with the spoils of the abbey lands in the time of Henry VIII.

Before the Diarist became known, one of the most distinguished members of the family was Richard Pepys, created Lord Chief Justice of Ireland by Charles I. When the King was executed, Richard resigned his office; but he enjoyed the favour of Cromwell, and resumed the place. As he did not die until 1678, it is strange that there should be no allusion to him in the "Diary."

The branch from which Samuel was descended had not much money; and his father, being a younger son, came to London and became a tailor. This descent in the social scale has caused much misapprehension, and his enemies did not forget to taunt him on his connection with tailoring; but it is a well-accredited axiom that trade does not injure gentry. Some remarks of Pepys himself upon his family have been greatly misunderstood. Referring to the non-appearance of any account of the Pepyses in Fuller's "Worthies," he writes:—"But I believe, indeed, our family were never considerable."[2] Dr. Doran paraphrased this into : "Let others say of his family what they might: he, for his own part, did not believe that it was of

---

[1] "Diary," ed. Mynors Bright, vol. iv. p. 366; vol. vi p. 306.   [2] "Diary," Feb. 10, 1661-62.

anything like gentle descent." [1] This is a pure blunder, for Pepys merely meant that none of the family had made much mark ; and he would have been very indignant had any one told him that they were not gentle.

Samuel, the fifth child of John and Margaret Pepys, was born on February 23rd, 1632, either at Brampton, a village near Huntingdon, or in London. There is something to be said in favour of each supposition, but, as the registers of Brampton church do not commence until the year 1654, [2] the question cannot now be definitely settled. We have Pepys's own authority for the statement that his father and mother were married at Newington, in Surrey, on October 15th, 1626. [3] The register of marriages of St. Mary, Newington, has been searched, but the name of Pepys occurs neither in the years 1625, 1626, nor in 1627, [4] and Mrs. John Pepys's maiden name is still unknown. In early youth, Samuel went to a school at Huntingdon, as appears by a passage in the "Diary" (March 15th, 1659-60), where he writes: "I met Tom Alcock, one that went to school with me at Huntingdon, but I had not seen him this sixteen years." He seems to have spent his youth pretty equally between town and country, for on one occasion, when he was walking over the fields to Kingsland, he re-

---

[1] " Habits and Men," p. 300.
[2] I am indebted to the kindness of the Rev. Herbert Bree, Rector of Brampton, for this information.
[3] " Diary," Dec. 31, 1664.
[4] "Notes and Queries," 1st S. vol. xii. p. 102.

membered the time when, as a boy, he lived there,
and "used to shoot with my bow and arrow in
these fields."[1] When he left Huntingdon he entered St. Paul's School, and remained there until
he had reached the age of seventeen. In after
life, on the occasion of an official visit to Mercers'
Hall, he remembered the time when he was a
petitioner for his exhibition.[2] He was a stout
Roundhead in his boyish days, and this fact was
remarked upon, to his great chagrin, in after
years, by his friend and schoolfellow Mr. Christmas. He went to see the execution of Charles I.
at Whitehall, and made himself conspicuous by
saying on his return that, were he to preach
upon the event of the day, he should select as
his text the verse : " The memory of the wicked
shall rot." He was in some fear that Mr.
Christmas might remember this also, but he was
happy to find that that gentleman had left
school before the incident occurred.[3] Pepys
always took a lively interest in the welfare of his
school, to which references are frequently made
in the " Diary."

In 1650, his name occurs as a sizar on the
boards of Trinity College, Cambridge ; but
before going to reside at the University, on
March 5, 1650-51,[4] he was entered at Magdalene College, having probably been led to make
the change by the greater inducements held out
to him by the latter college. Here he was elected

---

[1] " Diary," May 12, 1667.   [2] Jan. 22, 1660-61.
[3] Nov. 1, 1660.
[4] " Did put on my gown first, March 5, 1650-51," Dec. 31,
1664 (note).

into one of Mr. Spendluffe's scholarships in the following month ; and two years later, on October 14, 1653, he was preferred to one on Dr. John Smith's foundation. His father was at this time described as a citizen of London.

Little is known of Samuel's academic career, during which he does not appear to have gained much distinction ; and remarks in various parts of the " Diary " show that his conduct was not such as became a Puritan. The College books can be brought as a witness against him, for we learn from that source that, on October 21st, 1653, " Peapys and Hind were solemnly admonished .... for having been scandalously overserved with drink the night before." Still, we must not jump to the conclusion that his time was entirely wasted, for he evidently carried into his busy life a good stock of classical learning. It was while he was at the University that he made the acquaintance of the learned Selden, from whom he borrowed the collection of ballads which formed the basis of the famous Pepysian collection. He relates that, while at Cambridge, he wrote a romance entitled, " Love a Cheate," which he tore up on the 30th of January, 1663-64. This work of destruction must have been performed with some feelings of regret, for he tells us that he rather liked the tale, and wondered that he had ever been able to write so well. His previous literary performances had consisted in the concocting of some anagrams upon Mrs. Elizabeth Whittle, afterwards the wife of Sir Stephen Fox.[1] It is not recorded at what

---

[1] " Diary," Nov. 11, 1660.

time Pepys left college, but it must have been either in 1654 or 1655. He was made Master of Arts by proxy, in June, 1660, the grace being passed on the 26th of that month.

On the 1st of December, 1655,[1] when he was still without any settled means of support, Pepys married Elizabeth St. Michel, a beautiful and portionless girl of fifteen. Although there is extant a letter from Balthasar St. Michel to Pepys (dated from Deal, February 8th, 1673-74), in which the history of Mrs. Pepys's family is set forth, Lord Braybrooke was contented with the information on her monument, and merely added that she was educated in a convent, which in point of fact she was not. The letter alluded to was printed as far back as the year 1841,[2] and yet I cannot find that the history contained in it has ever been used by the biographers of Pepys. What is even more remarkable than Lord Braybrooke's silence respecting it, is the fact that the Rev. John Smith, who published the letter, overlooked it when he wrote his introduction. Mons. St. Michel was of a good family in Anjou, but having turned Huguenot at the age of twenty-one, when in the German service, his father disinherited him, and he was left penniless. He came over to England in the retinue of Henrietta Maria, on her marriage with Charles I., as one of her Majesty's gentleman carvers; but the Queen dismissed

---

[1] Lord Braybrooke says October, but the "Athenæum" (1848, p. 551) says December 1st.

[2] "Life, Journals, and Correspondence of S. Pepys," vol. i. p. 146.

him on finding out that he was a Protestant, and did not go to mass. Being a handsome man with courtly manners, he gained the affections of the daughter of Sir Francis Kingsmall (lately left a widow by an Irish squire), who married him against the wishes of her family, and, with £1,500 which they raised, the newly-married couple started for France, in the hope of recovering, if possible, some part of the family estates. Unhappily, they were taken prisoners at sea, with all their goods, by the Dunkirkers, and when released they settled at Bideford, in Devonshire. Here, or near by, Elizabeth and Balthasar and the rest of the family were born.

In course of time they all went to France, and the father, in command of a company of foot, assisted at the taking of Dunkirk. He occupied his time with propositions of perpetual motion and other visionary schemes, and consequently brought himself and all dependent upon him to the brink of poverty. While he was away from Paris, some devout Roman Catholics persuaded Madame St. Michel to place her daughter in the nunnery of the Ursulines. The father was enraged at this action, but managed to get Elizabeth out of the nunnery after she had been there twelve days. Thinking that France was a dangerous place to live in, he hurried his family back to England, and shortly afterwards Elizabeth married Pepys. Her father was greatly pleased that she had become the wife of a true Protestant; and she herself said to him, kissing his eyes, "Dear father, though in my tender years I was by my low fortune in this world deluded to popery by the fond dictates thereof, I have now (joined with my riper years, which give me more understanding) a man to my husband too wise, and one too religious in the Protestant religion, to suffer my thoughts to bend that way any more."

There are several references in the " Diary" to Mrs. Pepys's father and mother, who seem never to have risen out of the state of poverty into which they had sunk. On May 2, 1662, Mons. St. Michel took out a patent, in concert with Sir John Collidon and Sir Edward Ford,[1] for the purpose of curing smoky chimneys; but this scheme could not have been very successful, as a few months afterwards he was preparing to go to Germany in order to fight against the Turks.[2] Pepys gave him some work to do in 1666, and Mrs. Pepys carried the account-books that he was to rule; but such jobs as these must have given him but a sorry living, and in the following year he again proposed to go abroad. Pepys sent him three jacobuses in gold to help him on his journey.[3] We hear nothing more of either father or mother, with the exception of an allusion to their pleasure at seeing the prosperous state of their daughter [4]—a prosperity in which they certainly did not share.

This account of Mrs. Pepys's parentage has led us away from the early days of Pepys, when, with improvident passion, he married his young

---

[1] " Diary," Sept. 22, 1663. In the original patent (No. 138) St. Michel's name appears as Alexander Merchant of St. Michaell. (See Appendix.)   [2] Jan. 4, 1663-64.
[3] June 21, 1667.   [4] Dec. 28, 1668.

wife; and we will therefore return to the year
1655. Early marriages were then far from un-
common, and Mrs. Pepys's beauty was considered
as forming a very valid excuse for the improvi-
dence of the match. There seems to be some
reason for believing that she was of a dark complexion, for her husband on one occasion was
mad with her for dressing herself according to the
fashion in fair hair.[1] Sir Edward Montagu, who
was Pepys's first cousin one remove (Samuel's
grandfather and Sir Edward's mother being
brother and sister), gave a helping hand to the
imprudent couple, and allowed them to live in
his house. The Diarist alludes to this time,
when, some years afterwards, he writes of how
his wife "used to make coal fires, and wash" his
"foul clothes with her own hand," in their little
room at Lord Sandwich's.[2]

Samuel does not appear to have lived with
his father after he had grown up, and as old
John Pepys was not a very thriving tradesman,
it seems likely that Montagu had previously
assisted his young kinsman. Indeed, it was probably under his patronage that Samuel went to
the University.

The Diarist seems to have held some official
position in the year 1656, because on Thursday,
August 7th, a pass was granted "to John Pepys
and his man with necessaries for Holland, being
on the desire of Mr. Sam^ll. Pepys."[3] John Pepys
had probably long been in the habit of going

---

[1] "Diary," May 11, 1667. [2] Feb. 25, 1666-67.
[3] Entry-Book No. 105 of the Protector's Council of State,
p. 327 (*quoted*, "Notes and Queries," 5th S. vol. v. p. 508).

backwards and forwards to Holland, for Samuel writes (January 24th, 1665-66): "We went through Horslydowne, where I never was since a little boy, that I went to enquire after my father, whom we did give over for lost coming from Holland." Whether these journeys were undertaken in the way of business, or whether they had any connection with Montagu's affairs, we cannot now tell. That Samuel acted as a sort of agent for Montagu, we have evidence; and among the Rawlinson Manuscripts in the Bodleian Library is a memorandum of the payment to him on General Montagu's part for the ransom of the Marquis of Baydez (22nd January, 1656-57).

On March 26th, 1658, he underwent an operation for the stone, a disease that seems to have been inherited. The operation was successfully performed, and ever after he made a practice of celebrating the anniversary of this important event in his life with thanksgiving.

In 1659 he accompanied Sir Edward Montagu in the "Naseby," when that admiral made his expedition to the Sound; and he was very surprised to learn afterwards how negotiations had been carried on of which at the time he was quite ignorant. This is not the place for a history of the various stages that led to the Restoration, but a passing allusion to one of these may be allowed here, as the particulars are given in the "Diary." When Sir Edward Montagu left England for the Sound, he said to the Protector Richard, on parting with him, that "he should rejoice more to see him in his grave at his return home, than that he should give way to such things as were then in hatching, and afterwards did ruin him."[1] Finding the condition of affairs in England hopeless, Montagu took advantage of this expedition to correspond with Charles II.; but he had to be careful and secret, for his fellow-plenipotentiary, Algernon Sidney, who suspected him, was an enemy.[2] Pepys's remark on finding out what had been going on under his nose was, " I do from this raise an opinion of him, to be one of the most secret men in the world, which I was not so convinced of before."[3]

On Pepys's return to England he was employed in the office of Mr., afterwards Sir George, Downing, as a clerk of the Exchequer connected with the pay of the army, and soon afterwards commenced to keep the " Diary" which we now possess.

The account of the incidents of Pepys's early life must be more or less fragmentary, as they can be obtained merely from occasional allusions ; and it is only in the next chapter, in which we see Pepys in the " Diary," that we can obtain any full idea of the man as painted by himself. Before passing on to this part of our subject, it will be well to set down a few notes on the " Diary" as a book. The book has thrown such a flood of light upon the history and manners of the middle of the seventeenth century, that we are apt to forget the fact that before the year 1825 the world knew nothing of this man of gossip. Yet so ungrateful are we to our benefactors, that the publication of the

[1] "Diary," June 21, 1660. [2] March 8, 1664-65.
[3] Nov. 7, 1660.

"Diary" did an immense injury to the writer's reputation. Previously he was known as a staid, trustworthy, and conscientious man of business; as a patron of science and literature, and as a President of the Royal Society. Jeremy Collier says, he was "a philosopher of the severest morality." Since 1825 we have been too apt to forget the excellence of his official life, and to think of him only as a busybody and a *quidnunc.*

When Pepys's library was presented to Magdalene College, Cambridge, by his nephew, John Jackson, in 1724, there were, among the other treasures, six small volumes of closely-written MS. in shorthand (upwards of three thousand pages in all), which attracted little or no notice until after the publication of Evelyn's "Diary." Then it was that the Hon. and Rev. George Neville, Master of the College, drew them out of their obscurity, and submitted them to his kinsman, the well-known statesman, Lord Grenville, who had as a law student practised shorthand. Lord Grenville deciphered a few of the pages, and drew up an alphabet and list of arbitrary signs. These were handed to John Smith, an undergraduate of St. John's College, who undertook to decipher the whole. He commenced his labours in the spring of 1819, and completed them in April, 1822—having thus worked for nearly three years, usually for twelve and fourteen hours a day.[1]   What was remark-

---

[1] Smith afterwards took orders, and was presented to the rectory of Baldock in Hertfordshire by Lord Brougham in 1832, at the instigation of Harriet Martineau. In 1841 he published two octavo volumes, entitled, "The Life, Journals,

able in all this was, that in the Pepysian library there rested a little volume which contained the account of Charles II.'s escape after the battle of Worcester, taken down in shorthand by Pepys from the King's dictation, and written out by himself in long-hand. Here, therefore, was the key that would have unlocked the " Diary" quite overlooked. Lord Braybrooke made the statement that the cipher used by Pepys "greatly resembled that known by the name of Rich's system;" but this was misleading, as the system really adopted was the earlier one of Thomas Shelton. Mr. J. E. Bailey, F.S.A., communicated a very valuable paper, " On the Cipher of Pepys's Diary," to the Manchester Literary Club in 1876, in which he gave particulars of the various old systems of shorthand, and expressed the opinion that Pepys made himself familiar with Shelton's " Tachygraphy" [1] while a student at Cambridge. The earliest edition of Rich's "Pen's Dexterity" was published in 1654, while in 1642 Shelton could refer to twenty years' experience as a shorthand-writer. When the Rev. Mynors Bright was about to decipher the "Diary"

and Correspondence of Samuel Pepys, Esq., F.R.S." This wretchedly edited book contains the Tangier " Diary " and much valuable information ; but I cannot find that the information has been used by the successive editors of the "Diary." He died in 1870.

[1] " Tachygraphy. The most exact and compendious methode of short and swift writing that hath ever yet beene published by any. Composed by Thomas Shelton, author and professor of the said art. Approued by both Unyuersities. Ps. 45, 1, My tongue is as the pen of a swift writer." 1641.

afresh, he consulted Shelton's book, a copy of which, with other works on shorthand, is preserved in the Pepysian Library. Mr. Bright informs us that, " When Pepys wished to keep anything *particularly concealed*, he wrote his cipher generally in French, sometimes in Latin, or Greek, or Spanish. This gave me a great deal of trouble. Afterwards he changed his plan and put in *dummy* letters. I was quite puzzled at this, and was nearly giving up in despair the hope of finding out his device, but at last, by rejecting every other letter, I made out the words. It would have been better for Pepys's credit if these passages could not have been deciphered, as all of them are quite unfit for publication."

Pepys was a great lover of shorthand, and he was always ready to invent a character, as it was then called, for a friend. He used the art in drafting his public and private letters ; and although he was forced to discontinue his " Diary " in 1669, on account of the weakness of his eyesight, he continued its use throughout his life.

We learn from the " Diary " itself some particulars of how it was written. The incidents of each day were dotted down in short, and then the writer shut himself up in his office to fill up all the details. Sometimes he was in arrear : thus we read, on January 1st, 1662-63, " So to my office to set down these two or three days' journal ;" on September 24th, 1665, " Then I in the cabin to writing down my journal for these last seven days to my great content ;" and on November 10th, 1665, " Up and entered all my

journal since the 28th of October, having every
day's passage well in my head, though it troubles
me to remember it."

Lord Braybrooke, who first introduced the
"Diary" to the public, had no very accurate
notions of the duties of an editor ; and he treated
his manuscript in a very unsatisfactory manner.
Large portions were omitted without explanation, and apparently without reason; and although
much was added to succeeding editions, still the
reader might well say—

> "That cruel something unpossess'd
> Corrodes and leavens all the rest."

The third edition, published in 1848, contained
a large mass of restored passages, amounting, it
is said, to not less than one-fourth of the entire
work. Some fresh notes were added to the
fourth edition, published in 1854 ; but no alteration of the text was made beyond "the correction of a few verbal errors and corrupt passages
hitherto overlooked." Subsequent editions have
been mere reprints of these. In 1875 appeared
the first volume of the Rev. Mynors Bright's
entirely new edition, with about one-third of
matter never yet published, all of which was of
the true Pepysian flavour. Here was a treat for
the lovers of the "Diary" which they little expected.

Having traced the particulars of Pepys's life
to the year 1659, and described the way in which
the "Diary" was written, and the means by
which it first saw the light, I will now pass on
to notice, in the next chapter, the chief personal
incidents recorded in the book itself.

CHAPTER II.

PEPYS IN THE "DIARY."

"An exact Diary is a window into his heart that maketh
it : and therefore pity it is that any should look therein but
either the friends of the party or such ingenuous foes as will
not, especially in things doubtful, make conjectural com-
ments to his disgrace."—PRYNNE's *Remarks on Abp. Laud.*

N the 1st of January, 1659-60,
Samuel Pepys (then in his twenty-
seventh year) commenced to write
his famous "Diary." If, as seems
more than probable, he had pre-
viously kept a journal of some kind, all traces of
it are now lost; and our earliest glimpses of the
circumstances of his life are to be obtained only
from the "Diary," which is by far the most remarkable book of its kind in existence. Other
men have written diaries and confessions, but
they have been intended either for the public or
at least for a small circle of friends to see. This
" Diary " was only intended for the writer's eye.
He wrote it in secret, and when he unguardedly
told Sir William Coventry in the Tower that he

kept a diary, he was sorry for his indiscretion immediately afterwards. Pepys has been likened to the barber of King Midas, who relieved his mind by communicating to a bundle of reeds the fact that his master had the ears of an ass; and assuredly no other writer has so unreservedly stripped his soul bare. It is, therefore, only fair to bear in mind what is said in the motto at the head of this chapter, and not to forget that very few could bear the accusing witness of such a truthful record of thoughts as well as actions as is here. The "Diary" extends over nearly ten eventful years in the history of England, and contains a voluminous record of both public and private events. The fascination of Pepys's garrulity is so great, that most of those who have written about him have found it difficult to restrain their praise within bounds. A writer in the "Athenæum" (apparently the late Peter Cunningham) was quite carried away by his subject when he wrote—"He has the minuteness of Dee and Ashmole without their tediousness, the playfulness of Swift in his best moments without his prejudice and his party feelings, and a charm over Byron and Scott, and, indeed, above all other memorialists that we can call to mind, in that his Diary was kept without the slightest view to publication."[1]

I will now first note some of the chief circumstances of Pepys's life during the period covered by the "Diary," and then say something about his character as it is painted by himself.

When we are first introduced to Pepys he is

[1] "Athenæum," 1848, p. 669.

C

living in Axe Yard, Westminster, with very small means of support, but making so good a show that he is esteemed rich. His family consists of himself, his wife, and servant Jane. During the frosty weather they have not a coal in the house, and he is forced to dine at his father's, or make himself as comfortable as he can up in the garret. That the larder is not very plentifully supplied is seen by the fact that, on the 1st of February, he and his wife dine on pease pudding, and on nothing else. At one time he has not money enough in the house to pay the rent, but soon afterwards he finds himself worth £40 which he did not expect, and is therefore afraid that he must have forgotten something. On the 16th of January, Mr. Downing (in whose office he then was) asked our Diarist, in a half-hearted way, whether he would go to Holland, and gave him the impression that his services could be dispensed with. At this time political affairs were in the greatest confusion, and no one knew what opinions to hold with profit to himself. Thus, William Symons said that " he had made shift to keep in, in good esteem and employment through eight governments in one year, and then failed unhappy in the ninth, viz., that of the King's coming in."[1]

As in times of anarchy every one wishes to talk, the Rota, or Coffee Club founded by James Harrington, the author of " Oceana," was found to be a congenial resort by those who wished to express their opinions on passing events. The principle of the club was political, and the plan

[1] "Diary," Jan. 8, 1663-64.

formed there for the government of the country was, that every official should be chosen by ballot. Every year a third part of the House of Commons were to " rote out by ballot," and no magistrate was to continue in his position more than three years. Other than politicians attended the meetings, and many distinguished men, such as Dr. Petty, Dr. Croon, Sir William Poultney, and Cyriack Skinner, were to be found in the evening at the Turk's Head, in the New Palace Yard. The room was usually as full as it would hold, and Aubrey gives it as his opinion that the arguments heard in Parliament were flat as compared with those delivered at the Rota Club. The object of worship was the ballot-box, and the company sat round an oval table, which had a passage in the middle for Miles, the landlord, to deliver his coffee. Pepys paid his eighteen-pence on becoming a member of the club, on the 9th of January, 1659-60, and he frequently attended after this. If the following can be considered as a good illustration of proceedings, there must have been considerable divergence in the opinions of the members :—" I went to the Coffee Club and heard very good discourse ; it was in answer to Mr. Harrington's answer, who said that the state of the Roman government was not a settled government, and so it was no wonder that the balance of property was in one hand, and the command in another, it being therefore always in a posture of war ; but it was carried by ballot, that it was a steady government; so to-morrow it is to be proved by the opponents that the balance lay in one hand

and the government in another."[1] On the 20th of
February, Pepys writes: "After a small debate
upon the question whether learned or unlearned
subjects are best, the club broke up very poorly,
and I do not think they will meet any more."
After the Restoration Harrington was put in the
Tower, and then removed to Portsea Castle.
His imprisonment turned him mad, so that he
fancied his perspiration turned sometimes to flies
and sometimes to bees, but all his hallucinations
were inoffensive. One of the first steps taken
by Monk towards obtaining a free Parliament
was the admission of the secluded members
who had been previously purged out. Pepys
describes the marching-in of these men on the
21st of February, and specially notices Prynne's
"old basket-hilt sword." The editors of the
"Diary" might have illustrated this by an
amusing passage from Aubrey's "Lives." It
appears that as the members were going to the
House, Prynne's long rusty sword "ran between
Sir William Waller's short legs, and threw him
down;" which caused laughter, as Aubrey takes
care to add. About this time Pepys seems to
have discerned the signs of the times, for we find
him, on a visit to Audley End, drinking the
health of the King down in a cellar.[2] Sir Edward
Montagu now comes to the front, and is intent
upon benefiting his kinsman. Pepys hopes to
be made Clerk of the Peace for Westminster,
but finds the place already promised to another.
Montagu offers him the post of Secretary to
the Generals at Sea, which he joyfully accepts;

[1] "Diary," Jan. 17, 1659-60.   [2] Feb. 27, 1659-60.

and he receives his warrant on the 22nd of March. The following day sees the party on board the " Swiftsure" at Longreach, where Pepys receives a letter directed to "S. P., Esq.," and this superscription seems to have delighted him greatly, for he says, "of which God knows I was not a little proud." On the 30th inst. Montagu and his people went on board the "Naseby," which was the ship in which he had gone to the Sound in the previous year. They remain for a time in the neighbourhood of Deal, and on the 3rd of May the King's declaration and letter to the two generals is received by Montagu, who dictates to Pepys the words in which he wishes the vote in favour of the King to be couched. The captains all came on board the " Naseby," and Pepys read the letter and declaration to them ; and while they were discoursing on the subject he pretended to be drawing up the form of vote, which Montagu had already settled. When the resolution was read, it passed at once ; and the seamen all cried out, " God bless King Charles!" a cry that was echoed by the whole fleet. A little piece of Pepys's vanity (and perhaps shrewdness also) here peeps out, for he tells us that he signed all the copies of the vote of the Council of War, so that if it should by chance get into print his name might be attached to it.[1] The English fleet lies off the Dutch coast about the middle of May, and our Diarist avails himself of the opportunity to visit the Hague and some of the chief towns of Holland. The Dukes of York and Gloucester came on board the " Naseby " on the

[1] " Diary," May 4, 1660.

22nd inst., and the King followed them on the following day, when the opportunity of his visit was taken to change the objectionable names of the ships. The "Naseby" became the "Charles," the "Richard" the "James," the "Speaker" the "Mary," and the "Lambert" the "Henrietta."

> "The Naseby now no longer England's shame,
> But better to be lost in Charles his name."[1]

Pepys takes the opportunity, when the Duke of York is on board, to bespeak his favour; and is overjoyed at the Duke calling him Pepys. On the 25th the King lands at Dover, and is received by Monk. Pepys tells how the mayor presented the King with a handsome Bible, which he received, and told the people that "it was the thing he loved above all things in the world!"

The 5th of June was Pepys's last day on board, and he was awoke about three o'clock in the morning by the pouring into his mouth of the water with which the people above were washing the deck; and he was forced to rise and sleep leaning on the table. He returned to shore better off than he had originally left it, as he took care to make use of his opportunities by getting men made captains, and by obtaining gratuities for the favours. Fortune continued to smile upon him, for he had not been many days back in London when Sir Edward Montagu, now a Knight of the Garter, and in high favour with the King, obtained for him the promise of the place of Clerk of the Acts. On the

---

[1] Dryden, "Astræa Redux," ll. 230-31.

28th of June he clears himself of his old office under Sir George Downing, and is glad to part from this stingy fellow, as he calls him. On the following day he gets his warrant, but is much cast down when he learns that his predecessor, Mr. Barlow, is still alive, and coming up to town to look after the place. General Monk's wife wishes the clerkship to be given to Mr. Turner, of the Navy Office; but Montagu's influence secures it for Pepys. Turner then offers to give Pepys £150 to be joined with him in the patent, but this is refused. Pepys is kept in a great state of excitement respecting Barlow for a time. He hears that he is a sickly man, and on July 17th he agrees to give him £100 a year out of his raised salary. This payment continued until February, 1664-65, when Barlow died. Pepys's remarks on the death are particularly characteristic: "For which God knows my heart, I could be as sorry as is possible for one to be for a stranger, by whose death he gets £100 per annum, he being a worthy honest man; but when I come to consider the providence of God by this means unexpectedly to give me £100 a year more in my estate, I have cause to bless God, and do it from the bottom of my heart."[1]

---

[1] "Diary," Feb. 9, 1664-65. Thomas Barlow was appointed in 1638 Clerk of the Acts, jointly with Dennis Fleming, who had held the office for several years previously. Lord Braybrooke says in a note, that "Barlow had previously been Secretary to Algernon, Earl of Northumberland, when High Admiral;" but Colonel Pasley tells me this is a mistake, for Barlow had been appointed Clerk of the Acts two months before the Earl became Lord High Admiral. Barlow had, however, been in his service at an

Now, our Diarist has become a man of importance, as one of the principal Officers of the Navy, and Montagu consequently asks him to dinner for the first time.[1] Yet he has not much faith in his power to keep the place; and when a Mr. Man offers him £1,000 for it, his mouth waters, and he would gladly take the money if his patron would agree.[2] On the 23rd of July he takes the oaths as a Clerk of the Privy Seal, which he does not expect to be a very profitable office; but he soon finds himself making about £3 a day,[3] in addition to his regular salary at the Navy Office. Being settled at his house in Seething Lane, attached to the office, he is glad to get his little house in Axe Yard off his hands, which he does on the 17th of September, receiving £41 for his interest in it. About this time he is sworn as a justice of the peace, and he is "mightily pleased" at the honour, although he confesses that he is wholly ignorant of the duties.[4]

There were great doings at the coronation of Charles II. in the following year, and the "Diary" is full of particulars respecting it. Pepys and a party went to a shop in Cornhill to see the procession when the King passed from the Tower to Whitehall, and while they waited they partook of "wine and good cake."[5]

On the next day Pepys gets into Westminster

---

earlier date, and the Earl had appointed him Muster Master of the Fleet under his command in 1636.

[1] "Diary," July 2, 1660.   [2] Aug. 6, 10, 1660.
[3] Aug. 10, 1660.   [4] Sept. 23, 1660.
[5] April 22, 1661.

Abbey to see the coronation, and sits patiently in a scaffold from a little after four until eleven. Afterwards he goes into Westminster Hall, sees the banquet, and returns home to bed with the feeling that he will " never see the like again in this world." Next morning he wakes with his "head in a sad taking through the last night's drink."[1]

Sometimes the Clerk of the Acts has a great deal of business to get through, and he always sticks to his work manfully. By going to the office early and staying late he was often able to spare the afternoons for the theatre. Day after day he gets up and is at his desk at four o'clock in the morning;[2] but this hard work is varied by some idle days. On June the 5th the Officers of the Navy play at bowls and drink and talk. Pepys takes his flageolet, and plays upon the leads. Sir William Penn comes out in his shirt-sleeves, and there is more drinking and talking, the result of which is, that Pepys goes to bed nearly fuddled, and wakes up the next morning with an aching head.

A very important event in the life of the Diarist occurred in the following month. His uncle, Robert Pepys, dies, and a small property at Brampton, worth about £80 per annum,[3] comes into the possession of old John Pepys, not, however, without some litigation on the part of some members of the family. As his father has no money, Samuel takes all the business affairs into his own hands, and seems to consider the property as his own. When he

[1] "Diary," April 23, 1661.
[2] July 3, 1662; June 17, 1663.   [3] June 17, 1666.

learns the news, on the 6th of July, 1661, he posts down to Brampton, leaving London between eleven and twelve o'clock in the morning, and arriving there about nine o'clock at night. When he gets to his uncle's house he is very uncomfortable, from the badness of the food and drink, and the biting of the gnats; but although he is nearly out of his wits, he appears contented, so as not to trouble his father. He has much work of arrangement to get through, and he remains nearly sixteen days away from London. When he returns he gives out among his most distinguished friends and acquaintances that he has had an estate of £200 a year in land left him, beside money, " because he would put an esteem upon himself."[1]

Pepys acknowledged to two weaknesses, of which he tried to cure himself by means of vows—not, however, with a very successful result. The first weakness was a too great addiction to the bottle, and the second a too frequent attendance at theatres. On July 26th, 1661, we find him making this confession: " Having the beginning of this week made a vow to myself to drink no wine this week (finding it unfit me to look after business), and this day breaking of it against my will, I am much troubled for it; but I hope God will forgive me!" On Michaelmas Day, 1661, he took so much wine that he "was even almost foxed," so that he "durst not read prayers for fear of being perceived by my servants in what case I was." Next year, on the same day, he finds that his " oaths for drinking

[1] " Diary," July 24, 1661.

of wine and going to plays are out," and so he
resolves to take some liberty, "and then fall to
them again." On December 30th, 1662, we find
him writing : "After dinner drinking five or six
glasses of wine, which liberty I now take till I
begin my oathe again."[1]

On October 29th, 1663, he drinks some hippocras, which consists of wine mixed with sugar
and spices, under the belief that he is not breaking his vow, because it is "only a mixed compound drink, and not any wine." Sir Walter
Scott likened this piece of casuistry to that of
Fielding's Newgate chaplain, who preferred
punch to wine because the former was a liquor
nowhere spoken against in Scripture.

It is necessary now to return to the date at
which we broke off to follow our hero's vows
He sums up his blessings on February 23rd,
1661-62, in these words : "I am 29 years of
age, and in very good health, and like to live
and get an estate ; and if I have a heart to be
contented, I think I may reckon myself as happy
a man as any is in the world, for which God be
praised." Yet, on the next day, he is troubled
to part with £5 for five weeks' music-lessons ;
and soon afterwards he complains at his father
spending £100 a year.[2] Although he was of a
saving turn, he could clearly see that it was
wise to spend money while he could enjoy the
results of his spending, and alludes to this on two

---

[1] There are some amusing passages relating to the vow
on theatre-going under date of Feb. 23, 1662-63; Jan. 2,
1663-64.
[2] "Diary," April 23, 1663.

separate occasions. On May 20th, 1662, he writes: "But though I am much against too much spending, yet I do think it best to enjoy some degree of pleasure now that we have health, money, and opportunity, rather than to leave pleasures to old age or poverty when we cannot have them so properly." Four years after this we find the same idea in other words: "The truth is I do indulge myself a little the more in pleasure, knowing that this is the proper age of my life to do it; and out of my observation that most men that do thrive in the world do forget to take pleasure during the time that they are getting their estate, but reserve that till they have got one, and then it is too late for them to enjoy it with any pleasure." [1]

About this time Pepys is sworn a younger brother of the Trinity House, is made a burgess of Portsmouth, is troubled with a lawsuit by one Field, signs warrants as a justice of the peace, and is appointed one of the Commissioners for the Affairs of Tangier. This business with Field, which was connected with the office, gives him much annoyance. At one time he is in fear of being taken by the bailiffs,[2] and at another he is in such terror that the falling of something behind a door makes him start with fright.[3]

About the middle of the year 1662 he engages the services of Mr. Cooper, mate of the "Royal George," of whom he intends to learn mathematics; but his early attempts do not appear to have been very ambitious, for he begins by

[1] "Diary," March 10, 1666.   [2] Feb. 21, 1662-63.
[3] Feb. 23, 1662-63.

learning the multiplication-table. In the following year, he and Mrs. Pepys learn to dance, and he thinks he shall be able to manage the coranto well enough. He grudges the cost, however, particularly as he is forced by his oath to give half as much more to the poor.[1]

The mixture of extravagance and frugality that is constantly exhibited in the " Diary " is most amusing, particularly in the case of clothes. Thus, when he hears that the Queen is ill, he stops the making of his velvet cloak until he sees whether she lives or dies.[2] In spite of this forethought, he finds, on casting up his accounts, that he spent £55 on his own clothes, although, as a set-off against this large sum, Mrs. Pepys's clothes only cost £12. This love of fine clothes is continually peeping out, and it has been suggested that he inherited it with the tailor blood of his father. A better reason, however, may be found in the fact that at one time he was very poor, and " forced to sneak like a beggar " for want of clothes; so that, now he is in funds, he tries to make up for his former deficiency, and resolves to dress himself handsomely.[3]

A few years after this he expresses himself as ashamed of the shabbiness of his clothes, when he wished to speak to the King but did not like to do so, because his linen was dirty and his clothes mean.[4]

At the end of the year 1663, Pepys performed a duty in a way that did him great credit. Sir Edward Montagu, now Earl of Sandwich, is

[1] "Diary," May 4, 1663.　　[2] Oct. 22, 1663.
[3] Oct. 31, 1663.　　[4] March 20, 1667.

taken ill, and, on his recovery, he goes for change of air to Chelsea. After a time it gets abroad that he dotes upon one of the daughters of his landlady, and neglects his duties. On the 9th of September, 1663, Mr. Pickering tells Pepys of all this, and we therefore read in the " Diary :" " I am ashamed to see my lord so grossly play the fool, to the flinging-off of all honour, friends, servants, and everything and person that is good, with his carrying her abroad and playing on his lute under her window, and forty other poor sordid things, which I am grieved to hear." Pepys determines to be silent, as he learns that the Earl will not bear any allusion to his doings. Still his mind continually reverts to the matter, and in the end he decides to write a letter of counsel to his patron.[1] When this is sent, he continues for some time to be anxious as to the manner in which the Earl is likely to receive it. Nothing is, of course, said when the two meet, and there is for a time a coldness between them ; but at last they return to their old relations with each other, and Lord Sandwich, having left Chelsea, is seen in the world again.

Pepys's habit of sitting up late, reading and writing by candlelight, begins to tell upon his eyesight ; and in January, 1663-64, he finds it fail him for the first time. In October, 1664, he consults the celebrated Mr. Cocker as to the best glass to save his eyes at night ; but they continue to trouble him, and he proposes to get

[1] This letter is printed in the " Diary," under date Nov. 18, 1663.

some green spectacles.[1] How the eyesight got weaker, so that the "Diary" had to be discontinued, we all know to our great loss.

On one occasion Mr. Coventry talks with Pepys on the need for a history of the navy of England, and then suggests that he should write a history of the late Dutch war. Pepys likes the idea, as he thinks it agrees with his genius, and would recommend him much to the authorities ;[2] but he succeeded in doing this without writing the history. On the 10th of March, 1663-64, he was appointed one of the assistants of the Corporation of the Royal Fishery, of which the Duke of York was the Governor; his commission as Treasurer of the Tangier Committee is signed on the 18th of April, 1665; and in October of the same year he obtains the appointment of Surveyor-General of the Victualling Office. Besides these tangible proofs of his success in life were the expressions of esteem made use of in respect to him by men in authority. The Duke of York told him that he highly valued his services,[3] and the Duke of Albemarle said that he was the right hand of the navy.[4]

Pepys quite deserved these words of praise, and moreover continued to deserve them, for during the whole period of the Dutch war he did his best to provide what was required for the navy, and while the plague was devastating London he alone remained at his post. His straightforward common-sense shows out strongly during the course of the Great Fire. From the

---

[1] "Diary," Dec. 13, 1666.   [2] June 13, 1664.
[3] March 22, 1664-65.   [4] April 24, 1665.

2nd of September, 1666—when the servants
wake him to tell of the burning which they saw
in the city—to the 7th, when he visits the ruins,
we have a lively picture of the whole scene in
the pages of the " Diary." On the Sunday Pepys
goes to Whitehall, and tells the King and the
Duke of York of what he had seen. He says
that unless his Majesty will command houses to
be pulled down, nothing can stop the fire. On
hearing which, the King instructs him to go to
the Lord Mayor, and command him to pull down
houses in every direction. Sir Thomas Bludworth, the Lord Mayor, seems to have been but
a poor creature ; and when he heard the King's
message, "he cried like a fainting woman, ' Lord!
what can I do ? I am spent : people will not
obey me. I have been pulling down houses, but
the fire overtakes us faster than we can do it."
On the 4th inst. there seemed to be little hope
of saving the Navy Office, unless some extraordinary means were taken with that object.
Pepys therefore suggested that the workmen
from Woolwich and Deptford Dockyards should
be sent for to pull down the houses round them.
Sir William Penn went to see after the men, and
Pepys wrote to Sir William Coventry for the
Duke of York's permission. In the letter he
remarks that the fire is very near them, both on
the Tower Street and Fenchurch sides ; and that
unless houses are pulled down, there are little
hopes of their escape. The next day Penn
sends up the men, who help greatly in the
blowing-up of houses ; and to this action Pepys
mainly attributes the stoppage of the fire. He

then goes up to the top of Barking church, and there he saw " the saddest sight of desolation "—" everywhere great fires, oil-cellars, and brimstone and other things burning." He then walks through the town, the hot ground almost burning his feet, till he comes to Moorfields, which he finds full of people, " the poor wretches carrying their goods there, and everybody keeping his goods together by themselves."

During the period of fright, when he expected the office to be destroyed, he sent off his money, plate, and best things to Sir W. Rider, at Bethnal Green, and then he and Penn dug a hole in the garden, in which they put their wine and Parmezan cheese. On the 10th of September, Sir W. Rider lets it be known that, as the town is full of the report respecting the wealth in his house, he will be glad if his friends will provide for the safety of their property elsewhere.

About the time of the Great Fire, Pepys had saved a large sum of money, and was making a good income ; so we find his thoughts running on the advantage of keeping a private coach, as he is ashamed to be seen in a hackney coach.[1] It was not, however, until more than a year after this that he actually bought his carriage, and we find that he spent £53 on the coach,[2] and £50 on a fine pair of black horses.[3] He was very proud of the appearance of his carriage, but his enemies made some capital out of the proceeding, and protested that he throve on the distresses of others.

[1] " Diary," April 21, 1667.   [2] Oct. 24, 1668.
[3] Dec. 11, 1668.

In these days of banks and other means for the deposit of money, it is not easy to realize the difficulties of men who possessed money in the seventeenth century. Pepys sent some down to Brampton to be buried, but his wife and father did the business entrusted to them so badly that he was quite wild and uneasy with fears that it might be found by others.[1] Therefore, at the first opportunity, he goes down himself to see after his treasure; and the description of the hunt after it is certainly one of the most entertaining passages in the " Diary."[2] He and his father and wife go out into the garden with a dark lantern, and grope about a long time before they come on the trace. Then they find that the bags are rotten, and gold and notes are all spread about and covered with dirt, the latter being scarcely distinguishable. Then there is a gathering of it up to be washed, and in the end not much is lost, although throughout the proceedings Pepys is in dread that the neighbours will see and hear what is going on.

We now come to the consideration of one of the most important incidents in the life of the Diarist—that is, his great speech at the Bar of the House of Commons. When peace was concluded with the Dutch, and the people had time to think over the disgrace which this country had suffered by the presence of De Ruyter's fleet in the Medway, they naturally looked round for someone to punish. It was the same feeling, only in a much intensified degree, which found expression at the time of

---

[1] " Diary," June 19, 1667.   [2] Oct. 10, 1667.

the Crimean war in the cry, "Whom shall we
hang?" A Parliamentary Committee was appointed in October, 1667, to inquire into everything relating to this business, at Chatham.
Pepys is warned to prepare himself, as there is
a desire to lay the blame upon the Commissioners of the Navy, and a resolution "to lay
the fault heavy somewhere, and to punish it."[1]
He therefore gives as clear a statement as possible, and satisfies the Committee for a time;
but for months afterwards he is continually being
summoned to answer some charge, so that he is
mad to "become the hackney of this Office in perpetual trouble and vexation, that need it least."[2]
Then breaks out a storm in the House of Commons against the Principal Officers of the Navy,
and some members demand that they be put out
of their places. The result is, that they are
ordered to be heard in their own defence at the
Bar of the House. The whole labour of defence
falls upon Pepys, and he sets to work with a
will to collect his evidence, and to display it in
the most satisfactory manner. He is somewhat
annoyed that the other officers can do little to
help him; but he is proud that they, in spite of
themselves, must rely upon him. The eventful
day (5th March, 1667-68) at last arrives, and,
having first fortified himself with half a pint of
mulled sack and a dram of brandy, our Diarist
stands at the Bar with his fellow-officers. But
here we must use his own words, for it would be
presumptuous to paraphrase the vivid account
he himself gives:—"After the Speaker had told

[1] "Diary," Oct. 21, 1667.　　[2] Feb. 11, 1667-68.

us the dissatisfaction of the House, and read the Report of the Committee, I began our defence most acceptably and smoothly, and continued at it without any hesitation or loss, but with full scope, and all my reason free about me, as if it had been at my own table, from that time (about twelve o'clock) till past three in the afternoon; and so ended without any interruption from the Speaker; but we withdrew. And there all my Fellow-officers and all the world that was within hearing, did congratulate me, and cry up my speech as the best thing they ever heard; and my Fellow-officers were overjoyed in it." The orator was congratulated on every side, and the flattery he received is set down in the "Diary" in all good faith. Sir William Coventry addresses him the next day with the words, "Good morrow, Mr. Pepys, that must be Speaker of the Parliament-house;" and the Solicitor-General protests that he spoke the best of any man in England. One man says that he would go twenty miles to hear such another speech; and another, although he had sat six-and-twenty years in Parliament, had never heard anything like it before; and there is much more to the same effect.

I do not find that Pepys ever distinguished himself by another speech, although he sat for several years in the House of Commons; and there is therefore reason to doubt his oratorical powers. In fact, it is easy to explain the secret of his success, for he was speaking on a subject that he thoroughly understood to an audience that understood it but imperfectly. Still we

must give Pepys due credit for his achievement.
He had a bad case, and yet he seems to have con-
verted his audience. It was here that his clear-
headedness and remarkable powers of arrangement were brought into play, and having at the
same time his whole soul in the matter, he easily
carried his hearers with him.

The praises he received raised up a strong
desire in his breast to become a Parliament-
man. He hints at this design on the 5th
of December, 1668, and again, on the 19th of
February, 1668-69, he opens the matter to his
friend, Sir William Coventry, who likes the idea
mightily, and promises to speak about it to the
Duke of York. A few more months, and his
eyes—which already, as we have seen, had given
him trouble—become so much worse that he
begins to think seriously of taking rest. On the
16th of May, 1669, he draws up a rough copy
of a petition to the Duke of York for leave of
absence for three or four months. A few days
after, the Duke takes him to the King, who expresses his great concern at the state of his eyes,
and gives him the leave he desires.[1] On the
31st of May, 1669, the pen that has written so

---

[1] "Diary," May 24, 1669. "To Whitehall where I attended the Duke of York and was by him led to the King."
To this passage Lord Braybrooke added this note : " It
seems doubtful whether the expression of being led to the
King has any reference to the defective state of Pepys's
vision. Perhaps he might wish to make the most of this
infirmity, in the hope of strengthening his claim for leave of
absence." It is rather too absurd to think that the Duke of
York would lead Pepys by the hand through the corridors
of the palace. If a guide had been needed, the services of
a less august personage could surely have been obtained.

much to amuse us is put to the paper for the last time; and the " Diary " ends with these words of deep but subdued feeling :—"And thus ends all that I doubt I shall ever be able to do with my own eyes in the keeping of my Journal, I being not able to do it any longer, having done now so long as to undo my eyes almost every time that I take a pen in my hand; and therefore whatever comes of it I must forbear; and therefore resolve, from this time forward to have it kept by my people in longhand, and must be contented to set down no more than is fit for them and all the world to know; or if there be any thing, which cannot be much, now my amours are past, and my eyes hindering me in almost all other pleasures, I must endeavour to keep a margin in my book open, to add here and there, a note in short-hand with my own hand. And so I betake myself to that course, which is almost as much as to see myself go in to my grave: for which and all the discomforts that will accompany my being blind, the good God prepare me!" The "Diary" is one of the most curious of psychological studies, and surely no other man has so relentlessly laid bare his secret motives. When he does a good action from a good motive, he cannot forbear to add a dirty little motive as well. There is no posing for effect, such as the writers of confessions adopt, and herein consists the chief charm of the book.

I cannot pretend to draw the character of the Diarist, for he has done that himself in his own vivid manner; but a few of his leading character istics may be set down here. Two of the most prominent of these characteristics are his money-grubbing and his love of women.

1. *Money-grubbing.* His paramount anxiety is to get money, and we find him constantly making up his accounts in order to see how much better off he is this month than he was in the last. He takes care that no opportunity of money-getting shall be allowed to slip, and he certainly succeeds in his endeavours; for whereas, at the opening of the " Diary," he is only worth about £40, he makes £3,560 in the year 1665, while his salary as Clerk of the Acts remains at £350. In the following year he only made £2,986.[1]

The same prudent habits that made Pepys so careful in casting up his accounts induced him to

---

[1] The particulars of his accounts, as given in the " Diary," are very curious, and it may be worth while here to tabulate some of them.

On June 3, 1660, he was worth nearly £100
 „ Dec. 31, 1660,   „   £300
 „ May 24, 1661,   „   £500
 „ Aug. 31, 1662,   „   £686 19s. 2½d.

About this time he appears to have made but little extra money, for his monthly balances vary only a few pounds, sometimes more and sometimes less :—

Dec. 31, 1663 . . . . . . £800
 (Of which £700 was in Lord Sandwich's hands).
March 31, 1664 . . . . . . £900
July 31, 1664 . . . . . . £1,014
Feb. 28, 1664-65 . . . . . £1,270
Aug. 13, 1665 . . . . . . £2,164

This year he made money by prizes and fees for victualling, so that by Dec. 31 he had raised his estate to £4,400.

April 30, 1666 . . . . . . £5,200
Dec. 31, 1666 . . . . . . £6,200

After this he did not pay so much attention to these details, and on Jan. 23, 1668-69, he says that he is two years behind hand.

make a new will as changes were required. On the 17th of March, 1659-60, he bequeathed all that he possessed (but this was not very much at that time) to his wife, with his French books, the other books being left to his brother John. Another will was made on August 10th, 1665, because the town was so unhealthy "that a man cannot depend upon living two days." We have fuller particulars of the will of May 27th, 1666, by which Pall Pepys, the Diarist's sister, was to have £500, his father £2,000, and his wife the rest of his estate—"but to have £2,500 secured to her though by deducting out of what I have given my father and sister." Another will was prepared in the following year, by which Pepys left all he possessed to be equally divided between his wife and father.[1]

2. *Admiration for women.* Some of the oddest passages in the "Diary" grew out of this trait in Pepys's character; and one can only marvel that he thought it well to set down such passages on paper. When he came to Gravesend, after Charles II.'s landing, he kissed "a good handsome wench," because she was the first he had seen for a great while ;[2] and, at another time, the widow of a naval officer came to see him, apparently on business, when he had "a kiss or two of her, and a most modest woman she is."[3] His gallantry was so great as even to cause him to kiss the mouth of Katherine of Valois, whose body was exposed at Westminster Abbey. He seems to have performed this act

[1] "Diary," June 13, 1667.   [2] June 8, 1660.
[3] Dec. 21, 1665.

with great content, for he notes particularly that
on his birthday, February 23rd, 1668-69 (being
then thirty-six years of age), he "did first kiss a
queen." Although he was always ready to kiss
the ladies he met, his admiration was often quite
disinterested; this was peculiarly the case with
regard to the two Court beauties, the Duchess of
Richmond and the Countess of Castlemaine, to
neither of whom, apparently, he ever spoke.
There is an odd little entry which he made on
the 9th of September, 1668, that well illustrates
this feeling of his. The Duke of Richmond
wanted to consult Pepys about his yacht, and
sent for him to his lodgings in Whitehall. Pepys
hoped to have seen the Duchess, but found that
she was in the country; so he adds, "I shall
make much of this acquaintance, that I may live
to see his lady near." But the Clerk of the Acts'
chief admiration was lavished upon the worthless Countess of Castlemaine. He is always delighted when he can get a glimpse of her; and
he usually finds the play to be insipid if she does
not grace the theatre with her presence. Even
the sight of her clothes gives him pleasure, for
he tells us that one day, in passing the Privy
Garden at Whitehall, he saw her smocks and
linen petticoats hanging out to dry, and it did
him good to look upon them.[1]

Pepys was a pretty regular attendant at
church, and he seems to have enjoyed a good
sermon; but his chief delight was to look about
for pretty women: thus, on the 26th of May,
1667, he went (alone, by-the-bye) to St. Marga-

[1] "Diary," May 20, 1662.

ret's Church, Westminster, and there, he says,
" Did entertain myself with my perspective glass
up and down the church, by which I had the
great pleasure of seeing and gazing at a great
many very fine women ; and what with that, and
sleeping, I passed away the time till sermon was
done."

Our hero was very fond of pretty Betty
Michell, and would take some trouble to get a
sight of her ; and there is a most ludicrous passage in the " Diary " in which he describes a
mistake he made once at church. He went
again to St. Margaret's, in hopes of seeing
Betty, and stayed for an hour in the crowd,
thinking she was there " by the end of a nose "
that he saw ; but at last, to his great disgust, the
head turned towards him, and it was only her
mother ; he naturally adds, "which vexed me."[1]
Although he gave his wife much cause to be
jealous, he was inclined, without any cause, to be
jealous of her ; and, from his own account, he
seems often to have treated her in a very boorish
manner. One would have liked to have read
the lady's account of the constant little squabbles
which occurred ; but Pepys was not of the same
opinion, for on one occasion, when he found a
paper which his wife had written on the "disagree-
ables" of her life, he burnt it, in spite of her re-
monstrances.[2]

Pepys's nature was singularly contradictory,
and in summing up the chief points of his character, we can do little more than make a catalogue of
his various qualities, giving the bad ones first, and

[1] "Diary," Aug. 25, 1667.   [2] Jan. 9, 1662-63.

then enumerating the good ones as a set-off.
Thus, he was unfaithful to his wife, and a coward,
yet he knew his faults, and could try to amend
them. He was vain, ignorant, credulous, and
superstitious; yet he had scholarly tastes, and
his orderly and business habits were so marked
that they alone would point to him as a man
out of the common run. He was mean, and yet
he was also generous. This seems a harsh verdict, but it can easily be proved to be true, and
we will proceed to notice the several points
seriatim.

As to his unfaithfulness, his own description
of his conduct towards several women makes it
probable; but, in the instance of Deb Willett,
there can be no doubt. This episode, which
occurred in October and November, 1668, is by
far the most painful one in the " Diary."[1] Pepys
appears to have been infatuated, and, in spite of
his struggles, he fell. He repented, and prayed
fervently in his chamber that he might not fall
again. He resolved not to give any new occasion for his wife's jealousy, and he found great
peace in his mind by reason of this resolution.[2]

He was a coward, for on one occasion he was
so angry with the cookmaid that he kicked her.
He was not sorry for doing this, but he was
vexed that Sir William Penn's footboy saw him,
and would probably tell the family.[3]

His vanity may be taken for granted, as every
line of the " Diary" shows it. He was ignorant

[1] See particularly " Diary," Oct. 15, 1667 ; Oct. 25, Nov.
3, 13, 19, 20, 29, 1668.
[2] Dec. 5, 18, 1668.   [3] April 12, 1667.

of history, for he expected to find an account of England's dominion on the sea in "Domesday Book."[1]　As to his credulity, he appears to have believed everything that was told him, however absurd.　His superstition is shown in his belief in charms and in most of the popular delusions of his time; and also by his subterfuges, as when he opens a letter, and does not look at it until the money has fallen out, so that he may be able to say that he saw no money in the paper, if he should be questioned about it.[2]

He was mean, for he grudges money for his wife, while he spends liberally on himself; he is stingy to his father, and dislikes lending money to the benefactor from whom all his prosperity originally came.　Yet he could be singularly generous at times.　He gave £600 to his sister Paulina as her marriage portion;[3] and, after quarrelling with his wife because she had spent twenty-five shillings on a pair of earrings without his leave,[4] he pays £80 for a necklace which he presents her with.[5]　Of his scholarly tastes and business habits we shall have an opportunity of saying somewhat further on.

Perhaps, on the whole, the most remarkable characteristic of the man was his total want

---

[1] "Diary," Dec. 21, 1661. Each count in the above indictment is founded on many instances, but one will frequently be sufficient to give. The reader will easily find others for himself.

[2] April 3, 1663. On July 19, 1662, he makes the following odd remark : " Methought it lessened my esteem of a king, that he should not be able to command the rain."

[3] Feb. 10, 1667-68.　　　　　[4] July 4, 1664.

[5] April 30, 1666.

of the imaginative faculty. Here was one who had been well educated, and had kept up his learning through life; who had an artistic taste, and was a thorough musician; who could not so much as understand true wit or the higher poetry. "Midsummer Night's Dream" was insipid and ridiculous to him,[1] and he found " Hudibras " so silly that he was ashamed of it.[2]

I must leave my readers to answer the question why it is that, in spite of all that has been said, Pepys can stand the ordeal through which we have passed him; and why it is that, with all his faults, we cannot put his book down without some sort of affection for the man ?

[1] " Diary," Sept. 29, 1662.   [2] Dec. 26, 1662.

CHAPTER III.

PEPYS AFTER THE "DIARY."

" Truly may it be said that this was a greater and more grievous loss to the mind's eye of his posterity, than to the bodily organs of Pepys himself. It makes me restless and discontented to think what a Diary, equal in minuteness and truth of portraiture to the preceding, from 1669 to 1688 or 1690, would have been for the true causes, process, and character of the Revolution."—COLERIDGE'S MS. note in his copy of the "Diary" ("Notes and Queries," 1st S. vol. vi. p. 215).

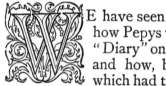E have seen in the previous chapter how Pepys wrote the last line of his "Diary" on the 31st of May, 1669; and how, by the physical defect which had then increased to alarming proportions, we have suffered what Coleridge calls "this grievous loss." In treating of Pepys's life after the "Diary," we at once find the difference between dealing with a few isolated facts and condensing from the living record of the man's own life. Moreover, Pepys as painted by his friends and as painted by himself, appears like two different men. The question is—would

the highly-respected Secretary of the Admiralty and the dignified President of the Royal Society have proved himself of the same nature as was the officious Clerk of the Acts if the "Diary" had been continued for some twenty or more years? or did time and domestic affliction mellow and settle the somewhat turbulent affections of the Diarist? There seems to be some reason for taking the latter view, and it is probable that, when he attained a more mature age, the dross of meanness was refined away, leaving the native ore of generosity pure and undefiled. When Pepys had obtained his leave of absence, he set out on a tour through France and Holland, accompanied by his wife. He carried with him on his journey the love which he always evinced for the occupation of his life, and he attempted to improve his knowledge of nautical affairs, making at the time collections respecting the French and Dutch navies. Some months after his return he spoke of his journey as having been "full of health and content," but no sooner had they returned to London than his wife became seriously ill with a fever. The disease took a fatal turn, and on the 10th of November, 1669, Elizabeth Pepys died, at the early age of twenty-nine years, to the great grief of her husband. She died at their house in Crutched Friars, and was buried in St. Olave's Church, where Pepys erected a tablet to her memory.

Mrs. Pepys occupies so prominent a position in the "Diary," and her husband, in spite of his faults, was so truly fond of her, that we must believe her death gave him a shock from which he would be long in recovering. He had no child nor near connection to be with him, and therefore, after this sad event, the whole current of his home life must have been changed.

In this same year, 1669, Sir Robert Brooke, member of Parliament for the borough of Aldborough, in Suffolk, died, and Pepys came forward as a candidate to fill his place. The Duke of York was favourable, and used all his influence to obtain the return of the Clerk of the Acts, but without success. When the election came on, Pepys was in distress, and his loss prevented him from taking part in the proceedings; so that, in spite of all that friends could do for him, he was defeated, and John Bence was elected on the 9th of November. In the following year he quarrelled with Sir James Barkman Leyenburg, the Swedish Resident in this country, and a duel between them was only prevented by an order from the King, given in a letter from Matthew Wren to Pepys, commanding him not to send or receive a challenge. This incident is not easy to be understood, as from what we know of Pepys he was not a man who would be very wishful to rush into a hostile encounter. Lord Braybrooke suggests that, as Leyenburg married the widow of Sir William Batten, the quarrel may have related to some money which was owed to Pepys by Batten, and for which the widow was liable ; but this suggestion can only be taken for what it is worth.

We do not know the exact date of Pepys's appointment to the Secretaryship of the Admiralty, but in a document found among his manuscripts, and dated November 3, 1672, he is described as holding that office.[1] When he was thus raised in his official position he was able to obtain his old place of Clerk of the Acts for his own clerk, Thomas Hayter, and his brother, John Pepys, who held it jointly. The latter does not appear to have done much credit to Samuel. He took holy orders in 1666,[2] and was appointed clerk to the Trinity House in 1670. When he died, in 1677, he was in debt £300 to the corporation, which Samuel had to pay.

Pepys's kind patron and kinsman the Earl of Sandwich died heroically in the naval action in Solebay, and on June 24, 1672, his funeral was performed with some pomp. There were eleven earls among the mourners, and Pepys, as the first among "the six Bannerrolles," walked in the procession. This same year there was some talk of the elevation to the peerage of Sir Robert Paston, M.P. for Castle Rising, and the Duke of York at once thought of Pepys as a candidate for his seat. The influence of Lord Howard, who had done what he could at Aldborough, was pre-eminent at Castle Rising; and James at once spoke to him to obtain his interest. Lord Howard was, however, in somewhat of a fix, for according to a letter which Thomas Povey wrote Pepys on August 31st, 1672, "he stands engaged to the King for Sir Francis North, to the Duchess of Cleveland for Sir John Trevor, her counsel and feoffee, and to the Duke

<hr>

[1] Smith's "Life, Journals, and Correspondence of S. Pepys," 1841, vol. i. p. 142.
[2] "Diary," Feb. 21, 1665-66.

E

for" Pepys. Time, however, got the peer out
of his dilemma. First of all, Sir Robert Stewart,
a Master of Chancery and the other member for
the borough, died, and Trevor was elected in his
place; then North was put in for King's Lynn;
and lastly, when Paston was created Viscount
Yarmouth, Pepys was chosen to succeed him,
on the 4th of November, 1673. Mr. Offley, his
unsuccessful opponent, petitioned against the
return, and the Committee of Privilege determined the election to be void; but Parliament
being prorogued shortly afterwards, before any
decision had been come to by the House, Pepys
was permitted to retain his seat. The journals
of the House [1] contain a full account of the proceedings, which chiefly consisted of evidence
respecting a frivolous charge made against
Pepys. It was reported that a person of quality
(who turned out to be Lord Shaftesbury) had
seen an altar with a crucifix upon it in his
house. When called upon, Shaftesbury denied
that he had ever seen "an altar in Mr. Pepys's
house or lodgings; as to the crucifix," he said he
had "some imperfect memory of seeing somewhat which he conceived to be a crucifix." [2]
Pepys stood up in his place and flatly denied
"that he had ever had any altar, or crucifix, or
the image or picture of any saint whatsoever in
his home from the top to the bottom of it." [3] He
further explained what might have given cause
for the aspersion. "Because he could not go
much abroad, he has made his home as pleasant
to himself as he could, embellishing it with

[1] Vol. ix.   [2] Vol. ix. p. 309.   [3] Vol. ix. p. 306

painting. He has a small table in his closet, with a Bible and Common Prayer-book upon it, and ' The Whole Duty of Man,' a bason and an ewer, and his wife's picture over it, done by Lombard. This is the whole thing talked of for an altar." [1]

It appears from the endorsement of a letter from Balthasar St. Michel to Pepys, to which allusion has already been made, that the latter was actually charged with having turned Mrs. Pepys from a Protestant to a Roman Catholic. Pepys therefore obtained from her brother an account of the fortunes of their family, which shows the utter absurdity of any such imputations.[2] He was always a true Protestant, although there is some reason for believing that Mrs. Pepys was a Catholic at heart.[3] On the passing of the Test Act, in 1673, the Duke of York resigned all his employments; and the Admiralty being put in commission, Pepys, as secretary, was brought in immediate correspondence with Charles II.

In 1677[4] he was elected Master of the Clothworkers' Company, when he presented a richly-chased silver cup, which is still used at their dinners. He was not long allowed to remain in peace, for the charge of popery, which was first made in 1673, was frequently repeated,

[1] Grey's "Debates."
[2] Smith's "Life, &c., of Pepys," vol. i. p. 147.
[3] "Diary," Nov. 29, Dec. 6, 1668.
[4] In this year was published "The Portugal History : or a Relation of the Troubles that happened in the court of Portugal in the year 1667 and 1668. By S. P. Esq. London (Richard Tonson)," 1677, which has been attributed to Pepys. There is a copy in the Pepysian Library.

and in 1679 he was accused, on the depositions
of Colonel John Scott, of betraying the navy, by
sending secret particulars to the French Government; and also of a design to dethrone the King
and extirpate the Protestant religion. He and
Sir Anthony Deane were committed to the
Tower under the Speaker's warrant on May
22nd, and Pepys's place at the Admiralty was
filled up by the appointment of Thomas Hayter.
When the two prisoners were brought to the
bar of the King's Bench on the 2nd of June,
the Attorney-General refused bail; but subsequently they were allowed to find security for
£30,000. At length, after several months of de-
lay, it was found that Colonel Scott refused to
acknowledge to the truth of the original deposi-
tion; and the prisoners were relieved from their
bail on February 12th, 1679-80. Scott turned
out to be a blackguard. He is said to have
cheated the States of Holland out of £7,000, in
consequence of which he was hanged in effigy
at the Hague, in 1672; and in 1681 he fled
from England to escape from the law, as he
had been found guilty of wilful murder for
killing a coachman. James, a butler, previously
in Pepys's service, confessed on his deathbed, in
1680, that he had trumped up the whole story
relating to his former master's change of religion
at the instigation of Mr. Harbord, M.P. for
Launceston, a leading enemy of Pepys.[1]

Evelyn visited Pepys in the Tower, and
expressed his belief in the unjustness of the
charge. While he was in custody Pepys kept

[1] Several letters relating to this affair will be found in
Smith's " Life, &c., of Pepys," vol. i.

up a correspondence with the Duke of York, who was then abroad, and he received an application from a Mr. D'Oyly for a loan of £50; but he was obliged to answer that he himself had been forced to borrow £100 from friends, to pay his fees and defray his expenses while in durance. It is impossible not to respect Pepys for his conduct towards James when the Royal Duke was in disgrace. He certainly made enemies by his action, and one of these was Andrew Marvell, who is reputed to have published a " Black Book " entitled, " A List of the principal labourers in the great design of Popery and arbitrary Power," which contains the following vituperative entry : " Castle Rising—Samuel Pepys Esquire, once a taylor, then a serving man to Lord Sandwich, now Secretary to the Admiralty, got by passes and other illegal wages £40,000." We know these assertions to be untrue, but they probably did the victim as much harm as if they had been true.

Pepys was chosen by the electors of Harwich as their member in the short Parliament that sat from March to July, 1679, his colleague being Sir Anthony Deane ; but both members were superseded in the next Parliament, that met on the 17th of October, 1679.

In 1680 Pepys attended on Charles II. at Newmarket, and there he took down, from the King's own mouth, the narrative of his escape after the Battle of Worcester, which now remains in the Pepysian Library, both in shorthand and longhand.

Sir Thomas Page, the Provost of King's College, Cambridge, died in August, 1681 ; and

S. Maryon, a Fellow of Clare, wrote at once, suggesting that Pepys was a fit and proper person for the post, and urging him to apply to the King for it. Pepys replied that he believed Colonel Legge (afterwards Lord Dartmouth) wanted to get the office for an old tutor. Although he pretended unfitness, he evidently liked the idea; and in a letter to Legge, while recommending an early application for the tutor, he expresses himself as willing to take the Provostship if the tutor cannot get it. He also promises, if he should be chosen, to give the whole profit of the first year, and at least half of that of each succeeding year, to " be dedicated to the general and public use of the college."[1] In the end Dr. John Copleston was appointed to the post.

In May, 1682, Pepys accompanied the Duke of York to Scotland, and narrowly escaped shipwreck by the way. Before letters could arrive in London to tell of his safety, the news came of the wreck of the "Gloucester" (the Duke's ship), and of the loss of many lives. His friends' anxiety was relieved by the arrival of a letter which Pepys wrote from Edinburgh to Hewer on the 8th inst., in which he detailed the particulars of the adventure. The Duke invited him to go on board the " Gloucester," but he preferred his own yacht, in which he had more room, and in consequence of his resolution he saved himself from the risk of drowning. On the 5th of May, about five in the morning, the frigate struck upon the sand called " The Lemon and the Oar," about sixteen leagues from the mouth

---

[1] Smith's " Life, &c., of S. Pepys," vol. i. pp. 265-72.

of the Humber, through the carelessness of the pilot, it was said. The Duke and his party were all asleep at the time, and after they were awoke it is supposed that they remained so long on board in the hope of saving the ship, that more men were drowned than otherwise need have been. It is said that the sinking sailors gave a loud huzza for the Duke, although they perhaps owed their deaths to an error of judgment on his part. Pepys writes that, had the said wreck occurred two hours earlier, and the accompanying yachts been at the distance they had previously been, not a soul would have escaped. Pepys on his arrival in Edinburgh was allowed by the Duke to attend one or two of the councils, and he was greatly struck with the union of absoluteness and gentleness by which James maintained his authority. He then made a tour through some of the Scottish towns with Colonel Legge, being most pleased with the "beauty and trade" of Glasgow. The people were not to his liking, for he writes to Hewer: "The truth is, there is so universal a rooted nastiness hangs about the person of every Scot (man and woman) that renders the finest show they can make nauseous, even among those of the first quality."[1]

The time was now coming when Pepys was to be again employed officially, and on July 30, 1683, he left London for Portsmouth, in order to join his old friend Colonel Legge (now Lord Dartmouth) in his expedition to Tangier for the purpose of demolishing that place. Pepys kept a journal of his proceedings, which is now

[1] Smith's "Life, &c., of Pepys," vol. i. p. 295.

in the Bodleian Library at Oxford, and has been printed by the Rev. John Smith in his "Life, Journals, &c., of Pepys." As the next chapter is devoted particularly to Tangier, it is not necessary to do more here than remark that, although this journal is of considerable interest, it falls very far short of the *naïveté* and charm of the original "Diary." On March 29th, 1684, Lord Dartmouth and his party (including Pepys) arrived in the English Channel.

Shortly after this, Charles II. made some further alterations at the Admiralty, and appointed Pepys to his old place of Secretary, possession of which he kept until the Revolution, when friends of the banished prince were not likely to be in favour. This same year he was elected President of the Royal Society, an office which he held for two years, apparently with credit to himself and general satisfaction to the Fellows. He certainly was not a scientific man, but at that period most of the subjects discussed could be understood by an intelligent man; and Pepys had a sincere love for curious learning which made him peculiarly fitted to act the part of an imitation Mecænas. In 1685 Charles II. died, and James came to the throne. We have already seen how Pepys was a spectator at Charles's coronation, now he was to take the position of an actor. We find that he marched in the procession at James's coronation, immediately behind the King's canopy, as one of the sixteen barons of the Cinque Ports. A Parliament was summoned to meet on the 19th of May, and Pepys was elected both by the burgesses of Harwich and by those of Sandwich. He chose to serve for Harwich, and Sir Philip Parker, Bart., was elected to fill his place at Sandwich. This Parliament was dissolved by proclamation, July 2nd, 1687, and on August 24th, the King declared in Council that another Parliament should be summoned for November 27th, 1688, the writs to bear date September 5th; but they were recalled on news being received of the Prince of Orange's design. On December 10th, James ordered those writs which had not been sent out to be burned ; and the same night, on his going away from Whitehall, he threw the Great Seal into the water. The Rev. Alexander Mills, a friend of Pepys, wrote to him from Sandwich in July, 1687, after the news of the dissolution had arrived, to say that he thought that Pepys might again be chosen if he felt inclined to stand for the town. In the next few months a great change had come over public affairs, and when the Convention Parliament was called together in January and February, 1689-90, Pepys found no place in it. In 1688 he had some correspondence with the Mayor of Harwich respecting the removal of the Custom-house from Ipswich to Harwich, and his chances of election seemed good at that time ; but a few months changed all that, and the corporation did not care to be represented by an official of the late King : so when the election came on, someone called out in the street, "No Tower men, no men out of the Tower!" His public career was closed soon after this, for an order was made out by the Commissioners of the Admiralty on the 9th of

March, 1688-89, commanding him to give up
his books, &c., to Phineas Bowles, the newly-
appointed Secretary of the Admiralty. He still
retained hopes of a return to public life, and on
the 8th of February, 1689-90, he wrote to the
proud Sir Edward Seymour for "his interest
anywhere, by which I might compass an election " for the new Parliament.[1] What Seymour's
answer was we do not know, but we do know
that a few months afterwards (June, 1690) Pepys
was committed to the Gate-house at Westminster, upon pretence of his being affected to King
James; but he was soon permitted to return to
his own home on account of ill-health. On this
occasion four stanch friends—Sir Peter Pala-
vicini, Mr. James Houblon, Mr. Blackburne, and
Mr. Martin—were bail for him. Soon after, he
published his " Memoirs of the Navy," to show
what he had done for its improvement and government, but although he was on all sides
looked up to as the greatest authority on naval
affairs, he continued, even in 1692, to apprehend
some fresh persecution.

Pepys had never been a healthy man, and as
years began to tell upon him he suffered much.
One day, when he was at Tangier, he was
frightened by the old swimming in the head
coming over him, and this made him melancholy.[2]
In December, 1686, he was again troubled with
pain night and day, caused by the complaint for
which he was successfully operated upon before
the " Diary " commences. In a letter to his

[1] Smith's " Life, &c., of Pepys," vol. ii. p. 246.
[2] *Ibid.* vol i. p. 452.

brother-in-law, St. Michel, he expresses the opinion that a general decay of his stomach and system will soon bring his life to an end; but he had several years still to live.

About this time Pepys secured the services of a Mrs. Fane as his housekeeper, and of her he wrote, in 1689 : " I do not believe that a more knowing, faithful, or vigilant person, or a stricter keeper at home (which is to me a great addition) —a person more useful in sickness as well as health, than Mrs. Fane is, can anywhere be found. As such I esteem and love her with all my heart, and should ever desire to keep her acquaintance, friendship, and neighbourhood." But—and this is a very important reservation— Mrs. Fane had a very disagreeable temper, as her victim goes on to say : " She hath a height of spirit, captiousness of humour, and bitterness and noise of tongue, that of all womankind I have hitherto had to do withal, do render her conversation and comportment as a servant most insupportable."[1] He parted with her once, but Mrs. Skinner prevailed upon him to receive her again. At last, after forbearance for three years and a-half, she was obliged to leave finally. Mr. James Houblon pleaded for her, but when he heard the above explanation, he was unable to say more.

In 1700, Pepys removed from York Buildings to what his friend Evelyn calls his " Paradisian Clapham." Here he lived with his old clerk and friend, William Hewer, but his infirmities kept him constantly in the house.

[1] Smith's " Life, &c., of Pepys," vol. ii. p. 219.

The eminent Dr. John Wallis, Savilian Professor of Geometry in the University of Oxford, was highly esteemed by Pepys, who had known him for many years as one of the most distinguished Fellows of the Royal Society. In 1701, therefore, the Diarist matured a scheme which did him the greatest credit. He sent Sir Godfrey Kneller down to Oxford to paint the old man's portrait; and, when it was finished, he presented the picture to the University of Oxford, and received in exchange a Latin diploma thanking him in gorgeous language for his munificence. Pepys explained to Kneller that it had long been his wish to provide from the painter's hands a means of "immortalizing the memory of the person—for his fame can never die—of that great man and my most honoured friend, Dr. Wallis, to be lodged as an humble present of mine, though a Cambridge man, to my dear aunt, the University of Oxford."

So much for the donor. The painter, on his part, was proud of his work, and assured Pepys that he had never done a better picture, if so good a one, in his life before.

In the following year all was over with both Wallis and Pepys. On the 26th of May, 1703, Samuel Pepys, after long-continued suffering, breathed his last, in the presence of the learned Dr. George Hickes, the non-juring Dean of Worcester, who writes as follows of the deathbed: "The greatness of his behaviour, in his long and sharp tryall before his death, was in every respect answerable to his great life; and I believe no man ever went out of this world with

greater contempt of it, or a more lively faith in
every thing that was revealed of the world to
come. I administered the Holy Sacrament
twice in his illnesse to him, and had administered it a third time but for a sudden fit of illness that happened at the appointed time of
administering of it. Twice I gave him the ab-
solution of the church, which he desired, and
received with all reverence and comfort, and I
never attended any sick or dying person that
dyed with so much christian greatnesse of mind,
or a more lively sense of immortality, or so
much fortitude and patience, in so long and
sharp a tryall, or greater resignation to the Will
which he most devoutly acknowledged to be the
wisdom of God : and I doubt not but he is now
a very blessed spirit, according to his motto,
mens cujusque is est quisque."

It was found necessary to have a post-mortem
examination of his body, when a nest of seven
stones, weighing about four and a-half ounces,
was found in the left kidney, which was entirely
ulcerated. His constitution generally, however,
appears to have been strong. The body was
brought from Clapham, and buried in St. Olave's
Church, Crutched Friars, on the 5th of June,
at nine o'clock in the evening, in a vault close
by the monument erected to Mrs. Pepys.

John Jackson, Pepys's nephew, sent a suit of
mourning to Evelyn, and expressed his sorrow
that distance and his correspondent's health
would prevent him from assisting at the holding-
up of the pall.

It appears from a list printed at the end of

Pepys's correspondence, that mourning was given
to forty persons, and that forty-five rings at 20*s.*,
sixty-two at 15*s.*, and sixteen at 10*s.* were dis-
tributed to relations, godchildren, servants, and
friends; also to representatives of the Royal
Society, of the Universities of Cambridge and
Oxford, of the Admiralty, and of the Navy
Office. The bulk of the property was bequeathed
to John Jackson, the son of Mrs. Jackson, the
Pall Pepys of the "Diary;" but the money which
was left was much less than might have been
expected.   In spite of all his public services,
which were universally acknowledged, he received neither pension nor remuneration of any
kind after his enforced retirement at the Revolution.   Public men in those days, without
private property, must have starved if they had
not taken fees, for the King had no idea of
wasting his money by paying salaries.   At the
time of Pepys's death there was a balance of
£28,007 2*s.* 1¼*d.* due to him from the Crown,
and the original vouchers still remain an heir-
loom in the family.

CHAPTER IV.

TANGIER.

" And with asphaltick slime broad as the gate
Deep to the roots of hell the gather'd beach
They fasten'd : and the *mole* immense wrought on
Over the foaming deep high-arch'd : a bridge
Of length prodigious."—*Paradise Lost*, x. 298-302.

EPYS was so intimately connected with the government of Tangier during the twenty-two years it remained in the possession of the English, that it seems necessary, in a memoir of him, to give some account of the history of the place during that period.

Tangier is a seaport, on a small bay or inlet of the Straits of Gibraltar, which affords the only good harbour for shipping on the sea-board of Morocco, an extent of coast of about 900 miles. The town was early coveted by the Portuguese, and in 1437 their army attacked it, but were defeated beneath the walls. On this occasion Dom Fernando, the King's brother, was left behind as a hostage. A treaty of peace

was concluded, but the stipulations not being
executed, the Moors threw Dom Fernando into
prison, where he died.   The prince's body was
treated with insult, and hung up by the heels
over the city walls.   A few years later this
unworthy conduct was revenged, for in 1463,
the Portuguese being successful in battle,
Alonzo V. took the town from the Moors.   For
two centuries the Portuguese kept possession,
but about the period of our Restoration they found
the place somewhat of an encumbrance, and were
anxious to obtain a desirable alliance against
their enemies the Spaniards, by transferring it
to another power.   In November, 1660, Thomas
Maynard, British Consul at Lisbon, writing to
Sir Edward Nicholas, says, that the King of
Portugal would part with Tangier to England
on reasonable terms.[1]

Shortly afterwards the Portuguese ambassador in London proposed the Infanta Katharine,
daughter of that Duke of Braganza who became
King of Portugal as Joam IV., as a wife for
Charles II., offering at the same time a portion
of half a million pounds sterling ("almost double
what any King [of England] had ever received
in money by any marriage "),[2] and in addition a
grant of a free trade in Brazil and the East
Indies, and the possession of Tangier and the
Island of Bombay.   The ambassador observed
that these two places "might reasonably be
valued above the portion in money." [3]   It was
supposed that the possession of Tangier would

[1] Lister's "Life of Clarendon," vol. iii. p. 113.
[2] Clarendon's Life, 1827, vol. i. p. 495.   [3] *Ibid.* p. 491.

be of infinite benefit to England and a security to her trade, and the Earl of Sandwich and Sir John Lawson were consulted respecting the proposed acquisition. Lord Sandwich said that if the town were walled and fortified with brass, it would yet repay the cost, but he only knew it from the sea. Lawson had been in it, and said that it was a place of that importance, that if it were in the hands of Hollanders they would quickly make a mole, which could easily be done. Then ships would ride securely in all weathers, and we could keep the place against the world, and give the law to the trade of the Mediterranean.[1] The Portuguese were delighted at the prospect of a marriage between the Infanta and Charles, and after a few hitches the treaty was concluded, but some murmurs were heard against the delivery of Tangier into the hands of heretics. Dom Fernando de Menezes, the Governor, entreated the Queen Regent to spare him the grief of handing over the city to the enemies of the Catholic faith. He was given to understand that, if he obeyed instructions, a marquisate would be conferred upon him, but if he continued to resist he would be dismissed. Upon this, Dom Fernando threw up his command.

Lord Sandwich was instructed to take possession of Tangier, and then convey the Infanta and her portion to England. Although the Queen Regent sent a governor whom she had chosen as one devoted to her interest, and sure to obey her commands, yet Clarendon affirms

---

[1] Clarendon's Life, 1827, vol. i. p. 494.

F

that he went to his government with a contrary resolution.[1] This resolution, however, was frustrated by the action of the Moors. A few days only before Lord Sandwich arrived, the Governor marched out of the town with all the horse and half the foot of the garrison, and fell into an ambush. The whole party were cut off, and the Governor and many of his chief men were killed. The town was so weak that, when Lord Sandwich arrived at this conjuncture, he was hailed as a deliverer from the Moors. He conveyed the remainder of the garrison into Portugal, and Henry, second Earl of Peterborough, with the English garrison, entered the town on the 30th of January, 1662, as the first Governor from England.

Now began a system of mismanagement worthy of the disorganized condition of public affairs. A commission was appointed for the purpose of carrying on the government of Tangier in London, and constant meetings were held. None of the commissioners knew anything of the place, and they were quite at the mercy of the governors and deputy-governors who were sent out. Pepys was placed upon the commission by the influence of Lord Sandwich, and John Creed was appointed secretary.[2] Thomas Povey, the treasurer, got his accounts into so great a muddle, that he thought it wise to surrender his office to Pepys, on condition of receiving half the profits, which he did on

---

[1] Clarendon's Life, 1827, vol. ii. p. 161.
[2] "Diary," Dec. 1, 1662. In Lord Braybrooke's "Life of Pepys" it is incorrectly stated that Pepys was secretary.

March 20, 1664-65. This treasurership and the
contract for victualling the garrison of Tangier
were sources of considerable profit to our
Diarist. At one of the earliest meetings of the
committee, the project of forming a mole or
breakwater was entertained. A contract for
the work to be done at 13s. the cubical yard
was accepted, although, as Pepys writes, none
of the committee knew whether they gave too
much or too little (February 16, 1662-63);
and he signed the contract with very ill will
on that score (March 30, 1663). When the accounts were looked into on April 3, 1663, it
was found that the charge for one year's work
would be as much as £13,000. Two years
after this, the committee agreed to pay 4s. a
yard more, and the whole amount spent upon
the mole was found to be £36,000 (March
30, 1665). The wind and sea exerted a very
destructive influence over this structure, although
it was very strongly built, and Colonel Norwood
reported in 1668 that a breach had been made
in the mole which would cost a considerable
sum to repair. As Norwood was an enemy of a
friend of his, Pepys at once jumps to the conclusion that he must be a bad man (February 22,
1668-69). The second Earl of Carnarvon said
that wood was an excrescence of the earth,
provided by God for the payment of debts, and
Sir W. Coventry, in a conversation with Pepys,
applied this saying to Tangier and its governors. It is not always safe to take for granted
all that our Diarist says against the persons he
writes about, but there must have been some

truth in the indictment he drew up against all those who undertook the government of Tangier. When Lord Peterborough received the place from the Portuguese, a book was given to him which contained a secret account of all the conduit-heads and heads of watercourses in and about the town. This book was always given from one governor to another, but was not to be looked at by anyone else. When Lord Peterborough left, he took the book away with him, and on being asked for it always answered that he had mislaid it and could not recover it. Colonel Kirke told Pepys in 1683 that the supply of water was greatly reduced by the want of this information.[1] In 1666 Pepys had applied the adjective "ignoble" to Lord Peterborough's name, on account of his lordship's conduct in regard to money matters. On December 15, 1662, Andrew Lord Rutherford and Earl of Teviot, Governor of Dunkirk until its surrender to the French, was appointed Governor of Tangier in succession to Lord Peterborough, who was recalled. He was a brave but rash man, and made a practice of going out of the town into the country without taking proper precautions. In May, 1664, he was surveying his lines after an attack by the Moors, when he and nineteen officers were killed by a party of the enemy in ambush. Pepys called him a cunning man, and said that had he lived he would have undone the place; but in 1683, Dr. Lawrence told Pepys that his

[1] "Tangier Diary" (Smith, vol. i. p. 444).

death was a great misfortune, for he took every opportunity of making the place great, but without neglecting himself.[1] John Lord Bellassis was the next governor, and he was said to be corrupt in his command. The deputy-governors were no better than their superiors. Of Colonel Fitzgerald, Pepys writes, on October 20th, 1664, he is "a man of no honour nor presence, nor little honesty, and endeavours to raise the Irish and suppress the English interest there, and offend every body." Certainly, when he sees him on August 7th, 1668, he is pleased with him and his discourse. Pepys's opinion of Colonel Norwood we have already seen; but none of the governors rose to the height of villany exhibited by Colonel Kirke, whose name is condemned to everlasting infamy in the pages of Macaulay.

The further history of Tangier, previous to its final destruction, can be put into a few words. In January, 1668-69, Lord Sandwich proposed that a paymaster should be appointed at Tangier, and suggested Sir Charles Harbord for the post; but the Duke of York said that nothing could be done without Pepys's consent, in case the arrangement should injure him in his office of treasurer. Our Diarist was much pleased at this instance of the kindness of the Duke, and of the whole committee towards him.[2]

Henry Sheres, who accompanied Lord Sandwich to Spain, and afterwards became a great

<hr />

[1] "Tangier Diary" (Smith, vol. i. p. 444).
[2] "Diary," Jan. 4, 1668-69.

friend of Pepys, was paid £100, on January
18th, 1668-69, for drawing a plate of the Tangier
fortifications. In the same year (1669), the
great engraver, Hollar, was sent to Tangier
by the King to take views of the town and
fortifications. Some of these he afterwards engraved, and the original drawings are in the
British Museum.

In 1673 a new commission was appointed,
and Pepys and Povey were among the commissioners.[1] Two years afterwards the vessel in
which Henry Teonge was chaplain anchored in
Tangier Bay; and in the "Diary" which he
left behind him he gives a description of the
town as it appeared to him. The mole was not
then finished, and he found the old high walls
much decayed in places. He mentions "a pitiful
palizado, not so good as an old park pale (for
you may anywhere almost thrust it down with
your foot);" but in this palisade were twelve forts,
well supplied with good guns.

In 1680, Tangier was besieged by the Emperor
of Morocco, and Charles II. applied to Parliament for money, so that the place might be properly defended. The House of Commons expressed their dislike of the management of the
garrison, which they suspected to be a nursery
for a Popish army. Sir William Jones said:
"Tangier may be of great importance to trade,
but I am afraid hath not been so managed as to
be any security to the Protestant religion;" and
William Harbord, M.P. for Thetford, added:

[1] Sir Joseph Williamson's "Letters" (Camden Soc.),
vol. i. p. 149.

"When we are assured we shall have a good Protestant governor and garrison in Tangier, I shall heartily give my vote for money for it."[1]

A most unworthy action was at this time perpetrated by the Government. Not having the support of Parliament, they were unable to defend the place with an adequate force; and they chose the one man in England whose brilliant career rivals those of the grand worthies of Elizabeth's reign to fight a losing game.

The Earl of Ossory, son of the Duke of Ormond, was appointed Governor and General of the Forces; but, before he could embark, he fell ill from brooding over the treatment he had received, and soon after died. Lord Sunderland said in council that "Tangier must necessarily be lost; but that it was fit Lord Ossory should be sent, that they might give some account of it to the world."

The Earl left his wife at their daughter's house, and came up to London. Here he made a confidant of John Evelyn, who records in his "Diary" his opinion of the transaction. It was not only "an hazardous adventure, but, in most men's opinion, an impossibility, seeing there was not to be above 3 or 400 horse, and 4000 foot for the garrison and all, both to defend the town, form a camp, repulse the enemy, and fortify what ground they should get in. This touch'd my Lord deeply that he should be so little consider'd as to put him on a business in which he should probably not only lose his reputation,

---

[1] Smith, vol. i. p. 390 (note).

but be charged with all the miscarriages and ill
success."[1] It was on this man that Ormond pronounced the beautiful eulogy, " I would not exchange my dead son for any living son in
Christendom ! "

In August, 1683, Lord Dartmouth was constituted Captain-General of his Majesty's Forces
in Africa, and Governor of Tangier, being sent
with a fleet of about twenty sail to demolish and
blow up the works, destroy the harbour, and
bring home the garrison; but his instructions
were secret.   Pepys received the King's command to accompany Lord Dartmouth, but without being informed of the object of the expedition.
In a letter to Evelyn, Pepys tells him, " What
our work is I am not solicitous to learn nor forward to make griefs at, it being handled by our
masters as a secret."   When they get to sea,
Lord Dartmouth tells Pepys the object of the
voyage, which the latter says he never suspected,
having written the contrary to Mr. Houblon.[2]
On September 17th they landed at Tangier,
having been about a month on their voyage.
All the doings on board ship, and the business
transacted on shore, are related with all Pepys's
vivid power of description in his " Tangier
Journal."   The writer, however, has become
more sedate, and only once " the old man " appears, when he remarks on the pleasure he had in
" again seeing fine Mrs. Kirke,"[3] the wife of the
Governor.   We are told that " the tyranny and
vice of Kirke is stupendous,"[4] and the " Journal"

[1] Evelyn's " Diary," July 26, 1680.
[2] Smith, vol. i. p. 331.   [3] P. 374.   [4] P. 403.

is full of the various instances of his enormities.
Macaulay, however, with that power of charac-
terization which he so eminently possessed, has
compressed them all into his picture of the leader
of " Kirke's lambs."

Pepys was now for the first time in the town
with the government of which he had been so
long connected, and he was astonished at its
uselessness. Day by day he finds out new disadvantages ; and he says that the King was kept
in ignorance of them, in order that successive
governors might reap the benefits of their position. He complains that even Mr. Sheres was
silent for his own profit, as he might have made
known the evils of the place ten years before.[1]

In a letter to Mr. Houblon, he gives his
opinion that "at no time there needed any more
than the walking once round it by daylight to
convince any man (no better-sighted than I) of
the impossibility of our ever making it, under
our circumstances of government, either tenable
by, or useful to, the crown of England." He
adds : "Therefore it seems to me a matter much
more unaccountable how the King was led to
the reception, and, afterwards, to so long and
chargeable a maintaining, than, at this day, to the
deserting and extinguishing it."[2]

On the other side Mr. Charles Russell wrote
to Pepys from Cadiz, deprecating the destruction
of Tangier, and pointing out the advantages of
possessing it.[3] Sheres also showed Pepys a
paper containing the ordinary objections made

[1] Smith, vol. i. p. 403. [2] P. 419.
[3] P. 385.

against the mole, " improved the most he could, to justify the King's destroying it," and added that he could answer them all.[1]

When the work of destruction was begun, it was found that the masonry had been so well constructed that it formed a protection as strong as solid rock. The mining was undertaken piecemeal, and it took six months to blow up the whole structure. The rubbish of the mole and the walls was thrown into the harbour, so as to choke it up completely. Still the ruined mole stands, and on one side the accumulated sand has formed a dangerous reef.

On the 5th of March, 1683-84, Lord Dartmouth and Pepys sailed out of Tangier Bay, and abandoned the place to the Moors. Shortly afterwards the Emperor of Morocco (Muly Ismael) wrote to Captain Cloudesley Shovel : " God be praised! you have quitted Tangier, and left it to us to whom it did belong. From henceforward we shall manure it, for it is the best part of our dominions. As for the captives, you may do with them as you please, heaving them into the sea, or destroying them otherways." To which Shovel replied : " If they are to be disowned because they are poor, the Lord help them! Your Majesty tells us we may throw them overboard if we please. All this we very well know ; but we are Christians, and they bear the form of men, which is reason enough for us not to do it. As to Tangier, our master kept it twenty-one years ; and, in spite of all your force, he could, if he had pleased, have continued it to the world's

[1] Smith, vol. i. p. 383.

end ; for he levelled your walls, filled up your harbour, and demolished your houses, in the face of your Alcade and his army; and when he had done, he left your barren country without the loss of a man, for your own people to starve in."[1]

According to Pepys's account Tangier was a sink of corruption, and England was well rid of the encumbrance. He describes the inhabitants as given up to all kinds of vice, "swearing, cursing and drinking," the women being as bad as the men; and he says that a certain captain belonging to the Ordnance told him that " he was quite ashamed of what he had heard in their houses; worse a thousand times than in the worst place in London he was ever in." Dr. Balaam, a former Recorder, had so poor an opinion of the people of the place, that he left his estate to a servant, with the caution that if he married a woman of Tangier, or one that ever had been there, he should lose it all.[2]

Yet Tangier was positively outdone in iniquity by Bombay, which Sir John Wyborne calls "a cursed place."[3] These were the two acquisitions so highly rated when Charles II. married the Infanta of Portugal.

In spite of all disadvantages, one of the greatest being that ships of any size are forced to lie out far from shore, Tangier is still a place of some importance as the port of North Morocco. The description of the town given by Sir Joseph

[1] Ockley's "Account of South-West Barbary," quoted in Smith's " Life, &c., of Pepys," vol. ii. p. 130 (note).
[2] Smith, vol. i. p. 446.   [3] Vol. ii. pp. 99-100.

Hooker[1] answers in most particulars to that written by Teonge two centuries before. It stands on the western side of a shallow bay, on rocky ground that rises steeply from the shore, and the cubical blocks of whitewashed masonry, with scarcely an opening to represent a window, which rise one above the other on the steep slope of a recess in the hills, give the place a singular appearance from the sea. On the summit of the hill is a massive gaunt castle of forbidding aspect, and the zigzag walls which encompass the city on all sides are pierced by three gates which are closed at nightfall.

[1] "Journal of a Tour in Marocco," by Sir Joseph D. Hooker and John Ball. London, 1878, p. 5.

CHAPTER V.

PEPYS'S BOOKS AND COLLECTIONS.

" A snapper-up of unconsidered trifles."
Winter's Tale, act iv. sc. iii.

EPYS desired that his name might go down to posterity, but he could little have foreseen the fame that it has attained in the nineteenth century. The mode he took to keep it alive was the bequeathment of his library and collections to a time-honoured foundation; and there is every reason to believe that he would have strongly objected to the publication of his "Diary." Now that that book has been published, we all see the full-length figure of the man; but his character might also have been read in the Pepysian library at Magdalene College, Cambridge; and this latter exhibition of him has been much longer before the public. Comparatively little interest was, however, taken in it until after the appearance of the deciphered "Diary," when his name at once sprang into fame.

The library was left, in the first instance, to the Diarist's nephew, John Jackson, but with a special proviso that it should on no account be dispersed. Pepys refers in his memorandum to " the infinite pains and time and cost employed in my collecting and reducing the same to the state it now is " in. He is particularly solicitous " for its unalterable preservation and perpetual security against the ordinary fate of such collections, falling into the hands of an incompetent heir and thereby being sold, dissipated or imbezzled." Jackson was allowed a certain latitude in the disposal of the collections after his death. They were to be placed at one of the Universities, but Cambridge was to be preferred to Oxford. A private college was to be chosen rather than the Public Library, and of colleges Trinity or Magdalene were to be given the preference over the others. Of these two colleges (on the boards of each of which Pepys's name had been entered), Magdalene, at which he received his education, was to have the preference. The college which did not receive the gift was appointed visitor, and if at the annual inspection any breach of covenant occurred, the library became forfeited to it.

A fair room was to be provided for the library, and no other books were to be added, save those which Jackson might add in distinct presses. The whole was to be called " Bibliotheca Pepysiana," and the sole power and custody over it was to be vested in the master of the college for the time being.[1]

[1] Harl. MS. 7,031, pp. 208, 209. "Samuel Pepys, his disposition and settlement of his Library."

Magdalene College was founded by Lord Chancellor Audley, who vested for ever the right of nominating to the mastership in the possessors of Audley End. At the time that Pepys was a student the buildings were far from extensive, and consisted of the first court alone. The foundation of the second court was laid in 1677, and Pepys's " Correspondence" contains a letter from Dr. Hezekiah Burton, asking for the contribution already promised towards the new buildings; and another from John Maulyverer in 1679, thanking for money lent for the same purpose, and referring to a bond. A fellow-collegian of Pepys was John Peachell, afterwards Vicar of Stanwick, Prebendary of Carlisle, and Master of the College in 1679. He does not appear to have been altogether an estimable man, for in 1677 (May 3) Pepys felt half ashamed to be seen in his company because of his red nose; and according to Lord Dartmouth's manuscript notes on Bishop Burnet's " History of his own Time," there was cause for this rubicundity, as Archbishop Sancroft rebuked him for setting an ill example in the University by drunkenness and other loose behaviour. Dr. Peachell had his good points, however, for in 1687 he was suspended from his mastership and deprived of his vice-chancellorship for refusing to admit Alban Francis, a Benedictine monk, to the degree of Master of Arts without taking the prescribed oaths. It appears from a letter to Pepys that he greatly feared the Earl of Suffolk, who was then owner of Audley End, would be content to have him removed in order to obtain the privilege of nominating a successor, but he was fortunate in being restored to his office in the following year.

Pepys never forgot a friend, and a month before this restoration he induced Lord Dartmouth, on his appointment to the command of the fleet, to ask Peachell to be his chaplain, with authority over all the other chaplains. In 1690 the Master of Magdalene died of starvation brought about by a four days' fast which he prescribed himself as a penance after the archbishop's admonition; and when he afterwards tried to eat he could not.

The master at the period of Pepys's death was Dr. Quadring, and in the college chest are two letters written by Jackson to him to inform him of the will of the deceased respecting the library. It was not, however, until 1724, on the death of Jackson, that the three thousand volumes of which the library consisted were, with the original bookcases, removed to the college, and deposited in the new buildings which Pepys had assisted to build. The old inscription, " Bibliotheca Pepysiana," which was set up at the time, is still to be seen on the front in the second courtyard.

The library is of the greatest interest, and a mere enumeration of some of the treasures contained in it is enough to whet the appetite of the least ardent among the lovers of old books. To mention first the manuscripts :— there are the various papers collected by Pepys for his proposed " Navalia ;" a " vast treasure of papers" lent by Evelyn, but never returned to their owner ; seventeen letters from Henry VIII to Anne Boleyn, copied at Rome from the originals in the Vatican, 1682 ; a collection of papers relating to Charles II.'s escape from Worcester ; a journal of the proceedings of the Duke of Monmouth in his invading of England, with the progress and issue of the rebellion attending it, kept by Mr. Edward Dummer, then serving the train of artillery employed by his Majesty for the suppression of the same; and a Survey (made by order of the Admiralty) of buildings and encroachments on the River of Thames, from London Bridge to Cuckold's Point, 1684-1687. The Maitland MS., which contains an excellent collection of Scottish poetry, and is named after Sir Richard Maitland of Lethington, Lord Privy Seal and Judge in the Court of Session (b. 1496, d. 1586), who formed it, is also worthy of special mention. How the two volumes of which it consists came into Pepys's possession is not recorded. Selections from them were printed by Pinkerton in 1786.

Among the choice articles that should have some notice, however inadequate, are the pocketbook constantly used by Sir Francis Drake, and that of James II., described as follows by Pepys himself :—" My Royal master K. James ye 2^d. Pocket Book of Rates and Memorandums during ye whole time of his serving at ye Seas as Lord High Admiral of England, vizt., from May, 1663, to his laying down his commission, May, 1673." Another great curiosity is the original " Libro de Cargos as to Provisions and Municõns of the Proveedor of the Spanish Armada, 1588," with a hole right through, for the purpose of hanging it up in the ship.

G

Besides all the papers on naval affairs in the Pepysian Library, there is a series of fifty volumes of Pepys's manuscripts in the Rawlin-son Collection in the Bodleian Library. How these papers came into the possession of Raw-linson is not known.

What gives a special interest to the Library is the fact that it still remains in exactly the same condition as Pepys left it, the books being in the original cases, arranged in the order which he had fixed. There are several entries in the " Diary" relating to the arrangement and cata-loguing of the books; thus on December 17th, 1666, we read :—" Spent the evening in fitting my books, to have the number set upon each, in order to my having an alphabet of my whole, which will be of great ease to me." He employs his brother John to write out the catalogue " perfectly alphabeticall,"[1] but he afterwards finishes it off with his own hand.[2] He was very particular as to the books he admitted into his catalogue, so when he bought in the Strand " an idle rogueish French book, ' L'escholle des filles,' " he resolved, as soon as he had read it, to burn it, " that it might not stand in the list of books nor among them, to disgrace them if it should be found."[3] He had, at a later time, a similar feeling with regard to Lord Rochester's poems, and in a letter dated Nov. 2, 1680, he directs Hewer to leave the volume in a drawer, as it is written in a style which he thought unfitted it for mixing with his other books. He

[1] " Diary," Jan. 8, 1666-67.   [2] Feb. 4, 1666-67.
[3] Feb. 8, 1667-68.

adds that as the author (who had just died) was past writing any more poems so bad in one sense, he despaired of any man surviving "to write so good in another."[1] When I was looking over the Library I made a point of seeing whether this book had found a place at last on the shelves, and I discovered it there ; but with sad hypocrisy it stood in false colours, for the lettering on the back was "Rochester's Life."

The books were numbered consecutively throughout the Library, and, therefore, when rearranged, they needed to be all renumbered. All hands were pressed into this service ; and we read that on the 15th of February, 1667-68, Pepys himself, his wife, and Deb Willett, were busy until near midnight "titleing" the books for the year, and setting them in order. They all tired their backs, but the work was satisfactory, though, on the whole, not quite so much so as the previous year's job had been.

On account of this constant changing, each book contains several numbers, sometimes as many as six ; and the last, which is the one by which the books are still found, is in red ink.

The books are arranged in eleven curious old mahogany bookcases, which are mentioned in the "Diary," under date August 24th, 1666, and which gave the Diarist so much pleasure, when they were sent home quite new by Mr. Sympson, the joiner and cabinet-maker. The presses are handsomely carved, and have handles fixed at each end ; the doors are formed of little panes of glass ; and, in the lower divisions, the glass

[1] Smith's "Life, &c., of Pepys," vol. i. p. 247.

windows are made to lift up. The books are all arranged in double rows; but, by the ingenious plan of placing small books in front of large ones, the letterings of all can be seen. Some have tickets on the outside, and this practice is mentioned in the "Diary," where we read: "To my chamber, and there to ticket a good part of my books, in order to the numbering of them for my easy finding them to read as I have occasion." [1]

The word "arranged" has been several times used in this chapter; but it must not be understood as implying any kind of classification, for the books are merely placed in order of size. This arrangement, however, has been very carefully attended to; and, in one instance, some short volumes have been raised to the required height by the help of wooden stilts, gilt in front.

The classification was to be found in the catalogues; and, as Pepys increased in substance, he employed experts to do this work for him. One of these was Paul Lorrain, the author of several tracts and sermons, who was employed in copying manuscripts, and making catalogues of books and prints. A letter from this man, written on October 12th, 1700, to explain the nature of the work he then had in hand, is printed in the correspondence of Pepys.

There are numerous entries in the "Diary" relating to the binding of certain books; and a single glance at the Library as it now exists would show any one experienced in the matter that Pepys paid great attention to this most important point in the proper preservation of a

"Diary," Dec. 19, 1666.

library. As early as May 15th, 1660, he showed
this taste by buying three books solely on account of the binding; and on January 18th,
1664-65, he went to his bookseller to give directions for the new binding of a great many of his
old books, in order that his whole studyful
should be uniform. Nearly all the books are
bound in calf, although some are in morocco and
some in vellum.

Pepys came to the resolution in the year 1667
that he would not have any more books than his
cases would hold; so when, on the 2nd of February, 1667-68, he found that the number of
books had much increased since the previous
year, he was forced to weed out several inferior
ones to make room for better. He had previously written : " Whereas, before, my delight
was in multitude of books, and spending money
in that, and buying alway of other things, now
that I am become a better husband, and have
left off buying, now my delight is in the neatness
of everything." [1] This plan he continued to
practise throughout his life, generally to the improvement of the character of his library, but
not always so.

When I was allowed the privilege of looking
through the Library, I came upon a list of books
headed " Deleta, 1700." The entries in this list
are most curious. To each title is added a note,
such as these : " Ejected as a duplicate," " Removed to a juster place," " To give way to the
same reprinted," " To give way to a fairer
edition."

As the " Diary" is full of notices of books

[1] " Diary," Aug. 10, 1663.

purchased, I felt interested to know which of them had been weeded out after they had been bought, and which had been thought worthy to remain on to the end.

The following is the result of these inquiries in a few instances, chosen from the poets :—On the 8th of July, 1664, Pepys went to his bookseller about some books; from his shop he went on to the binder, to give directions as to the binding of his "Chaucer;" "and thence to the claspmakers, to have it clasped and bossed." Reposing in a quiet corner of the Pepysian Library is Speght's edition of 1602, which is the identical copy referred to, and here, therefore, we have an example of the books that remained. It is in a plain calf cover, unlettered, "full neat enough," with brass clasp and bosses.

This evident attempt to do honour to the memory of

> "That renownmed Poet
> Dan Chaucer, well of English undefyled,
> On Fame's eternall beadroll worthie to be fyled,"

is an incident of the more interest, in that Chaucer is almost the only great poet that Pepys was able to appreciate. Sir John Minnes, the wit, taught him to love England's grand old singer. These two men were constantly brought together in the fulfilment of business duties, and Pepys writes "among other things Sir J. Minnes brought many fine expressions of Chaucer, which he doats on mightily." To this he adds as his own opinion, "and without doubt he is a very fine poet." [1]

[1] "Diary," June 14, 1663.

That this is not a mere passing remark is evident, for on August 10th, 1664, he actually quotes a line from "Troilus and Cressida," a most unusual practice with this "matter-of-fact" man. He goes to visit the famous Cocker, and has an hour's talk with him on various matters. "He (Cocker) says that the best light for his life to do a very small thing by (contrary to Chaucer's words to the Sun, 'that he should lend his light to them that small seals grave')¹ it should be by an artificial light of a candle, set to advantage, as he could do it."

I very much fear that the quotation did not spring up into Pepys's own mind, but that it was suggested by Cocker, who was "a great admirer, and well read in all our English poets." More than thirty years after this, Pepys still remained one of Chaucer's warmest admirers, and we have it on the best authority that we owe Dryden's modernization of the "Character of a Good Parson" to his recommendation.²

---

¹ "Allas! what hath this lovers the agylte?
Dispitous Day, thyn be the pyne of Helle!
For many a lover hastow slayn, and wilt;
Thi pourynge in wol nowher lat hem dwelle:
What? profrestow thi light here for to selle?
Go selle it hem that smale seles grave,
We wol the nought, as nedeth no day have!"
Troylus and Cryseyde, book iii. ll. 1408-14.

² This is so interesting a fact that I think Dryden's letter to Pepys on the subject may well appear in full at this place:—

"July 14, 1699.

"Padron Mio,
"I remember last year when I had the honour of dining with you, you were pleased to recommend to me the

To return, however, to the Pepysian Library. On the 7th of July, 1664 (the day before he went to the binder about Chaucer), Pepys bought " Shakespeare's Plays." This probably was the third edition, which had just appeared; though it might have been either the first folio of 1623, or the second folio of 1632; but whichever of these three it happened to be, it was replaced in after years by the fourth folio of 1685, which is now in the collection. Although " Paradise Lost " was first published in 1667, we find no notice either of it or of its author in the " Diary."

The Library contains the collected edition, in three folio volumes, of Milton's Works, pub-

character of Chaucer's " Good Parson." Any desire of yours is a command to me, and accordingly I have put it into my English, with such additions and alterations as I thought fit.

" Having translated as many fables from Ovid, and as many novels from Boccace, and tales from Chaucer, as will make an indifferent large volume in folio, I intend them for the press in Michaelmas term next. In the mean time my Parson desires the favour of being known to you, and promises if you find any fault in his character, he will reform it. Whenever you please, he shall wait on you, and for the safer conveyance, I will carry him in my pocket, who am

" My *Padron's* most obedient servant,

" JOHN DRYDEN.

" For Samuel Pepys, Esq.,
    At his house in York Street, These."

In Pepys's answer, dated on the same day, he writes: " You truly have obliged me, and, possibly, in saying so, I am more in earnest than you can readily think, as verily hoping from this your copy of one ' Good Parson ' to fancy some amends made me for the hourly offence I bear with from the sight of so many lewd originals."—Smith's " Life, &c., of Pepys," vol. ii. pp. 254-55.

lished at London by John Toland in 1698, but
stated in the title-page to be published at Amsterdam. Pepys probably thought it wise to
have nothing to do with any of the publications
of so dangerous a man as Milton before the
period of the Revolution ; and a curious letter
from Daniel Skinner to Pepys, dated from Rot
terdam, November 19th, 1676, shows that a man
might be injured in his public career by the rumour
that he had the works of Milton in his possession. Skinner agreed with Daniel Elzevir, the last
of that learned race, to print at Amsterdam certain
of Milton's writings which the poet had left to
him. In the meantime a surreptitious edition of
some State Letters appears, or as Skinner puts
it, "creeps out into the world." When Sir
Joseph Williamson, the Secretary of State, is
informed of this, and is asked to give a licence
for the proposed authentic edition, he replies
that "he could countenance nothing of that
man's (Milton) writings." Upon this, Skinner
gives up his scheme, and lends the papers to
Williamson, but he gets shabby treatment in
return, for on his arrival in Holland he finds
that those likely to employ him have been
warned against him as a dangerous character.[1]

The last instance of Pepys's weeding-out process shall be "Hudibras," and it is the most
curious of all. On the 26th of December, 1662,
we read in the "Diary:" "To the Wardrobe.
Hither come Mr. Battersby; and we falling into
a discourse of a new book of drollery, in verse,
called ' Hudebras,' I would needs go find it out,

[1] Smith's " Life, &c., of Pepys," vol. i. pp. 169-81.

and met with it at the Temple : cost me 2*s.* 6*d.*
But when I came to read it, it is so silly an
abuse of the Presbyter Knight going to the
warrs, that I am ashamed of it ; and by and by
meeting at Mr. Townsend's at dinner, I sold it
to him for 18*d.*" The book is dated 1663, and
could only have been published a few days when
Pepys bought and sold it at a loss of one shilling.

Warned by his previous experience, he would
not buy the second part when it came out, but
borrowed it " to read, to see if it be as good as
the first, which the world cry so mightily up,
though it hath not a good liking in me, though
I had tried but twice or three times reading to
bring myself to think it witty." [1]

He still remained uneasy, and tried to appreciate the fashionable poem, so that on December
10th, 1663, he thought it well to buy both parts
and place them in his library. Twenty years
after this he was still doing his best to find
" where the wit lies," for we find by the " Tangier
Diary" that he read the first two books on
board ship during the voyage out. [2]

The edition of " Hudibras " in the Library is
that of 1689, so that the earlier editions must
have been exchanged for it.

It does not say much for the literary taste of
the man who tried in vain to appreciate " Hudibras," that he found Cotton's " Scarronides, or
Virgile Travestie," " extraordinary good." [3]

The Library contains many very valuable

[1] " Diary," Nov. 28, 1663.
[2] Smith's " Life, &c., of Pepys," vol. i. p. 343.
[3] " Diary," March 2, 1663-64.

volumes ; as, for instance, there are nine Caxtons, and several Wynkyn de Wordes and Pynsons, but the chief interest centres in the various collections.

First and foremost among these are the five folio volumes of old English Ballads, which contain the largest series of broadside ballads ever brought together; the next in size being the well-known Roxburghe Collection, now in the British Museum.

Pepys has written on the title-page of his volumes : " Begun by Mr. Selden : Improved by ye addition of many Pieces elder thereto in Time, and the whole continued down to the year, 1700, When the Form till then peculiar thereto, vizt., of the Black Letter, with Picturs, seems (for cheapness sake) wholly laid aside, for that of the White Letter, without Pictures."

The Ballads are arranged under the following heads :—1. Devotion and Morality. 2. History, true and fabulous. 3. Tragedy, viz. murders, executions, judgements of God. 4. State and Times. 5. Love, pleasant. 6. Love, unfortunate. 7. Marriage, cuckoldry. 8. Sea : love, gallantry, and actions. 9. Drinking and good fellowship. 10. Humorous frolics and mirth. The total number of Ballads is 1800, of which 1376 are in black letter. Besides these there are four little duodecimo volumes, lettered as follows : Vol. 1. Penny Merriments. Vol. 2. Penny Witticisms. Vol. 3. Penny Compliments ; and Vol. 4. Penny Godlinesses.

Other collections are lettered " Old Novels," " Loose Plays," and " Vulgaria." There are six folio volumes of tracts on the Popish Plot, four quarto volumes of Sea Tracts, and a collection of News-Pamphlets for six years, that is, from January 1st, 1659-60, to January 1st, 1665-66, the time of the commencement of the Gazettes. Pepys was the first person to collect prints and drawings in illustration of London topography. These he left to his nephew, who added to the collection, and two thick folio volumes therefore came to the College with the other treasures.

Pepys's collections have a special interest, because he collected his books himself, knew all about them, and registered them with loving care. His various catalogues and indexes are marvels of neatness, and living as he did in a pre-bibliographical age, he deserves the greatest credit for the judgment exercised in their production. In the fifth volume of the little collection of books on Shorthand, there is an index of authors, with dates of publication and references to the volume in which each will be found; and the following, which is the title of one of the appendixes to the catalogue, will show how much labour was willingly expended in the production of these helps to research :" A chronological Deductions of the Variations of Stile (to be collected from yᵉ Alphabet of my books) in yᵉ language of England between ann. 700 & yᵉ attempt last made towards its refinement by Sir Philᵖ Sidney in his ' Arcadia,' between 1580 and 1590."

Neatness and the love of accuracy were ruling passions with Pepys, and when a catalogue was filled up with additional entries he had it re-

arranged and copied out. On "A Catalogue
and Alphabet to my books of Geography and
Hydrography, 1693-95," is the following memorandum : " Before this Index be transcribed far
to collect and alphabet the particulars contained
in the List of additional Books inserted at the
end, and that being done To incorporate both
them and the four particular Indexes preceding
into the Principal, and so as to unite the whole."

This is an interesting list : " Bibliotheca Nau-
tica, 1695. Catalogue of Authors (the perfectest
I can arrive at) upon the art and practice of
Navigation, with a Chronological Catalogue of
the most eminent Mathematicians of this Nation,
Antient and Modern, to the year 1673." Some
papers show how all this was arrived at, thus :
" Memorandum, to look over y\u1d49 Epistles and
Prefaces to all the Bookes in this Collection, of
which I am not maister, and y\u1d49 other allsoe, and
apply what is usefull through y\u1d49 whole." Mr.
Mount, "son-in-law and successor to the late
Mr. Fisher, master of the ancient shopp and our
only magazine of English Books of Navigation
at the Postern on Tower Hill," prepared a list,
and tried to answer Pepys's queries. The Diarist
was well known to all the booksellers, and he
doubtless was a good customer, although he
must have troubled them sometimes with his
fastidiousness. A note intended for Mr. Mount
may be looked upon as a good sample of many
more such memorandums, " To get me the ' Invention of y\u1d49 Art of Navigation,' a fair one for
y\u1d49 dirty one I bought of him."

Robert Scott, the famous bookseller of Little

Britain, when sending Pepys four scarce books, the total cost of which was only £1 14*s*., writes, " But without flattery I love to find a rare book for you." Herringman, of the " Blue Anchor," at the New Exchange in the Strand, Joseph Kirton, of St. Paul's Churchyard, who was ruined by the Fire of London, and Bagford, the title-robber, were some among the booksellers with whom Pepys had dealings.

Pepys was not a producer of *marginalia*, but some of his books contain an occasional note of interest; thus, in Cotton's "Compleat Gamester" (1674), " cocking " is described at page 206 as a "game of delight and pleasure," and Pepys added a manuscript note in the margin, " of barbarity." Not only does this give us Pepys's opinion of the sport very pithily, but it also illustrates a passage in the " Diary," where he describes his visit to the cock-fighting in Shoe Lane, and says he soon had enough of it.[1]

All the books in the Library have a bookplate in the inside cover. These are of different design, two having Pepys's portrait (one large and the other small), and one having S. P. and two anchors interlaced. Dr. Diamond writes in " Notes and Queries," that he once met with a large quantity of these bookplates in four varieties. Two were beautifully engraved by Faithorne, as is supposed, and two were by White. Some of them had a rough margin, and others were cut close up to the mantle on the arms.[2]

The motto which Pepys adopted, *Mens cujusque is est quisque*, was criticized by some of the

---

[1] " Diary," Dec. 21, 1663.
[2] " Notes and Queries," 1st S. vi. 534.

Admirals in 1690, and the Diarist desired his friend Hewer to point out to them, through Mr. Southerne, that it was a quotation from Cicero's " Somnium Scipionis," and that the thought was derived from Plato and wrought upon by St. Paul. The whole passage is, "Tu vero enitere, et sic habeto te non esse mortalem, sed Corpus hoc. Nec enim is est quem forma ista declarat; sed *mens cujusque is est quisque,* non ea figura quæ digito monstrari potest."

In concluding this notice of the Pepysian Library, it will be necessary to say a few words about the Musical collections. Pepys was not a mere amateur in music, but understood both theory and practice thoroughly, and he found consolation from it when troubles came upon him.[1] On November 2nd, 1661, he tried "to make a song in praise of a liberal genius," which he took his own to be, but the result did not prove to his mind; and on March 20th, 1668, he endeavoured to invent "a better theory of music than hath yet been abroad."

We have references in the "Diary" to four songs which he composed, and a notice of one which he only attempted.[2] On January 30th, 1659-60, he sang Montrose's verses on the execution of Charles I. beginning,—

"Great, good, and just, could I but rate,"

which he had set to music. He composed "Gaze not on Swans," on the 11th of February,

---

[1] "The little knowledge in music which I have, never was of more use to me than it is now, under the molestations of mind which I have at this time more than ordinary to contend with."—Smith's "Life, &c., of Pepys," vol. i. p. 199.

[2] "Diary," Nov. 30, 1667.

1661-62; but his grand achievement was the setting to music of the song,

> "Beauty retire ; thou doest my pitty move,
> Believe my pitty, and then trust my love," &c.,

from Davenant's Second Part of "The Siege of Rhodes," (act iv. sc. 2). Mrs. Knipp sang the song so well that the composer is forced to exclaim, that it seems to be a very fine song, and Captain Downing, "who loves and understands music," "extols it above everything he had ever heard."[1] Further evidence of the pride of the composer is seen in the fact that he had his portrait painted with the music of "Beauty retire" in his hand.

On April 6th, 1666, he began "putting notes" to Ben Jonson's song,

> "It is decreed—nor shall thy fate, O Rome!
> Resist my vow, though hills were set on hills,"

but he did not finish it until November 11th, 1666. He thought himself that it was even better than "Beauty retire," but the opinion of others is not given.

In the Pepysian Library is a volume of music, entitled, "Songs and other Compositions, Light, Grave and Sacred, for a single voice adjusted to the particular compass of mine ; with a thorough base on ye ghitare, by Cesare Morelli," which contains, among others, "Beauty retire," "It is decreed," and "To be or not to be." We find in the "Diary" that on November 13th, 1664, Pepys was learning to recite this speech of Hamlet.

[1] "Diary," Dec. 6, 1665 ; Feb. 23, 1665-66 ; Nov. 9, 1666.

In the present day, when few instruments besides the piano are heard in private houses, it is somewhat surprising to find how many were familiar to our ancestors in the seventeenth century, and a note of some of these will perhaps be thought interesting.

The lute was a favourite instrument when Pepys was young, and a good lutenist was in high esteem among his fellows. Lady Wright's butler gave Pepys a lesson or two, and in the first two years of the " Diary," there are several references to the hours the Diarist spent in practising; but for a time he was unable to play, as his lute was in pawn. Various forms of the violin were much used by Pepys, who rose by candlelight on the 3rd of December, 1660, and spent his morning in fiddling, till it was time to go to the office.

He and Mr. Hill were engaged for an hour or two in stringing a theorbo; and, on another occasion, he had it mended at a cost of twenty-six shillings. The flute and flageolet were always handy, as he could put them in his pocket, and use them as occasion required, particularly if he were in the neighbourhood of an echo. He mentions the guitar twice in the " Diary," but did not play on it, as he thought it a bauble. He afterwards altered his opinion, for he expressly charges Morelli, the arranger of his musical papers, to set a certain French song to the guitar; and, as may be seen above, many others were treated in the same way.[1] He is at one

[1] Letter dated Sept. 25, 1679, in Smith's "Life, &c., of Pepys," vol. i. p. 200.

time angry with The. Turner because she will not give him a lesson on the harpsichord ; and afterwards he buys a spinet.[1]

I here end the portion of this book which deals with the life of Pepys himself. The "Correspondence" discovers a more dignified character than the " Diary," but we cannot say for certain whether, if we had a diary of the later years, we should not read such a confession as this on the 27th of January, 1666-67:—" Went down and sat in a low room (at Sir Philip War-

---

[1] References to the "Diary" where the several instruments are mentioned :—

Lute, Jan. 25, 31, Feb. 4, March 18, 1659-60; Oct. 21, Nov. 9, 21, 1660; May 26, 1662.

Viol, Jan. 4, March 4, 6, Feb. 17, 1662-63 ; Sept. 28, 1664.

Lyre viol, Nov. 17, 1660; Oct. 16, Nov. 20, 1666.

Bass viol, July 5, 1662 ; April 17, 1663.

Arched viol, Oct. 5, 1664.

Treble, April 23, 1660.

Violin, March 6, 1659-60 ; April 6, 10, Nov. 21, 1660; April 23, June 6, 1661 ; June 15, 1663.

Theorbo, March 5, 1569-60; Nov. 24, Dec. 30, 1660; Oct. 9, 28, Dec. 7, 1661; Aug. 21, 1663 ; July 30, 1666.

Guitar, June 8, 1660; July 27, 1661.

Cittern, June 5, 1660 ; Jan. 17, 1660-61.

Bandore, Oct. 15, 1662.

Recorder, April 8, 1668.

Flageolet, Jan. 16, 30, Feb. 8, 9, 27, 1659-60; May 14, June 21, 1660 ; June 5, 1661; Jan. 20, 1667-68.

Triangle, March 18, 1662-63 ; April 1, 15, June 21, 1663.

Triangle virginal, June 14, 1661.

Virginals, Dec. 8, 1660 ; Sept. 2, 1666.

Spinet (espinette), April 4, July 10, 13, 1668.

Harpsichord, March 17, 1659-60 ; Feb. 26, 1660-61 ; April 31, June 18, 1661 ; Sept. 9, 1664 ; April 4, 1668.

Dulcimer, June 23, 1662.

Trumpet marine, Oct. 24, 1667.

wick's), reading 'Erasmus de scribendis epis-
tolis,' a very good book, especially one letter
of advice to a courtier, most true and good,
which made me once resolve to tear out the two
leaves that it was writ in, but I forbore it."

CHAPTER VI.

LONDON.

"I have vow'd to spend all my life in London. People do really live no where else; they breathe and move and have a kind of insipid dull being, but there is no life but in London. I had rather be Countess of Puddle-dock than Queen of Sussex."—T. SHADWELL'S *Epsom Wells*, 1676.

AVING concluded that portion of our subject which relates more particularly to the personal character of Pepys, we now pass on to the general consideration of the component parts of the world he lived in. As Pepys was a thorough Londoner, and as most of the circumstances related in the "Diary" refer to London, I propose to commence with a notice of some parts of the capital at the time of the Restoration.

The almost constant use of the River as a highway is a marked feature of the habits of the time, which is illustrated by the fact that Pepys makes a point of mentioning that he went to a place "by land," when from some cause or other he did not take a boat; thus, on March 8th, 1659-60, we read, " Home about two o'clock, and took my wife *by land* to Paternoster Row, to buy some paragon for a petticoat, and so home again." When Pepys was appointed Clerk of the Acts, and he was settled in his house in Seething Lane, he found that a constant communication was necessary between the Navy Office in the City, and the Admiralty at Whitehall. In his frequent journeys by boat from place to place, he often stopped at Blackfriars, in order to visit Lord Sandwich at the "Wardrobe," where the royal clothes were kept. Sometimes, when there were shows and pageants on the Thames, it was no easy matter to get a boat, and on the occasion of the Queen's coming to town from Hampton Court, when her barge was attended by ten thousand barges and boats, Pepys in vain tempted the watermen with a bribe of eight shillings.[1] One of the chief dangers of boat traffic was found in "shooting" London Bridge, and it was generally considered good policy to get out of the boat and pass from side to side on foot instead of going through the arches. One Sunday night,[2] however, our Diarist passed through the "rapids," and did not like the sensation he experienced. "And so to Whitehall to Sir G. Carteret, and so to the Chappell, where I challenged my pew as Clerke of the Privy Seale, and had it, and then walked home with Mr. Blagrave, to his old house in the Fishyard, and there he had a pretty kinswoman that sings, and we did sing some holy things, and afterwards others

[1] "Diary," Aug. 23, 1662.   [2] April 20, 1662.

came in, and so I left them, and by water through the bridge (which did trouble me) home, and so to bed." It was not, however, much safer on the bridge than under it, for on one occasion Pepys nearly broke his leg there. He had been in Southwark, spending the evening at the well-known inn, the " Bear at the bridge foot," and when he wished to get home he could not find his coach, so he was forced to go over the bridge through the darkness and the dirt. His leg fell into a hole, although there was a constable standing by to warn persons away from the dangerous spot. At first he thought his leg was broken, but when he was pulled up he was found not to be much hurt.[1]

One of the advantages which our forefathers possessed over us, was to be found in the nearness of the fields and country lanes to their offices and shops. Pepys often indulged himself in a walk or a romp over the grass, in places that are now covered with bricks. On July 29th, 1669, he writes : " I dined, and in the afternoon, with Dick Vines and his brother Payton, we walked to Lisson-greene and Marybone and back again." On October 9th, 1660, he says, " I met with Sir W. Pen again, and so with him to Redriffe by water, and from thence walked over the fields to Deptford, the first pleasant walk I have had a great while." One Sunday he goes to Clerkenwell Church, and walks home across the fields.[2] At another time he takes the air in the fields beyond St. Pancras.[3] There

---

[1] " Diary," Oct. 26, 1664.   [2] Oct. 2, 1664.
[3] April 23, 1665.

is, however, another side to this pleasing picture; for these places were not always safe, and the pleasure-seekers were sometimes alarmed. One day Pepys and a friend were walking from Chelsea into town, when they were joined by a companion, and we read that, "coming among some trees near the Neate houses he began to whistle, which did give us some suspicion, but it proved that he that answered him was Mr. Marsh (the Lutenist) and his wife, and so we all walked to Westminster together."[1] In the following year Pepys walked from Woolwich to Rotherhithe on a fine moonshiny night, but he was accompanied by three or four armed men.[2] It gave him much satisfaction to be thought of enough importance to have such an escort provided for him unasked.

So much for the country parts near the town, but the streets appear to have been even less safe after dark. Those who wanted to find their way had to carry links,[3] as those without them fared but badly. The gates of the City were shut at night, but this had the effect of shutting in some of the ill-disposed as well as in shutting out others. Pepys and his party on coming home one night from the play found the gates closed. He goes on to say in the "Diary," "At Newgate we find them in trouble, some thieves having this night broke open prison. So we through and home; and our coachman was fain to drive hard from two or three fellows which he said were rogues,

[1] "Diary," Aug. 19, 1661.   [2] Sept. 19, 1662.
[3] Sept. 10, Nov. 15, 1661.

that he met at the end of Blowbladder Street." [1]

A London mob has never been famed for politeness, and we do not gain a very pleasing view of those in Pepys's day from some of the entries in the " Diary." On the 27th of November, 1662, the Russian Ambassador entered the city, and the trained bands, the King's Life Guards, and wealthy citizens clad in black velvet coats with gold chains were ready to receive him. Pepys did not see the Ambassador in his coach, but he was pleased with the " attendants in their habits and fur caps, very handsome, comely men, and most of them with hawks upon their fists to present to the King." He adds, however, " But, Lord! to see the absurd nature of Englishmen, that cannot forbear laughing and jeering at everything that looks strange."

The high road of Newgate Street was formerly crowded in a most inconvenient degree by the shambles of the butchers, and our Diarist once got into trouble while driving past them. The account of this adventure is amusing, from the ease with which he got out of his difficulty. " My coach plucked down two pieces of beef into the dirt, upon which the butchers stopped the horses, and a great rout of people in the street, crying that he had done him 40s. and £5 worth of hurt; but going down I saw that he had little or none ; and so I give them a shilling for it, and they were well contented." [2]

The following is a good sample of the quarrels that were constantly occurring ; there being no authority to put a stop to such exhibitions.

[1] " Diary," Aug. 1, 1667.   [2] Dec. 15, 1662.

"Great discourse of the fray yesterday in
Moorfields; how the butchers at first did beat
the weavers (between whom there hath been
ever an old competition for mastery), but at last
the weavers rallied and beat them. At first the
butchers knocked down all for weavers that had
green or blue aprons, till they were fain to pull
them off and put them in their breeches. At last
the butchers were fain to pull off their sleeves,
that they might not be known, and were soundly
beaten out of the field, and some deeply wounded
and bruised ; till at last the weavers went out
triumphing, calling £100 for a butcher."[1] Moorfields, now occupied by Finsbury Square and
Circus and the surrounding streets, was at this
time one of the chief recreation grounds outside
the City walls. It was partly given up to the
laundresses and bleachers; and boxers and cudgel-
players found in it a congenial sphere for their
amusements. On an emergency, the troops
were mustered on the fenny ground.

None of Pepys's days passed without a visit to
some tavern, for a morning draught, or a pint of
wine after dinner. The notice of these little
jovialities has preserved to us the names of
several old inns, such as the Star, Half Moon,
Harp and Ball, Swan, Bull Head, Plough, Lion,
Cock, Greyhound, Globe, Mitre, Cardinal's Cap,
King's Head, Hercules Pillars, Trumpet, &c.
We read in the "Diary," that on March 6th,
1659-60, there was a friendly meeting at one of
these places : "While we were drinking, in comes
Mr. Day, a carpenter in Westminster, to tell me
that it was Shrove tuesday, and that I must go

[1] "Diary," July 26, 1664.

with him to their yearly club upon this day, which,
I confess, I had quite forgot. So I went to the
Bell, where were Mr. Eglin, Veezy, Vincent, a
butcher, one more, and Mr. Tanner, with whom
I played upon a viall and viallin, after dinner,
and were very merry, with a special good dinner,
a leg of veal and bacon, two capons and fritters,
with abundance of wine." On January 10th,
1659-60, Pepys "drank a pint of wine at the
Star, in Cheapside," and on May 24th, 1662, he
took his "morning draft" at the same house.
These entries show how rapidly our forefathers
went from place to place, and how little they
thought of the distance between the City and
Westminster; this facility being evidently caused
by the water carriage. On a certain day Pepys
starts from Axe Yard, drinks his morning draught
with a friend, at the Sun, in Chancery Lane, and
then goes to Westminster Hall. At noon he visits
the Swan, in Fish Street; then goes back to
Westminster, looking in at the Coffee Club and
the Hall before going home.[1] The Swan, in Old
Fish Street, is mentioned in an inquisition held
before the mayor and aldermen in 1413, as
"The Swan on the Hoop." The house was destroyed in the Great Fire, but was rebuilt and
advertised to be let in the "Spectator" of April
25th, 1712.

King Street, Westminster, was full of inns.
Pepys's favourite haunt was the Leg, where an
ordinary was held. On December 6th, 1660, he
and Mr. Moore went there, and "dined together
on a neat's tongue and udder." Again, on April

[1] "Diary," Jan. 20, 1659-60.

6th, 1661, "with Mr. Creed and More to the Leg, in the Palace, to dinner, which I gave them, and after dinner I saw the girl of the house, being very pretty, go into a chamber, and I went in after her and kissed her." Two other King Street taverns were visited by Pepys, in July and August, 1660—viz., the Sun and the Dog. These houses of entertainment are both noted as haunts of Ben Jonson, in Herrick's Address to the Shade of "Glorious Ben."

> "Ah, Ben!
> Say how or when
> Shall we, thy guests,
> Meet at these lyric feasts
> Made at the Sun,
> The Dog, the Triple Tun?
> Where we such clusters had
> As made us nobly wild, not mad!
> And yet such verse of thine
> Outdid the meat, outdid the frolic wine."

Another Sun, that behind the Exchange, was a famous house frequented by Pepys; it was re-built after the Fire by John Wadlow, the host of the Devil Tavern, and son of the more famous Simon Wadlow whom Ben Jonson dubbed "Old Sym, the King of Skinkers." Pepys often went with his colleagues to the Dolphin, and drank "a great quantity of sack" there. On April 25th, 1661, he "went to an ordinary at the King's Head, in Tower Street, and there had a dirty dinner." On June 21st, of the same year, we read, "This morning, going to my father's, I met him, and so he and I went and drank our morning draft at the Samson, in Paul's Churchyard." On October 9th, he went after

the theatre " to the Fleece tavern, in Covent
Garden, where Luellin, and Blurton, and my old
friend, Frank Bagge, was to meet me, and there
staid till late, very merry." This was the chief
tavern in Covent Garden, but being the resort
of bullies, it obtained a very unenviable noto-
riety. The Green Dragon, on Lambeth Hill, the
Golden Lion, near Charing Cross, the Old Three
Tuns at the same place, and the Pope's Head,
in Chancery Lane, are among the other taverns
mentioned by Pepys. The Rhenish Wine-house,
in the Steelyard, Upper Thames Street, was a
favourite resort, and is frequently mentioned by
the old dramatists. Pepys went there sometimes, but he more often visited another house
so called in Cannon Row. All kinds of drinks
were alike agreeable to our Diarist, and he did
not even disdain "mum," a strong beer brewed
from wheat, which was once popular and sold
at special mum-houses.

These constant visits to taverns were not
very conducive to temperate habits of life, and
we therefore read much of the midday revellings
of the business men. One day, Pepys being a
little more sober than Sir W. Penn, has to lead
that worthy knight home through the streets,
and on another occasion he resolves not to drink
any more wine,—a rash vow which he forthwith
breaks. Sometimes with amusing casuistry he
tries to keep his vow to the letter while he breaks
it in the spirit; thus, to allude again to the
characteristic entry, on October 29th, 1663, we
read, "Went into the Buttery, and there stayed
and talked, and then into the Hall again ; and

there wine was offered, and they drunk, I only
drinking some hypocras,[1] which do not break my
vow, it being, to the best of my present judge-
ment, only a mixed compound drink, and not
any wine. If I am mistaken, God forgive me!
but I hope and do think I am not."

We have seen Pepys dividing his time pretty
equally between the City and Westminster, and
doing official work in both places. In Westminster Hall he was on friendly terms with all the
shopkeepers who formerly kept their little stalls
in that place, and most of the watermen at the
different stairs, who recognized his genial face,
were emulous of the honour of carrying him as
a fare. There is an entry in the " Diary " which
records a curious custom amongst the stationers
of the Hall. Pepys went on January 30th,
1659-60, to "Westminster Hall, where Mrs.
Lane and the rest of the maids had their white
scarfs, all having been at the burial of a young
bookseller."

Two of the most important events in the history of Old London,—viz., the Plague and the
Fire,—are very fully described in the " Diary."

On the 7th of June, 1667, Pepys for the first
time saw two or three houses marked with the
red cross, and the words " Lord have mercy
upon us " on the doors; and the sight made him
feel so ill at ease that he was forced to buy some
roll tobacco to smell and chew. Then we read
of the rapid increase in the numbers of those
struck down; of those buried in the open Tuttle-

Hippocras, a drink composed of red or white wine, with
the addition of sugar and spices.

fields at Westminster; and of the unfriendly feelings that were engendered by fear.

Pepys remained either in town or in its neighbourhood during the whole time of the raging of the pestilence; and on the 4th of September, 1665, he wrote an interesting letter to Lady Carteret, from Woolwich, in which he said: "The absence of the court and emptiness of the city takes away all occasion of news, save only such melancholy stories as would rather sadden than find your ladyship any divertissement in the hearing. I have stayed in the city till above 7,400 died in one week, and of them above 6,000 of the plague, and little noise heard day or night but tolling of bells; till I could walk Lumber Street and not meet twenty persons from one end to the other, and not fifty upon the Exchange; till whole families, ten and twelve together, have been swept away; till my very physician, Dr. Burnet, who undertook to secure me against any infection, having survived the month of his own house being shut up, died himself of the plague; till the nights, though much lengthened, are grown too short to conceal the burials of those that died the day before, people being thereby constrained to borrow daylight for that service; lastly, till I could find neither meat nor drink safe, the butcheries being everywhere visited, my brewer's house shut up, and my baker, with his whole family, dead of the plague."

He then relates a romantic incident which had just occurred, and a note of which he also inserted in his "Diary:" "Greenwich begins

apace to be sickly; but we are, by the command
of the king, taking all the care we can to prevent its growth; and meeting to that purpose
yesterday, after sermon with the town officers,
many doleful informations were brought us, and,
among others, this, which I shall trouble your
ladyship with the telling. Complaint was brought
us against one in the town for receiving into his
house a child brought from an infected house in
London. Upon inquiry, we found that it was
the child of a very able citizen in Gracious
Street, who, having lost already all the rest of
his children, and himself and wife being shut up,
and in despair of escaping, implored only the
liberty of using the means for the saving of this
only babe, which, with difficulty, was allowed,
and they suffered to deliver it, stripped naked,
out at a window, into the arms of a friend, who,
shifting into fresh cloathes, conveyed it thus
to Greenwich, where, upon this information from
Alderman Hooker, we suffer it to remain."

On the 20th of this same month of September
we read in the "Diary:" "But, Lord! what a
sad time it is to see no boats upon the River,
and grass grows all up and down White Hall
court, and nobody but poor wretches in the
streets." And on October 16th, Pepys is told
that, in Westminster, "there is never a physician, and but one apothecary left,—all being
dead."

In the following January, the question of attending to the overcrowded churchyards had
begun to agitate the public mind; and those
who lived in their immediate neighbourhood

were anxious that they should be covered with lime.[1] Not many months after this the greater portion of the city had become a void.

On the 2nd of September, 1666, Pepys was called up at three o'clock to see a fire; but not thinking much of it, he went to bed again. When, however, he got up, he found that about 300 houses had been burnt in the night. All were now busy in moving their property from place to place; and the women worked as hard as the men in doing what was needed. Some almost incredible instances of meanness are recorded in the "Diary," respecting those rich men who gave shillings grudgingly to those who saved their all. Alderman Starling, whose house was saved by the Navy Office men, while the next house was burning, gave 2s. 6d. to be divided among thirty of them, and then quarrelled with some that would remove the rubbish out of the way of the fire, on the score that they came to steal. Sir William Coventry told Pepys of another case which occurred in Holborn. An offer was made to one whose house was in great danger, to stop the fire for a sum that came to about 2s. 6d. a man, but he would only give 1s. 6d.[2]

Clothworkers' Hall burnt for three days and nights, on account of the oil in the cellars; and so intense was the heat caused by extension of the fire over a large space, that the ground of the City continued to smoke even in December.[3]

Moorfields was the chief resort of the house-

[1] "Diary," Jan. 31, 1665-66.   [2] Sept. 8, 1666.
[3] Dec. 14, 1666.

less Londoners, and soon paved streets and two-storey houses were seen in that swampy place, the City having let the land on leases of seven years.

It was said that this national disaster had been foretold, and the prophecies of Nostrodamus and Mother Shipton were referred to. Sir Roger L'Estrange, the Licenser of Almanacs, told Sir Edward Walker that most of those that came under his notice foretold the fire, but that he had struck the prophecy out.[1] Lady Carteret told Pepys a curious little fact, which was, that abundance of pieces of burnt papers were driven by the wind as far as Cranborne, in Windsor Forest; "and, among others, she took up one, or had one brought her to see, which was a little bit of paper that had been printed, whereon there remained no more nor less than these words : ' Time is, it is done.'"[2]

It is well known that the unfortunate Roman Catholics were charged with the crime of having set London on fire, and there appears to have been a very sufficient reason why the people should persist in affirming this fable. The judges determined, in the case of disputed liability between landlord and tenant, that the tenants should bear the loss in all casualties of fire arising in their own houses or in those of their neighbours; but if the fire was caused by an enemy they were not liable. As one poor man was convicted and hanged for the crime, it was held that the landlords must be mulcted.[3]

[1] Ward's " Diary," p. 94.   [2] " Diary," Feb. 3, 1666-67.
[3] Nov. 5, 1666.

I

Public opinion shifted about in this matter, for we read that on September 16th, 1667, Pepys saw "a printed account of the examinations taken, touching the burning . . . . showing the plot of the Papists therein, which it seems hath been ordered to be burnt by the hands of the hangman, in Westminster Palace." [1]

London remained in ruins for many months, and as late as April 23rd, 1668, Pepys describes himself as wearily walking round the walls in order to escape the dangers within. At last new streets of houses arose from the ruins, but, unfortunately, in spite of the proposals of Wren, Hooke, and Evelyn for erecting a handsome and well-arranged city, the old lines were in almost every case retained.

A passage in the " Diary" in which Pepys remarks on the great streets "marked out with piles drove in the ground," and expresses the opinion that, if ever so built, they will form " a noble sight," would seem to show that at one time a better plan of building was contemplated. [2]

Had the plan suggested in Parliament by Colonel Birch been carried out, great difficulties would have been avoided. His proposal was, that the whole ground should be sold and placed in trust. Then the trustees were to sell again, with preference to the former owners, by which

[1] The title of this very rare pamphlet is—" A true and faithful account of the several Informations exhibited to the Honourable Committee appointed by the Parliament to inquire into the late dreadful burning of the City of London. Printed in the year 1667." 4to. pp. 35.

[2] "Diary," March 29, 1667.

means a general plan of building might have been adopted ; but an unequalled opportunity of making London into a fine city was let slip.[1]

At one time it was supposed that the Fire would cause a westward march of trade, but the City asserted the old supremacy when it was rebuilt.

Soon after the conclusion of the " Diary," Pepys left the Navy Office, and the latter years of his life were spent partly in York Buildings and partly at Clapham. It was after the Restoration that the West End grew into importance, and the house at the foot of Buckingham Street, from the windows of which Pepys could look out upon the river, was not built when the Diarist was settled in Crutched Friars. It was erected upon part of the site of York House, whose last resident was the worthless Buckingham :—

> " Beggar'd by fools, whom still he found too late,
> He had his jest, and they had his estate."

This house, in which Pepys was pleased to find " the remains of the noble soul of the late Duke of Buckingham appearing, in the door-cases and the windows,"[2] was sold by his son and demolished in 1672.

As Pepys left London so it remained in its chief features for more than one hundred years, and it was not until the beginning of the present century that the vast extension of the town to the north and south began to make itself felt.

[1] " Diary," Feb. 24, 1666-67.   [2] June 6, 1663.

CHAPTER VII.

PEPYS'S RELATIONS, FRIENDS, AND ACQUAINTANCES.

"If a man does not make new acquaintances as he advances through life he will soon find himself left alone; a man should keep his friendship in constant repair."—DR. JOHNSON.

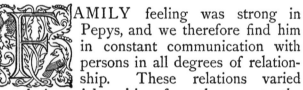

AMILY feeling was strong in Pepys, and we therefore find him in constant communication with persons in all degrees of relationship. These relations varied greatly in social position, from the peer to the little shopkeeper. Thus we find that one Pepys was a Lord Chief Justice of Ireland; another a Member of Parliament; another a Doctor of Divinity; another a goldsmith, and another a turner.

In later life, when Pepys had risen greatly in social importance, the relations were not so much associated with, and a more distinguished circle of friends make their appearance. This gradual dropping away of the relations may have been caused by decrease of the family, for the Diarist on one occasion writes : " It is a sad consideration how the Pepys's decay, and nobody almost that I know in a present way of increasing them."[1] The members of Pepys's immediate family have already been alluded to, and we have seen how his father, John Pepys, the tailor, retired to Brampton in 1661. The old man died in 1680, and desired by his will that all the lands and goods left him by his brother Robert should be delivered up to his eldest son. He also left £5 to the poor of Brampton, and 40s. to the poor of Ellington, and the remainder of his property to be divided amongst his three children—Samuel and John and Paulina Jackson. John, however, died before him.

Of the numerous cousins who figure in the " Diary," the Turners and the Joyces are the most frequently referred to. Serjeant John Turner and his wife Jane, who lived in Salisbury Court, were not very highly esteemed by Sir William Baker, who called the one a false fellow and the other a false woman, and Pepys does not appear altogether to have disliked hearing him say so.[2]

Their daughter Theophila was, however, a favourite with Pepys, and on March 3, 1662-63, she showed him his name on her breast as her valentine, "which," he observes, "will cost me 20s." Four days afterwards he bought her a dozen pairs of white gloves.

The Joyces were never much liked by Pepys, but at one time he thought it well to be friends

[1] " Diary," April 26, 1664.   [2] Oct. 10, 1664.

with them, as he writes on the 6th of August, 1663,—"I think it convenient to keep in with the Joyces against a bad day, if I should have occasion to make use of them." William Joyce was good-natured, but Pepys wearied of his company because he was "an impertinent coxcomb" and too great a talker. As is often the case with our Diarist, he gives a different character of the man on another occasion. He writes, "A cunning, crafty fellow he is, and dangerous to displease, for his tongue spares nobody."[1]

Anthony Joyce was in business, and on one occasion he supplied Pepys with some tallow, payment for which he was unduly anxious about, so that the purchaser was vexed.[2] Anthony gave over trade in 1664, but was ruined by the Fire; and afterwards kept the "Three Stags" at Holborn Conduit. William was greatly disgusted when his brother became a publican. Pepys says he ranted about it "like a prince, calling him hosteller and his sister hostess."[3]

In January, 1667-68, Anthony threw himself into a pond at Islington, but being seen by a poor woman, he was got out before life was extinct. "He confessed his doing the thing, being led by the devil; and do declare his reason to be, his trouble in having forgot to serve God as he ought since he came to this new employment."[4] He died soon after this, and his friends were in great fear that his goods would be seized upon on the ground that he was a suicide. Pepys

[1] "Diary," Aug. 14, 1664.   [2] May 31, 1662.
[3] Dec. 6, 1666.   [4] Jan. 21, 1667-68.

used all his influence to save the estate, and obtained the King's promise that it should not be taken from the widow and children. Those who were likely to benefit by the confiscation gave much trouble, and managed to stop the coroner's verdict for a time. At last, however, the widow's friends on the jury saved her from further anxiety by giving a verdict that her husband died of a fever. " Some opposition there was, the foreman pressing them to declare the cause of the fever, thinking thereby to obstruct it ; but they did adhere to their verdict, and would give no reason." [1]

Kate Joyce (Anthony's widow) was a pretty woman, and caused Pepys some trouble. She had many offers of marriage, and after a short period of widowhood she married one Hollingshed, a tobacconist. [2] Pepys was disgusted, and left her to her own devices with the expression, " As she brews let her bake."

Mrs. Kite, the butcher, was another of Pepys's aunts whose company he did not greatly appreciate. He was, however, her executor, and at her death he calls her daughter ugly names, thus : " Back again with Peg Kite, who will be I doubt a troublesome carrion to us executors." [3] A few days after she is called " a slut," [4] and when she declares her firm intention to marry " the beggarly rogue the weaver," the executors are " resolved neither to meddle nor make with her." [5]

---

[1] " Diary," Feb. 18, 1667-68. [2] May 11, 1668.
[3] Sept. 15, 1661. [4] Oct. 2, 1661.
[5] Nov. 7, 1661.

Few of these family connections were left
when Pepys himself died, for in the long list of
persons to whom rings and mourning were given
the following relations only are noticed:—Samuel
and John Jackson, sons of Pall Jackson (born
Pepys), the two nephews ; Balthazar St. Michel,
brother-in-law, and his daughter Mary ; Roger
Pepys, of Impington, Edward Pickering, Tim
Turner, the minister of Tooting ; Mr. Bellamy,
Mr. and Mrs. Mathews, Dr. Montagu, Dean of
Durham ; and the Earl of Sandwich.

Dr. Daniel Milles, the minister of St. Olave's,
Hart Street, was one of Pepys's life-long acquaintances—we can hardly call him friend, for
the Diarist never seems to have cared much for
him.   We read how he " nibbled at the Common
Prayer," then how he took to the surplice, and
gradually changed from the minister under the
Commonwealth to the Church of England rector
under Charles.   A year or two after he ought to
have been accustomed to the Prayer-Book, he
made an extraordinary blunder in reading the
service.   Instead of saying, "We beseech Thee
to preserve to our use the kindly fruits of the
earth," he said : " Preserve to our use our gracious Queen Katherine."[1]   In 1667 he was presented to the rectory of Wanstead, in Essex,
and in order to qualify him for holding two
livings at the same time, he was made one of
the Duke of York's chaplains.[2]

It is often amusing to notice how frequently
Pepys changed his opinion of certain persons :
for instance, in 1660, he calls Mr. Milles "a very

[1] "Diary," April 17, 1664.   [2] May 29, 1667.

good minister,"[1] while in 1667 he styles him "a lazy fat priest."[2]

Two men who occupy a considerable space in the "Diary" are the two clerks, Thomas Hayter and William Hewer. Most of those who were in any way connected with Pepys were helped on by him in the struggle of life, and his clerks were no exception to this rule. Hayter was appointed Clerk of the Acts in 1674, and Secretary of the Admiralty in 1679; and subsequently Hewer was a Commissioner of the Navy and Treasurer for Tangier. Some of those whose fortunes had been made by Pepys turned out ungrateful when their patron was out of power ; but Hewer continued to be a comfort to the old man to the last.

Allusion has already been made to Pepys's helpers in the arrangement of his books and papers, and therefore much need not be said about them here. While the "Diary" was being written, Pepys obtained help from his wife and brother-in-law and servants ; but when he became more opulent he employed educated men to write for him. One of these was Cesare Morelli, an Italian, recommended by Thomas Hill. He arranged Pepys's musical papers, and in 1681 he acknowledged the receipt of £7, which made a total of £85 17s. 6d. received from Pepys during a period extending from November 4th, 1678, to August 13th, 1681.[3] This friendship, which does Pepys much credit, caused him some trouble, as Morelli was a Ro-

[1] "Diary," Aug. 19, 1660.   [2] June 3, 1667.
[3] Smith's "Life, Journals, &c., of Samuel Pepys," vol. i. p. 270.

man Catholic, and the zealots falsely affirmed that he was also a priest.

Pepys early made the acquaintance of Dr. Petty, who was a member of the Rota Club; and he frequently mentions him and his double-bottomed boat (named " The Experiment ") in the " Diary." Many anecdotes are told of Petty by Aubrey—how he was poor at Paris, and lived for a week on three pennyworth of walnuts; how, while teaching anatomy at Oxford, he revived Nan Green after her execution, and how he obtained the Professorship of Music at Gresham College by the interest of Captain John Graunt, author of " Observations on the Bills of Mortality." At the Restoration Petty was knighted, and made Surveyor-General of Ireland, where he gathered a large fortune. Pepys considered Sir William Petty to be one of the most rational men that he ever heard speak with tongue;[1] and he was also an excellent droll. The latter character was proved when a soldier knight challenged him to fight. He was very short-sighted; and, having the privilege of nominating place and weapon for the duel, he chose a dark cellar for the place, and a great carpenter's axe for the weapon. This turned the challenge into ridicule, and the duel never came off.

Petty was a prominent Fellow of the Royal Society, and about 1665 he presented a paper on " The Building of Ships," which the President (Lord Brouncker) took away and kept to himself, according to Aubrey, with the remark, that " 'twas too great an arcanum of State to be

[1] " Diary, Jan. 27, 1663-64.

commonly perused." Aubrey also relates an excellent story *apropos* of the Royal Society's anniversary meeting on St. Andrew's Day. The
relater had remarked that he thought it was not
well the Society should have pitched upon the
patron of Scotland's day, as they should have
taken St. George or St. Isidore (a philosopher
canonized). "No," said Petty, "I would rather
have had it on St. Thomas's Day, for he
would not believe till he had seen and put his
fingers into the holes, according to the motto,
Nullius in verba."

Among the City friends of Pepys, the Houb-
lons stand forward very prominently. James
Houblon, the father, died in 1682, in his ninetieth
year, and was buried in the church of St. Mary
Woolnoth, his epitaph being written in Latin by
Pepys. His five sons are frequently mentioned
in the "Diary," but James and Wynne were
more particularly his friends, and were among
those who received mourning rings after his
death. In 1690, when Pepys was committed to
the Gate-house, and four gentlemen came forward to bail him, James Houblon was one of
these four.[1]

Alderman Backwell, the chief goldsmith of his
time, had many dealings with Pepys, who went
to him at one time to change some Dutch money,
and at another to weigh Lord Sandwich's cru-
sados.[2] Probably our Diarist was rather trouble-

---

[1] Smith's "Life, &c., of Pepys," vol. ii. p. 352.
[2] A Portuguese coin worth from 2*s.* 3*d.* to 4*s.* :—
   " Believe me, I had rather lost my purse
   Full of cruzados."—*Othello*, iii. 4.

some at times, for once he bought a pair of candlesticks, which soon afterwards he changed for a cup, and at last he obtained a tankard in place of the cup.   In 1665 there was a false report that Backwell was likely to become a bankrupt; but in 1672, on the closing of the Exchequer, the King owed him £293,994 16s. 6d., and he was in consequence ruined by Charles's dishonest action. On his failure many of his customers' accounts were taken over by the predecessors of the present firm of Child and Co., the bankers.

We shall have occasion to allude in the next chapter to some of those who were brought in contact with Pepys in the way of business; but it is necessary to say a few words here about two men who were both official acquaintances and personal friends.   Sir Anthony Deane was one of the most accomplished shipbuilders of his time, and a valuable public servant, but he did not escape persecution.   A joint charge of betraying the secrets of the British navy was made against Pepys and Deane in 1675.   In 1668 Deane had held the office of shipwright at Portsmouth, and afterwards he was appointed a Commissioner of the Navy.   In 1680 he resigned his post, but in 1681 he again formed one of the new Board appointed by James II., and hoped to help in improving the condition of the navy, which was then in a very reduced state.   After the Revolution he sought retirement in Worcestershire, and the two old men corresponded and compared notes on their states of mind.   Deane wrote to Pepys: " These are only to let you know I am alive.   I have nothing to do but read, walk and prepare for all chances, attending this obliging world. I have the old soldier's request, a little space between business and the grave, which is very pleasant on many considerations. As most men towards their latter end grow serious, so do I in assuring you that I am," &c. [1] Pepys replied : " I am alive too, I thank God! and as serious, I fancy, as you can be, and not less alone. Yet I thank God too! I have not within me one of those melancholy misgivings that you seem haunted with. The worse the world uses me, the better I think I am bound to use myself. Nor shall any solicitousness after the felicities of the next world (which yet I bless God! I am not without care for) ever stifle the satisfactions arising from a just confidence of receiving some time or other, even here, the reparation due to such unaccountable usage as I have sustained in this." [2]

Mr. (afterwards Sir Henry) Sheres is frequently referred to in the latter pages of the " Diary," but the friendship which sprang up between him and Pepys dates from a period subsequent to the completion of that work. Sheres accompanied the Earl of Sandwich into Spain, where he acquired that Spanish character which clung to him through life. He returned to England in September, 1667, carrying letters from Lord Sandwich. Pepys found him "a good ingenious man," and was pleased with his discourse.

In the following month Sheres returned to·

[1] Smith's "Life, &c. of Pepys," vol. ii. p. 291.
[2] Ibid., vol. ii. p. 238.

Spain, being the bearer of a letter from Pepys to Lord Sandwich.[1] Subsequently he was engaged at Tangier, and received £100 for drawing a plate of the fortification, as already related.[2] He was grateful to Pepys for getting him the money, and had a silver candlestick made after a pattern he had seen in Spain, for keeping the light from the eyes, and gave it to the Diarist.[3] On the 5th of April, 1669, he treated the Pepys household, at the Mulberry Garden, to a Spanish *olio*, a dish of meat and savoury herbs, which they greatly appreciated.

On the death of Sir Jonas Moore, Pepys wrote to Colonel Legge (afterward Lord Dartmouth) a strong letter of recommendation in favour of Sheres, whom he describes " as one of whose loyalty and duty to the King and his Royal Highness and acceptance with them I assure myself; of whose personal esteem and devotion towards you (Col. Legge), of whose uprightness of mind, universality of knowledge in all useful learning particularly mathematics, and of them those parts especially which relate to gunnery and fortification ; and lastly, of whose vigorous assiduity and sobriety I dare bind myself in asserting much farther than, on the like occasion, I durst pretend to of any other's undertaking, or behalf of mine."[4] Sheres obtained the appointment, and served under Lord Dartmouth at the demolition of Tangier in 1683. He appears to have been knighted in the following year, and

[1] Smith's " Life, &c. of Pepys," vol. i. p. 117.
[2] " Diary," Jan. 18, 1668-69.   [3] Jan. 28, 1668-69.
[4] Smith's " Life, &c. of Pepys," vol. i. p. 303.

to have devoted himself to literature in later life. He translated "Polybius," and some "Dialogues" of Lucian, and was the author of a pretty song. His name occurs among those who received mourning rings on the occasion of Pepys's death.

Raleigh said, "There is nothing more becoming any wise man than to make choice of friends, for by them thou shalt be judged what thou art." If so, it speaks well for Pepys that the names of most of the worthies of his time are to be found amongst his correspondents. Newton and Wallis stand out among the philosophers; the two Gales (Thomas and Roger), Evelyn, and Bishop Gibson among antiquaries and historians; Kneller among artists; and Bishop Compton and Nelson, the author of the "Festivals and Fasts," among theologians.

The letters of some of these men have been printed in the "Correspondence" appended to the "Diary," and in Smith's "Life, Journals, and Correspondence of Samuel Pepys;" but many more still remain in manuscript in various collections.

CHAPTER VIII.

THE NAVY.

"Our seamen, whom no danger's shape could fright,
Unpaid, refuse to mount their ships for spite,
Or to their fellows swim on board the Dutch,
Who show the tempting metal in their clutch."
MARVELL'S *Instructions to a Painter.*

OUR literature is singularly deficient in accounts of the official history of the navy. There are numerous books containing lives of seamen and the history of naval actions, but little has been written on the management at home. The best account of naval affairs is to be found in the valuable "Tracts" of the stout old sailor Sir William Monson, which are printed in "Churchill's Voyages."[1]

Sir William was sent to the Tower in 1616, and his zeal in promoting an inquiry into the state of the navy, contrary to the wishes of the Earl of Nottingham, then Lord High Admiral,

[1] Vol. iii. There is a MS. copy of these "Tracts" in the Pepysian Library.

is supposed to have been the cause of his trouble.

The establishment of the navy, during a long period of English history, was of a very simple nature. The first admiral by name in England was W. de Leybourne, who was appointed to that office by Edward I., in the year 1286, under the title of "Admiral de la Mer du Roy d'Angleterre," and the first Lord High Admiral was created by Richard II. about a century afterwards. This word "admiral" was introduced into Europe from the East, and is nothing more than the Arabic *amir-al*[1] (in which form the article is incorporated with the noun). The intrusive *d*, however, made its appearance at a very early period. The office of "Clerk of the King's Ships," or "of the Navy," afterwards "Clerk of the Acts of the Navy," is in all probability a very ancient one, but the first holder of the office whose name Colonel Pasley, R.E.,[2] has met with, is Thomas Roger or Rogiers, who lived in the reigns of Edward IV., Edward V., and Richard III. In the third volume of Pepys's MS. "Miscellanies" (page 87)

[1] Thus *Amir-al-moumenim* is the Arabic for Commander of the Faithful.

[2] It is to Colonel Pasley's kindness that I owe the greater portion of the information contained in this chapter. That officer, who is Director of Works at the Admiralty, has made large collections relating to the early history of the administration of the navy, and to him I am also indebted for the valuable lists in the Appendix, which he has compiled for me with great labour from original sources. No such lists were previously in existence. Colonel Pasley has further kindly supplied me with the notes that follow which are signed in each instance "C. P."

K

is an entry of an order, dated 18th May, 22
Edw. IV. (1482), to the Treasurer and Chamberlain of the Exchequer, to examine and clear the
account of "our well beloved Thomas Roger,
Esq., Clerk of our Ships." In Harleian manuscript 433, which is believed to have belonged
to Lord Burghley, there is a register of grants
passing the Great Seal during the reigns of
Edward V. and Richard III., and No. 1690
contains the appointment of "Thomas Rogiers
to be clerc of all maner shippes to the King
belonging." It has no date, but is very probably a reappointment by Richard III. on his
assumption of the crown.

The navy owes much to Henry VIII., who
reconstituted the Admiralty, founded the Trinity
House, and established the dockyards at Deptford, Woolwich, and Portsmouth. The origin
of the board of "Principal Officers and Commissioners of the Navy," commonly called in later
times "the Navy Board," dates from his reign.
His predecessors had usually themselves managed
whatever naval force they possessed, assisted by
their Privy Council, and by the officer already
alluded to, who was styled "Clerk" or "Keeper"
of the King's ships, but in Henry's time the
rapidly increasing magnitude and importance of
the navy rendered a more complete and better
organized system of management necessary. To
supply this want several new offices were created,
and before Henry's death we find, in addition to
the Lord High Admiral and the Clerk of the
Ships, a Lieutenant (or Vice-Admiral), a Treasurer, a Comptroller, and a Surveyor of the

Navy,[1] as well as a Keeper of the Naval Store-
houses at Erith and Deptford.[2] A few years
later we meet with a " Master of the Ordnance
of the Ships." This last office, which had been
held by Sir William Woodhouse, was granted
by Philip and Mary in 1557 to William (afterwards Sir William) Winter in addition to that
of Surveyor, to which he had been appointed by
Edward VI.[3]

Each of these officers must have received
some sort of instructions for his guidance, but
no general code of rules for the administration
of the navy was framed until after the accession
of Elizabeth, who issued, about 1560, a set of
regulations for " the Office of the Admiralty and
Marine Causes," with the following preamble :[4]—
"Forasmuch as since the erection of the said
office by our late dear father Henry VIII., there
hath been no certain ordinance established so as
every officer in his degree is appointed to his
charge : and considering that in these our days
our navy is one of the chiefest defences of us
and our realm against the malice of any foreign
potentate : we have therefore thought good by
great advice and deliberation to make certain
ordinances and decrees, which our pleasure and
express commandment is that all our officers
shall on their parts execute and follow as they

---

[1] Harl. MS. 249.
[2] Letters and Papers, Henry VIII. vol. iv. pt. 1, p. 309.
[3] Add. MS. 5752, fol. 6[b] (Brit. Mus.).
[4] State Papers, Dom. Eliz. vol. xv. No. 4. There is a
copy of these regulations in the British Museum, Add. MS.
9295, fol. 17.

tender our pleasure, and will answer to the contrary."

Then follows a list of the several officers at that time forming the Board, viz. :—

1. The Vice-Admiral.
2. The Master of the Ordnance and Surveyor of the Navy : one officer.
3. The Treasurer.
4. The Comptroller.
5. The General Surveyor of the Victuals.
6. The Clerk of the Ships.
7. The Clerk of the Stores.[1]

The officers were to meet at least once a week at the office on Tower Hill, to consult, and take measures for the benefit of the navy, and were further directed to make a monthly report of their proceedings to the Lord Admiral.

The particular instructions which follow are brief, and by no means explicit :—

1. The Master of the Ordnance is to take care to make the wants of his department known to the Lord Admiral in good time, and he is to obtain the signatures of three of his colleagues every quarter to his books and accounts, which are then to be submitted to the Court of Exchequer.

2. The Treasurer is to make no payments except on the warrant of at least two of his colleagues, and his books are to be made up and certified by a similar number of the officers every quarter.

[1] The number of principal officers was afterwards fixed at four, viz. :—1. Treasurer; 2. Comptroller; 3. Surveyor; 4. Clerk of the Acts.

3. The Surveyor-General of the Victuals is to have his issues warranted, and his accounts certified in the same manner. He is to take care always to have in store a sufficient stock of victuals to supply a thousand men at sea for one month at a fortnight's notice.

4. The Surveyor, Comptroller, Clerk of the Ships, and Clerk of the Stores are to see the Queen's ships grounded and trimmed from time to time, and to keep them in such order that upon fourteen days' warning twelve or sixteen sail may be ready for sea, and the rest soon after. They are to make a monthly report of the state of the ships to the Vice-Admiral and the other officers.

5. The Clerk of the Ships is to provide timber and other materials for building and repairing ships.

6. The Clerk of the Stores is to keep a perfect record of receipts and issues : the latter to be made on the warrant of at least two of the officers.

This most interesting and important document is concluded in the following words :—

"Item, our pleasure and commandment is that all our said officers do agree in one consultation, and all such necessary orders as shall be taken amongst them from time to time to be entered in a ledger book for the whole year, to remain on record.

"The assistants not to be accounted any of our head officers, but yet to travel in our courses when they shall be thereunto commanded or appointed by our Lord Admiral or Vice Admiral, or other our officers.

" Item, our mind and pleasure is that every
of our said officers shall see into their fellows'
offices, to the intent that when God shall dispose
His will upon any of them they living may be
able, if we prefer any of them, to receive the
same.

" These our ordinances to be read once a
quarter amongst our officers, so as thereby every
of them may the better understand his duty, and
to be safely kept in our Consultation house at
Tower Hill."

We will now return to Sir William Monson,
who, in his " Naval Tracts," answers the question
what kind of men are to be chosen for the various
offices. He suggests that "the Comptroller's
and Clerk's places be reduced into one, who
should be an experienced clerk, *long bred in
the office* . . . . Provided always, that besides
their experience and abilities to perform the
active part of His Majesty's service, these men
be of good substance and esteem in their
estates."

Such a rule as this would have excluded Pepys
from the service, as he knew nothing of the
navy when he was made Clerk of the Acts.
He soon, however, made himself master of his
business, and at the time of his death he was
esteemed the greatest authority on naval affairs.
In illustration of Monson's recommendation, it
may be remarked that in 1585 the two offices of
Clerk and Comptroller were held by the same
man, William Borough.

The salaries received by the various officers
are set down by Monson as follows :—

	£	s.	d.
Treasurer	220	13	4
Comptroller	155	6	8
Surveyor	146	6	8
Clerk	102	3	4[1]

Although the salary of the Clerk of the Acts is here put at over one hundred pounds, yet the ancient "fee out of the Exchequer," which was attached to the office, did not amount to more than £33 6s. 8d. per annum, and this sum is specially set forth in Pepys's patent.

In July, 1660, the salaries of the officers of the navy (with the exception of that of the Treasurer) were advanced, Pepys's being raised to £350.[2] The salary of the Treasurer remained the same, but this was but a small part of his emoluments, which amounted in all to several thousand pounds a year.[3]

In the Pepysian Library there is preserved the pocket-book of James II., from which I have been allowed to extract the following memorandum of salaries:—

	£	s.	d.
Treasurer of the Navy	220	13	4
Comptroller	500	0	0
Surveyor	490	0	0

[1] These amounts were made up of the "Fee out of the Exchequer" (or salary proper); the Allowance for one or more Clerks; "Boat-hire," and "Riding Costs" (or travelling expenses).—C. P.   [2] "Diary," July 7, 1660.

[3] The emoluments of the Treasurer arose chiefly from "poundage" on all sums passing through his hands. In time of war his profits were often very large.—C. P.

	£	s.	d.
Clerk of the Acts . .	350	0	0
Three Commissioners at £500 and one at	350	0	0
Messenger to the Admiralty	20	0	0

When the Duke of Buckingham was assassinated, in 1628, the office of Lord High Admiral was for the first time put into commission. All the great officers of State were Commissioners, and Edward Nicholas, who had been secretary to Lord Zouch and to the Duke of Buckingham, was appointed Secretary of the Admiralty.

During the Commonwealth both the Admiralty and the Navy Office were administered by bodies of Commissioners. The offices of Comptroller, Surveyor, and Clerk of the Acts were abolished, and although the Treasurer remained, he was not a member of the Navy Board. Robert Blackburne, who was Secretary to most of the Commissions of the Admiralty, entertained Pepys after the Restoration with an account of the doings of the members. He told him that Sir William Penn got promotion by making a pretence of sanctity; and he then mimicked the actions of the Commissioners, who, he affirmed, would ask the admirals and captains respecting certain men, and say with a sigh and a casting up of the eyes, "Such a man fears the Lord;" or, "I hope such a man hath the Spirit of God."[1]

At the Restoration the Duke of York was

[1] "Diary," Nov. 9, 1663.

appointed Lord High Admiral, and all powers formerly granted to the Admiralty and Navy Board were recalled.[1] By the Duke's advice a committee was named to consider a plan proposed by himself for the future regulation of the affairs of the navy; and at a court held on July 4th, 1660, three new commissioners (John Lord Berkeley, Sir William Penn, and Peter Pett) were appointed to assist the four principal officers. Pett was to be employed at Chatham dockyard, but the other two had no special duties assigned to them, although their appointment gave them equal power with the original members when they attended at the Board. As there was at this time no half-pay, these appointments were considered as affording a convenient means of granting a comfortable subsistence to an admiral when not at sea. Lord Clarendon strongly disapproved of this innovation, and attributed the idea to Sir William Coventry, who wished

[1] In the "Succession of the Lords High Admiral," &c., in Pepys's "Naval Collections," it is stated that on the Restoration the existing Commissioners of the Admiralty and of the Navy respectively were temporarily continued in office by order in council of the 31st May, 1660. By a subsequent order (7th July following) a Board of Principal Officers and Commissioners of the Navy on the ancient model was appointed, and the Duke of York was directed to revoke the authority *he* had granted "unto the former Treasurer, Officers, and Commissioners of the Navy." It would appear, therefore, that the Admiralty Commissioners had been suppressed, and the Duke appointed Admiral at some intermediate date between the 31st May and the 7th July, 1660; although, according to Pepys's list, quoted above, his patent under the Great Seal bore date the 29th January, 1660-61.—C. P.

to reduce the power and emoluments of the Treasurer.[1]

In January, 1661-62, James Duke of York issued Instructions which were founded on those drawn up by the Earl of Northumberland, Lord High Admiral from 1638 to 1644, and remained in force until the reorganization of the Admiralty at the beginning of the present century.

It is here necessary to stop a moment for the purpose of noticing Pepys's relation to these Instructions. Before the publication of the " Diary" it was supposed that he was the chief author of the Rules. In the first Report of the Commissioners of Naval Revision (13th June, 1805) it is distinctly stated that he drew them up under the direction of the Duke, and even Lord Braybrooke makes the claim in regard to Pepys's authorship. This is an error, and Colonel Pasley points out that at the date of the issue of the Regulations Pepys was by no means on intimate terms with James. Even two years later (4th March, 1633-34) he writes, " I never had so much discourse with the Duke before, and till now did ever fear to meet him;" but what really settles the matter is, that under date February 5th, 1661-62, Pepys writes : " Sir G. Carteret, the two Sir Williams, and myself all alone reading of the Duke's institutions for the settlement of our office, whereof we read as much as concerns our own duties, and left the other officers for another time." The latter of these important passages was not printed by Lord

[1] Life of Clarendon, 1827, vol. ii. p. 331.

Braybrooke, and is only to be found in the Rev. Mynors Bright's transcript.[1]

The Navy Office, as we see from the "Diary," was by no means a happy family. Each officer was jealous of his fellow, and this jealousy was somewhat fostered by the duties enjoined. Pepys constantly complains of the neglect by his colleagues of their several duties, and when the Duke of York returned from his command at the end of the first great Dutch war, he found the office in the greatest disorder. This caused the preparation of the Diarist's "great letter" to the Duke, which is referred to in the "Diary," on November 17th, 1666. A still more important letter, on the same subject, written by Pepys, but purporting to come from the pen of the Duke of York, was not prepared until nearly two years after this.[2] We learn from the "Diary" all the stages of progress of this letter, the effect it produced when read out at the office,[3] and the way in which the officers prepared their answers.[4] In his allusion to this letter, Lord Braybrooke again does some injustice to James, for he writes : "We even find in the 'Diary,' as early as 1668, that a long letter of regulation, produced before the Commissioners of the Navy by the Duke of York *as his own composition*, was entirely written by the Clerk of the Acts."

[1] The Regulations were printed in 1717, under the title of "The Œconomy of His Majesty's Navy Office . . . . By an Officer of the Navy."

[2] *See* "Diary," Aug. 16, 21, 23, 25, 30, 1668.

[3] Aug. 29, Sept. 8th, 1668.   [4] Sept. 12, 18, 1668.

Colonel Pasley very justly observes, in commenting on this view of the Lord High Admiral's position :—" There is nothing unusual or improper in a minister, or head of a department, employing his subordinates to prepare documents for his signature, and in this particular instance it was evidently of importance that the actual author should remain unknown. Not only was Pepys himself most anxious to avoid being known in the matter, but it is obvious that the authority and effect of the reprimand and warning would have been much lessened, if the other members of the Board had been aware that the Duke had no other knowledge of the abuses of the office than what Pepys told him. It seems from the ' Diary,' that about 1668 Pepys first obtained the complete confidence of the Duke—a confidence which he always after retained and never abused. It is evident from numerous remarks in his manuscripts that Pepys had the highest respect for James's opinion in naval matters. In fact, the mutual respect and friendship of these two men was equally honourable to both, and it is a mistake to endeavour to magnify one at the expense of the other."

The letter referred to is in the British Museum,[1] and as it is of considerable interest in the life of Pepys, it will be worth while to devote a small space to a few notes on its contents.

James refers to his former letter of January

---

[1] " The Duke's Reflections on the severall Members of the Navy Boards Duty," dated " St. James, 28 Aug., 1668." " The Duke's Answer to their severall Excuses," dated " Whitehall, 25 Nov., 1668 " (both in Harleian MS. 6003).

2nd, 1661, sent with the "Instructions," as well as
to that of March 22nd, 1664, and, after some
general remarks, he points out the particular
duty of each officer, finishing with remarks on
their joint duties as a Board. The letter is
drawn up in so orderly a manner, and discovers
so thorough a knowledge of the details of the
office, that there is little cause for surprise that
the officers suspected Pepys to be the author.
Article by article of the "Instructions" are set
down, and following each of them are remarks
on the manner in which it had been carried out.
It is very amusing to notice the tact with which
our Diarist gets over the difficulty of criticizing
his own deeds. The Duke is made to say that
although he has inquired as to the execution of the office of Clerk of the Acts, he cannot
hear of any particular to charge him with failure
in his duty, and as he finds that the Clerk had
given diligent attendance, he thinks that the
duty must have been done well, particularly
during the time of the war, when, in spite of the
work being greater, the despatch was praise-
worthy. Yet he would not express further satisfaction, but would be willing to receive any
information of the Clerk's failures which otherwise might have escaped his knowledge. The
officers were informed that an answer was required from each of them within fourteen days.
When these answers were received, Pepys set to
work to write a reply for the Duke to acknowledge. Matthew Wren, the Duke's secretary,
smoothed down the language of this letter [1] a

[1] *See* "Diary," Nov. 2ᵉ 1668.

little, but it still remained a very stinging reprimand. These two letters form, probably, the most complete instance of a severe "wigging" given by the head of an office to his staff.

We will now return to the consideration of the business management of the navy, and it is necessary for us to bear in mind that the offices of the Admiralty and of the Navy Board were quite distinct in their arrangements. The Navy Board formed the Council of the Lord High Admiral, and the Admiralty was, originally, merely his personal office, the locality of which changed with his own change of residence, or that of his secretary. It was at one time in Whitehall, at another in Cannon Row, Westminster; and when Pepys was secretary, it was attached to his house in York Buildings.

When, however, there was a Board of Admiralty in place of a Lord High Admiral, the Admiralty Office became of more importance, and the Navy Office relatively of less.

According to Pepys, there was some talk of putting the office of Lord High Admiral into commission in the year 1668,[1] but it was not so treated until June, 1673, when the Duke of York laid down all his offices. The Commissioners on this occasion were Prince Rupert, the three great officers of State, three dukes, two secretaries, Sir G. Carteret, and Edward Seymour (afterwards Speaker of the House of Commons); and Pepys was the secretary. Before the commission passed the Great Seal, the King did the business through the medium of Pepys.[2]

[1] " Diary," Nov. 5, 1668.
[2] Williamson Letters (Camden Society), vol. i. pp. 47, 51, 56.

Lords of the Admiralty were occasionally appointed to assist the Lord High Admiral, or to fill his place while he was abroad. Pepys refers to such Lords on November 14th, 1664, and in March of the following year he remarks : " The best piece of news is, that instead of a great many troublesome Lords, the whole business is to be left with the Duke of Albemarle to act as Admiral." [1]

These lords were not properly commissioners, as a commission was only appointed by the King when the office of Lord High Admiral was vacant, but they formed a deputation or committee appointed by the Admiral to act as his deputies.

Pepys was with the Duke of York previous to the reinstatement of the latter as Lord High Admiral, he returned to the office with his patron, and he continued secretary until the Revolution, when he retired into private life. On the Duke's accession to the throne a new board was formed and the navy was again raised to a state of efficiency.

Pepys was Clerk of the Acts from 1660 to 1672, that is, during the whole period of the " Diary," and three years afterwards. He was succeeded by his clerk, Thomas Hayter, and his brother John Pepys, who held the office jointly. As already stated, Pepys was promoted to be Secretary of the Admiralty in 1672, and continued in office until 1679, when he was again succeeded for a time by Hayter. We know comparatively little of him in the higher office, and it is as Clerk of the Acts that he is

[1] " Diary," March 17, 1664-65.

familiar to us. With regard to this position
it is necessary to bear in mind that the "so-
called" clerk, as well as being secretary, was also
a member of the Board, and one of the "principal officers." On one occasion Pepys met Sir
G. Carteret, Sir J. Minnes, and Sir W. Batten
at Whitehall, and when the King spied them
out, he cried, " Here is the Navy Office!"[1]

I have already mentioned that the principal
officers were superseded during the Commonwealth. Again, in 1686, they were suspended,
and the offices were temporarily placed under a
body of equal commissioners.

The Navy Office, where Pepys lived during
the whole period over which the " Diary" ex·
tends, was situated between Crutched Friars
and Seething Lane, with an entrance in each of
these places. The ground was originally occupied by a chapel and college attached to the
church of Allhallows, Barking, but these buildings were pulled down in the year 1548, and the
land was used for some years as a garden plot.

In Elizabeth's reign, when the celebrated Sir
William Wynter, Surveyor of Her Majesty's
Ships, brought home from sea much plunder of
merchants' goods, a storehouse of timber and
brick was raised on this site for their reception. In
course of time the storehouse made way for the
Navy Office, a rather extensive building, in which
the civil business of the navy was transacted until
the last quarter of the eighteenth century. On
July 4th, 1660, Pepys went with Commissioner
Pett to view the houses, and was very pleased

[1] " Diary," Nov. 2, 1663.

with them, but he feared that the more influential officers would shuffle him out of his rights. Two days afterwards, however, he went with Mr. Coventry and Sir G. Carteret to take possession of the place; still, although his mind was a little cheered, his hopes were not great. On July 9th, he began to sign bills in his office, and on the 18th he records the fact that he dined in his own apartments.

Pepys's house was a part of the Seething Lane front, and that occupied by Sir William Penn was on the north side of the garden, a house which was afterwards occupied by Lord Brouncker.[1] When the new Somerset House was finished, the Navy Office was removed there, and the old buildings in the city were sold and destroyed.

In course of time the work of the navy could not be properly carried out with the old machinery, and, at last, the Admiralty Office, which had largely grown in importance, swallowed up the Navy Office. By an Act of Parliament, 2 William IV., the principal officers and commissioners of the navy were abolished, as were also the commissioners for victualling the navy; and all power and authority was vested in the Admiralty.

I have attempted to give in a few pages as clear an account as possible of the kind of machinery by which the navy was governed, and I now propose to pass rapidly in review a few of the points raised by Pepys. To do more than glance at some of these would

[1] P. Gibson in "Life of Penn," ii. 616.

L

require a volume. The "Diary" is filled with information respecting the office and the petty squabbles of the officers, and we obtain from it a gloomy notion of the condition of the navy. In fact, it would be hardly possible to believe the wretched details if we had them from a less trustworthy authority. The whole system of money-getting was unsatisfactory in the extreme, and the officers of the navy were often expected to perform the task of making bricks without straw. The Treasurer, not being able to get money from the Treasury, floated bills, and these were often in very bad repute. We read in the "Diary," that on August 31st, 1661, the bills were offered to be sold on the Exchange at 10 per cent. loss; and on April 14th, 1663, things were even worse, for it was reported that they were sold at a reduction of 15 per cent. In December of the latter year Pepys could hardly believe the evidence of his ears when he learned the "extraordinary good news," that the credit of the office was "as good as any merchant's upon Change;" but these bright days did not last long. Parliament being very dissatisfied with the way in which the money was spent by the officers of the navy, appointed, a few years afterwards, a commission to look into the accounts. This gave Pepys much trouble, which he did not relish, and we find him busy in making things as pleasant as possible during the latter part of 1666. He was in "mighty fear and trouble" when called before the committee, the members of which appeared to be "in a very ill humour." Three years after this he drew up a letter to the Commissioners of Accounts on the state of the office, a transcript of which, addressed to " H.R.H. the Lord High Admiral," and dated January 8th, 1669-70, is now in the library of the British Museum.[1]

One of the most unsatisfactory divisions of the naval accounts related to the pursers. Pepys was early interested in the Victualling Department, out of which he afterwards made much money; and on September 12th, 1662, we find him trying "to understand the method of making up Purser's Accounts, which is very needful for me and very hard." On November 22nd, 1665, he remarks that he was pleased to have it demonstrated " that a Purser without professed cheating is a professed loser twice as much as he gets." Pepys received his appointment of Surveyor-General of the Victualling Office chiefly through the influence of Sir William Coventry, and on January 1st, 1665-6, he addressed a letter and " New Yeares Guift" on the subject of pursers to his distinguished friend. He relates in the " Diary" how he wrote the letter, and how Sir William praised his work to the Duke.[2]

The want of money led to other evils that brought the greatest discredit upon the Navy Office. The tickets that were given to the men in place of money, were received with the greatest disgust, and during the time of the Dutch war the scarcity of sailors was so great

---

[1] Sloane MS. 2751.

[2] The letter, signed " S. Pepyes," and dated " Greenwich, 1st January, 1665," is in the British Museum (Add. MS. 6287). There is also a copy in Harl. MS. 6003.

that a wholesale system of pressing was resorted
to. We learn that on June 30th, 1666, Sir
Thomas Bludworth, the Lord Mayor, impressed
a large number of persons wholly unfit for sea,
and when we are further told that some of them
were "people of very good fashion," it is not
surprising that Pepys should call the Mayor "a
silly man."

So great was the disgust of the unpaid men,
that during the war with Holland English sailors
positively preferred to serve in the ships of the
enemies of England rather than fight for their
own country, and when the Dutch were in the
Medway English voices were heard from Dutch
ships.[1]

The seamen were not likely to learn much
good from their superiors, for throughout the
whole fleet swearing, drinking, and debauchery
were rampant.[2]

A great part of the evils arose from the appointment of so-called "gentlemen captains,"
men who were unacquainted with maritime
affairs, and treated the sailor captains with contempt, calling them tarpaulins, a name which
now only remains to us in the reduced form of
tar. This evil was well known in the reign of
Elizabeth, and was pointed out by Gibson, who
wrote memoirs of the expeditions of the navy
from 1585 to 1603,[3] and all readers are familiar

---

[1] The "Englishmen on board the Dutch ships" were
heard to say, "We did heretofore fight for tickets; now we
fight for dollars!"—"Diary," June 14, 1667.

[2] "Diary," Oct. 20, 1666.

[3] Gibson was a contemporary of Pepys, and a clerk in

with Macaulay's remarks on the same subject. Captain Digby, a son of the Earl of Bristol, and one of these " ornamental officers," after he had been in the fleet about a year expressed the wish that he might not again see a tarpaulin have the command of a ship.[1] These useless captains, who could make bows, but could not navigate a ship, raised the ire of old Nan Clarges, otherwise Duchess of Albemarle, who " cried out mightily against the having of gentlemen captains with feathers and ribbands, and wished the king would send her husband to sea with the old plain sea captains that he served with formerly, that would make their ships swim with blood, though they could not make legs as captains now-a-days can."[2]

The common custom of employing indiscriminately land officers as admirals, and naval officers as generals, often led to disasters. There can be no doubt of the bravery of Monk and Rupert, but when on shipboard they made many blunders and endangered the safety of the fleet.

All this confusion caused dire disasters, which culminated in the presence of the hostile Dutch fleet in our rivers ; a national disgrace which no Englishman can think of even now without a feeling of shame. While reading the " Diary,"

the Navy Office. He was somewhat of a *laudator temporis acti*, and fonder of drawing his illustrations from events of Queen Elizabeth's time than from those of more recent days. See his paper in praise of "Seamen Captains," printed in the preface to Charnock's " History of Marine Architecture," pp. lxxiv.-xcv.—C. P.

[1] " Diary," Oct. 20, 1666.　　　　[2] Jan. 10, 1665-66.

we are overwhelmed with the instances of gross mismanagement in naval affairs. Many of the men whose carelessness helped to increase the amount of rampant blundering were, however, capable of deeds of pluck and bravery. In one of the engagements with the Dutch, Prince Rupert sent his pleasure-boat, the "Fanfan," with two small guns on board, against the Dutch admiral, De Ruyter. With great daring, the sailors brought their little boat near, and fired at De Ruyter's vessel for two hours, but at last a ball did them so much damage that the crew were forced to row briskly to save their lives.[1]

Another instance of bravery more deserving of honour is that recorded of Captain Douglas, of the "Royal Oak," who had received orders to defend his ship at Chatham. This he did with the utmost resolution, but, having had no order to retire, he chose rather to be burnt in his ship than live to be reproached with having deserted his command. It is reported that Sir William Temple expressed the wish that Cowley had celebrated this noble deed before he died.[2]

Pepys tells us that on July 21st, 1668, he went to his "plate-makers," and spent an hour in contriving some plates for his books of the King's four yards, and that on the 27th of the same month the four plates came home. They cost him five pounds, and he was in consequence both troubled and pleased.

No account of the state of the navy in Charles

[1] Campbell's "Naval History," 1818, vol. ii. p. 165.
[2] Ibid. p. 177.

II.'s time, however short, would be complete without some notice of the four dockyards (Chatham, Deptford, Portsmouth, and Woolwich), which necessarily occupy a very prominent place in the "Diary." Chatham yard was founded by Queen Elizabeth, and it remained under the special charge of the Surveyor of the Navy until a Special Commissioner was appointed in 1630. This explains a passage in the " Diary" which has not hitherto been illustrated. When, in April, 1661, Sir William Batten, the Surveyor of the Navy, and Pepys were on a visit to Chatham, they went "to see Commissioner Pett's house, he and his family being absent, and here I wondered how my Lady Batten walked up and down, with envious looks, to see how neat and rich everything is, saying that she would get it, for it belonged formerly to the Surveyor of the Navy.[1] The first Commissioner was Phineas Pett, who died in 1647, and was succeeded by his son, Peter Pett, who figures so frequently in the " Diary." Peter was continued in office at the Restoration, but he was suspended in 1667 in consequence of the success of the Dutch attack upon Chatham. He was sent to the Tower and threatened with impeachment, but, although the threat was not carried out, he was never restored to office. The appointment remained in abeyance for two years after, when, in March, 1669, Captain John Cox, the master

---

[1] "Diary," April 10, 1661. This house (of which there is a plan in King's MS. 43) was pulled down in 1703, and the house now occupied by the Admiral Superintendent of Chatham Dockyard was built in its place.—C. P.

attendant at Deptford, was made resident Commissioner at Chatham. In January, 1672, he was appointed flag captain to the Duke of York, in the " Prince," without vacating his office at Chatham, was knighted in April, and killed at the battle of Solebay in May, all in the same year.

The Hill-house that Pepys visited for the first time on the 8th of April, 1661, is frequently mentioned on subsequent pages of the " Diary."[1] The "old Edgeborrow," whose ghost was reported to haunt the place, was Kenrick Edisbury, Surveyor of the Navy from 1632 to 1638. Pepys does not seem quite to have appreciated the story of the ghost which was told him as he went to bed after a merry supper, although he affirms that he was not so much afraid as for mirth's sake he seemed.[2]   In the " Memoirs of English Affairs, chiefly Naval, from the year 1660 to 1673, written by James, Duke of York," there is a letter from James to the principal officers of the navy (dated May 10th, 1661), in which he recommends that the lease of the Hill-house should be bought by them, if it can be obtained at a reasonable rate, as the said house "is very convenient for the service of his Majesty's Navy."[3]

After the defeat of the Spanish Armada, Sir Francis Drake and Sir John Hawkins advised

[1] A plan, with front and side elevations of the Hill-house as it was in 1698, is in King's MS. 43.   The ground on which it stood is now included in the Marine Barracks.— C. P.
[2] " Diary," April 8, 1661.   [3] 1729, p. 23.

the establishment of a chest at Chatham for the
relief of seamen wounded in their country's service, and the sailors voluntarily agreed to have
certain sums "defalked" out of their wages in
order to form this fund. In July, 1662, Pepys
was told of the abuse of the funds, and advised
to look into the business.[1] At the end of the
same year a commission was appointed to in-
spect the chest,[2] but the commissioners do not
seem to have done much good, for in 1667
there was positively no money left to pay the
poor sailors what was owed to them.[3] After a
time the property became considerable, but unfortunately the abuses grew as well. In 1802
the chest was removed to Greenwich, and in
1817 the stock is said to have amounted to
£300,000 consols.

Deptford dockyard was founded about the
year 1513. Pepys made occasional visits to it,
and on one occasion he and Coventry took the
officers (of whose honesty he had not a very
high opinion) by surprise. On June 16th, 1662,
he mentions going to see "in what forwardness
the work is for Sir W Batten's house and mine."
He found the house almost ready, but we hear
no more of it in the subsequent pages of the
"Diary."

Portsmouth dockyard was established by
Henry VIII., but it did not hold a foremost
position until, in the reign of William III.,
Edmund Dummer contrived a simple and
ingenious method of pumping water from dry

[1] "Diary," July 3, 1662.   [2] Nov. 13, 1662.
[3] June 18, 1667.

docks below the level of low tide, which enabled
Portsmouth for the first time to possess a dry
dock capable of taking in a first-rate man-of-war.
It was Dummer who also designed and constructed the first docks at Plymouth.[1]

Sir Edward Montague first chose Portsmouth
as the place from which to draw his title, but
he afterwards gave the preference to Sandwich.

When Pepys visited Portsmouth in May, 1661,
he was very pleased with his reception by the
officers of the dockyard, who treated him with
much respect.

Although the date of the foundation of Woolwich dockyard is not recorded, it is known to
have been of considerable importance in Henry
VIII.'s reign.　It figures very frequently in the
" Diary." [2]

Very soon after Pepys was settled in his office,
he thought it advisable to give his attention to
the question of the British dominion of the seas,

---

[1] Dummer was Assistant to the Surveyor of the Navy
when he designed these works.　The improvement of Portsmouth and the foundation of a dockyard at Plymouth were
called for by the political changes arising out of the Revolution.　Previously our great naval wars had been waged
against the Dutch, and the Thames and Medway were then
the most convenient localities for fitting and repairing ships
of war.　After the Revolution, the Dutch became our allies,
and the French our most formidable enemies.　The naval
ports on the Channel then became more important than
those on the east coast.—C. P.

[2] King's MS. 43 (Brit. Mus.) contains plans of all the
dockyards in 1688 and 1698, and detailed drawings of the
principal buildings as they were in the latter year, as well
as of the Navy Office in Seething Lane, and the Hill-house
at Chatham.—C. P.

and he made a special study of Selden's "Mare Clausum." He intended to write a treatise on the rights of the English flag, and present it to the Duke of York. His reason for doing this was that it promised to be a good way to make himself known.[1] The right of making foreign vessels strike their sails to the English flag had been insisted upon from early times. Selden's work, in which the case was strongly urged, met therefore with great favour. Charles I. made an order in council that a copy should be kept in the council chest, another in the Court of Exchequer, and a third in the Court of Admiralty. The upholders of this right triumphed when, in the treaty of peace with the Dutch (February 9th, 1674), the States-General confessed that to be a right which before had been styled courtesy, and they agreed that not only separate ships, but whole fleets should strike sails to any fleet or ship carrying the king's flag.[2] John Evelyn argued strongly in favour of England's right to the dominion of the sea in his "Navigation and Commerce" (1674), but he privately confessed to Pepys that he did not consider there was any sufficient evidence of the right.[3]

We must now turn our attention to the Diarist's colleagues at the Navy Office, and it is here very needful to caution the reader against putting implicit faith in all the adverse remarks that fill

[1] "Diary," Nov. 29, 1661.

[2] Campbell's "Naval History," 1818, vol. ii. p. 217.

[3] "Evelyn's Diary," ed. 1879, vol. iii. p. 414. (Letter dated Sept. 19, 1682.)

the " Diary." It is a curious fact that, with the exception of Sir William Coventry, scarcely any of the officers come off with a good character. Pepys held Coventry in profound respect, and was never prouder than when he received a word of praise from him, and yet we do not obtain a very favourable idea of the secretary to the Duke of York from other writers, and in the pages of Clarendon we are presented with a very adverse character of him.

Those officers with whom Pepys came most in contact were Sir George Carteret, the Treasurer; Sir Robert Slingsby and Sir John Minnes, successive Comptrollers; Sir William Batten and Colonel Thomas Middleton, successive Surveyors; and Sir William Penn and Lord Viscount Brouncker, additional Commissioners.

Pepys did not hold Carteret in much esteem, and we read constant disparaging remarks respecting him, such as that on one occasion he wanted to know what the four letters S. P. Q. R. meant, " which ignorance is not to be borne in a Privy Counsellor,"[1] but after Sir George's son had married a daughter of Lord Sandwich, and he had thus become a near connection of Pepys's family, we read of "his pleasant humour," and are told that he is "a most honest man." Sir Robert Slingsby died in 1661, and therefore does not occupy a very prominent position in the " Diary," but Pepys grieved for his loss.

Sir John Minnes was better known as a wit than as a sailor, and it was he who taught Pepys to appreciate Chaucer. He does not, however,

[1] " Diary," July 4, 1663.

come off very handsomely in the "Diary." Captain Holmes called him "the veriest knave and rogue and coward in the world,"[1] and Sir William Coventry likened him to a lapwing, who was always in a flutter to keep others from the nest.[2] Pepys himself, after a few quarrels, hints pretty plainly that he was an old coxcomb, a mere jester or ballad-monger, and quite unfit for business.

We are told of Sir William Batten's corruption and underhand dealing,[3] of his knavery,[4] and of his inconsequent action in objecting to lighthouses generally, and then proposing one for Harwich;[5] but Pepys's two chief enemies were Sir William Penn and Lord Brouncker.

Sir William Penn and Pepys were much thrown together, and were alternately very friendly and very jealous of each other. When Pepys first associated with Penn, he found him sociable but cunning, and ever after the pages of the "Diary" are filled with vituperation respecting this successful admiral. Considering the eminent position of William Penn the son, as a leader among the Quakers, it is curious to note that before the Restoration, and when Monk was coming from the North, it was reported that Penn, the father, had turned Quaker.[6] In May, 1660, Charles II. wrote to Monk: "I have so good an opinion of General Penn, that if you had not recommended him to me I would have taken care of all his interests;"[7] and we cannot

[1] "Diary," Dec. 7, 1661. [2] Nov. 4, 1664.
[3] June 13, 1663. [4] May 5, 1664.
[5] Nov. 4, 1664. [6] Nov. 9, 1663.
[7] Lister's "Life of Clarendon," vol. iii. p. 107.

doubt that he possessed some eminent qualities of which we learn nothing in the " Diary."

Lord Brouncker was a good mathematician in his own day, and his name has come down with credit to ours as the first President of the Royal Society, but his portrait as painted by Pepys is far from a pleasing one—let us hope that it was not a true likeness. He was not a rich man, for his mother was a gamester, and his father a land-lacking peer, and he was probably not over particular as to the means he took to obtain money. We may believe this, however, without agreeing with Pepys that he was " a rotten-hearted, false man." [1] Aubrey says that the following lines were written on his parents :—

" Here's a health to my Lady Brouncker, and the best card in her hand ;
And a health to my Lord her husband, with ne'er a foot of land." [2]

These were some of the men who helped to carry on the work of the English navy. It would have been well for the fame of most of them if Pepys had never put pen to paper.

[1] " Diary," Jan. 29, 1666-67.
[2] Aubrey's " Lives," 1813, vol. ii. p. 260.

CHAPTER IX.

THE COURT.

" And when he was beat,
He still made his retreat
To his Clevelands, his Nells, and his Carwells."
MARVELL'S *Ballad on the Lord Mayor and
Aldermen.*

THE Court of Charles II. was not unlike that of Comus, for drunkenness and vice reigned supreme in both. Pepys's "Diary" forms a valuable antidote to the Grammont " Memoirs," because in the latter work the pictures are drawn in rose colour, while in the former we see the squalid poverty that accompanied the wasteful extravagance. In the courts of most of our sovereigns statesmen have borne an important part, but at the Restoration the court was formed of wits and beautiful women only. Then statesmen moved in the outer circles, and were laughed at by those who dwelt in the inner ones. Grammont relates that the Earl of Arlington was one day offering his humble ser-

vices and best advice to Miss Stewart, to assist
her in conducting herself as King s mistress, a
situation "to which it had pleased God and her
virtue to raise her!" He had only just begun
his speech, " when she recollected that he was at
the head of those whom the Duke of Buckingham used to mimic ; and as his presence and
his language exactly revived the ridiculous ideas
that had been given her of him, she could not
forbear bursting out into a fit of laughter in his
face, so much the more violent as she had for a
long time struggled to suppress it." It is not to
be supposed that Pepys could know much of the
inner circle of the court, but still there was much
gossip about those who composed it, and he sets
down many tales in his " Diary " respecting the
doings of the too celebrated ladies. Several
of the stories which were supposed to have
owed much to the lively imaginations of Counts
Hamilton and Grammont, are corroborated by
Pepys.[1] The wild frolic of Miss Jennings and
Miss Price, to which allusion will be made later
on in this chapter, is not overlooked by Pepys.[2]
Miss Jennings was not singular in her freak, and
Bishop Burnet relates that about the year 1668,
the King and Queen and all the court went
about disguised in sedan chairs to houses where
they were not known. On one occasion the
Queen's chairmen, not knowing who she was,
left her alone, and she had to get back to White-

[1] Peter Cunningham has a note in his "Story of Nell
Gwyn," "on the Chronology of the English portion of
De Grammont's Memoirs."
[2] " Diary," Feb. 21, 1664-65.

hall as best she could in a hackney coach or in a cart. The same masqueradings went on in the country as in town ; and in 1670 the Queen, the Duchess of Richmond, the Duchess of Buckingham, and some others, disguised themselves as country lasses, in red petticoats, waistcoats, &c., in order to visit the fair at Audley End. The grand ladies and their companions overacted their parts, and were soon discovered, so that they were glad to escape as best they could from the crowd that gathered round them.

Pepys seems to have held the vulgar opinion that the great people ought to converse in a more distinguished tone than ordinary mortals, and he constantly remarks on the commonplace character of the King's talk. On October 26th, 1664, there was a launch at Woolwich, attended by the King and his Court, which is fully described by our Diarist, who remarks : " But Lord ! the sorry talke and discourse among the great courtiers round about him, without any reverence in the world, but so much disorder. By and by the Queene comes and her Mayds of Honour ; one whereof M^{rs}. Boynton, and the Duchesse of Buckingham had been very sicke coming by water in the barge (the water being very rough) ; but what silly sport they made with them in very common terms, *methought was very poor and below what people think these great people say and do.*"

On the 15th of November, 1666, there was a grand ball at court, that day being the Queen's birthday ; and Pepys and his wife went to see the dancing, which they found very tiresome.

M

The ladies, however, were pleasant to look upon, and their dresses very rich ; so we read in the " Diary :" " Away home with my wife, between displeased with the dull dancing and satisfied with the clothes and persons."

These ladies owe much of their fame to the series of portraits which still exists to show a later age the outward forms that charmed the men of two centuries ago. We are told in the Grammont " Memoirs" that, " the Duchess of York being desirous of having the portraits of the handsomest persons at court, Lely painted them, and employed all his skill in the performance ; nor could he ever exert himself upon more beautiful subjects. Every picture appeared a masterpiece ; and that of Miss Hamilton appeared the highest finished : Lely himself acknowledged that he had drawn it with a particular pleasure." Next to the deshabille, in which most of these ladies are arranged, the most noticeable feature in these portraits is the soft, sleepy eye—a supposed beauty that was attained to after a considerable amount of practice :—

> "—— on the animated canvas stole
> The sleepy eye, that spoke the melting soul."

Mrs. Hyde, the first wife of Henry Hyde, afterwards second Earl of Clarendon, had by long practice given such a languishing tenderness to her looks, that we are told by Hamilton, "she never opened her eyes but like a Chinese." In spite of all this softness, many of these women were in the habit of swearing "good mouth-filling oaths"—a practice thoroughly in character with the general grossness of manners and language at Charles's court. When looking at these portraits of the beauties, we must not think of them all as the mistresses of the King and Duke of York, for some remained pure in this corrupt atmosphere. " La belle Hamilton " was one of these, and the description both of her mind and person by her husband, the Count de Grammont, forms such an exquisite portrait in words that, although well known, I venture to transfer it to my pages :—" Miss Hamilton was at the happy age when the charms of the fair sex begin to bloom ; she had the finest shape, the loveliest neck, and most beautiful arms in the world ; she was majestic and graceful in all her movements ; and she was the original after which all the ladies copied in their taste and air of dress. Her forehead was open, white, and smooth ; her hair was well set, and fell with ease into that natural order which it is so difficult to imitate. Her complexion was possessed of a certain freshness, not to be equalled by borrowed colours : her eyes were not large, but they were lively, and capable of expressing whatever she pleased : her mouth was full of graces, and her contour uncommonly perfect : nor was her nose, which was small, delicate, and turned up, the least ornament of so lovely a face. In fine, her air, her carriage, and the numberless graces dispersed over her whole person, made the Chevalier de Grammont not doubt but that she was possessed of every other qualification. Her mind was a proper companion for such a form : she did not endeavour to shine in conversation

by those sprightly sallies which only puzzle; and
with still greater care she avoided that affected
solemnity in her discourse, which produces stu-
pidity; but without any eagerness to talk, she
just said what she ought, and no more. She had
an admirable discernment in distinguishing between solid and false wit; and far from making
an ostentatious display of her abilities, she was
reserved, though very just in her decisions : her
sentiments were always noble, and even lofty to
the highest extent, when there was occasion;
nevertheless, she was less prepossessed with her
own merit than is usually the case with those who
have so much. Formed as we have described,
she could not fail of commanding love ; but so
far was she from courting it, that she was scru-
pulously nice with respect to those whose merit
might entitle them to form any pretensions to
her."

On the 25th of July, 1666, Pepys went to
Whitehall to see the King at dinner, and thought
how little he should care to have people crowd-
ing about him as they were round his Majesty.
He adds, "Among other things it astonished me
to see my Lord Barkeshire waiting at table, and
serving the King drink, in that dirty pickle as I
never saw man in my life."

There is a good story told of Grammont which
is *apropos* of the above. One day, when the
King dined in state, he made the Count remark
that he was served upon the knee, a mark of
respect not common at other courts. " I thank
your Majesty for the explanation," answered
Grammont; " I thought they were begging par-
don for giving you so bad a dinner."

I have already remarked on the poverty that went hand-in-hand with extravagance, and this is well illustrated by one or two entries in the "Diary." In April, 1667,[1] the King was vexed to find no paper laid for him at the Council table. Sir Richard Browne called Wooly, the person who provided the paper, to explain the reason of the neglect. He told his Majesty that he was but a poor man, and was already out of pocket £400 or £500, which was as much as he was worth; and that he could not provide it any longer without money, not having received a penny since the King's coming in. Evelyn corroborated this, and told Pepys that several of the menial servants of the court lacked bread, and had not received a farthing of wages since the Restoration.[2]

Shortly afterwards the King was found to want personal linen, and Mr. Ashburnham, one of the Grooms of the Bedchamber, rated the wardrobe-man very severely for this neglect. Mr. Townsend pleaded that he wanted money, and owed the linendraper £5,000. He further told Pepys that the grooms took away the King's linen at the end of the quarter as their fee, whether he could get more or not.[3] Hence the great want.

Charles II. was one of the most worthless of our monarchs, and the most beloved. The responsibility of all evils, troubles, or crimes, was laid upon his advisers, his mistresses, and anyone but upon himself, by his loving subjects. His readiness of access, and good-humoured freedom of manner charmed all who came in

---

[1] "Diary," April 22, 1667.   [2] April 26, 1667.
[3] Sept. 2, 1667.

contact with him. " Unthinkingness" was said by Halifax to be one of his characteristics, and Rochester uses the expression, " Unthinking Charles ;" yet this was more an apparent than a real characteristic. Like most indolent men, he tried to get his own way, and he was one of the earliest to find out that if the people are allowed their way when they are in earnest, they will let their governors do as they wish at other times. It has been said that the strongest resolve he ever formed was a determination not to go on his travels again ; therefore he never opposed a strong popular movement. He sought, however, every opportunity of turning the movement to his own advantage, if there were any possibility of doing so.

Charles was fit to be the head of his court, for he was among the wittiest there. He was a good teller of a story, and fond of exhibiting his talent. Walpole proposed to make a collection of his witty sayings, and Peter Cunningham carried out this idea in " The Story of Nell Gwyn."

Curiously enough, Pepys held a very poor opinion of the King's power in this respect. On one occasion he says Charles's stories were good, although "he tells them but meanly."[1] At another time he alludes to "the silly discourse of the King."[2]

The Diarist must surely have been prejudiced, for the general opinion on this point, and the stories that have come down to us, are against him. That was a happy distinction

[1] "Diary," Jan. 2, 1667-68.   [2] Dec. 2, 1668.

made by Charles when he said of Godolphin, then a page at court, that he was never *in* the way, and never *out* of the way. Of the King's natural abilities there can be no doubt. He took an intelligent interest in the formation of the Royal Society, and passed many hours in his own laboratory. Pepys visited this place on January 15th, 1668-69, and was much pleased with it. He saw there "a great many chymical glasses and things, but understood none of them."

The King was fond of seeing and making dissections,[1] and the very month he died he was engaged in some experiments on the production of mercury.

His greatest fault was want of faith, for he believed neither in the honour of man nor the virtue of woman ; and, as a consequence, he lived down to his debased views. His religion always sat lightly upon him, but such as it was it was not that of a Protestant. James II. told Pepys, in a private conversation, that Charles had been a Roman Catholic' some long time before his death.[2]

Charles's relations with women were singularly heartless. His conduct towards his wife was abominable, although when in her company he was usually polite. On the occasion of her serious illness, when she was like to die, he conjured her to live for his sake, and Grammont hints that he was disappointed when she took him at his word.

The Queen, although not beautiful, was pleas-

---

[1] "Diary," May 11, 1663.   [2] Smith, vol. ii. p. 264.

ing in appearance, and the King appears to have been satisfied with her when she arrived in England, for he wrote to Clarendon, that her eyes were excellent and her voice agreeable, adding, " If I have any skill in physiognomy, which I think I have, she must be as good a woman as ever was born." A few days after he wrote to the Chancellor in these words, " My brother will tell you of all that passes here, which I hope will be to your satisfaction. I am sure 'tis so much to mine that I cannot easily tell you how happy I think myself, and I must be the worst man living (which I hope I am not) if I be not a good husband. I am confident never two humors were better fitted together than ours are." [1] Yet shortly after writing thus, he thrust his abandoned mistress, Lady Castlemaine, upon this virtuous wife; so that from his own mouth we can condemn him. Pepys reports a sharp answer ("a wipe," he calls it) which the Queen made to the favourite. Lady Castlemaine came in and found the Queen under the dresser's hand, which she had been for a long time. " I wonder your Majesty," says she, "can have the patience to sit so long adressing?" —" I have so much reason to use patience," says the Queen, "that I can very well bear with it." [2]

Clarendon was charged with choosing Katherine because he knew that she could not bear children to the King, but this was a most foul calumny. She was naturally most anxious to be a mother, and in her delirium she fancied that

[1] Lister's " Life of Clarendon," vol. iii. p. 197.
[2] " Diary," July 3, 1663.

she had given birth to a boy, but was troubled
because he was ugly. The King, being by, said,
"No, it is a very pretty boy." "Nay," says
she, "if it be like you it is a fine boy indeed, and
I would be very well pleased with it." [1]

The Duke of York was pre-eminently a man
of business, and there remains little to be added
here to what has been already said in the
chapter on the Navy. He did not shine at
Court, and his conduct there is amusingly described in the Grammont "Memoirs," *apropos*
of his fancy for "la belle Hamilton:"—"As hunt-
ing was his favourite diversion, that sport employed him one part of the day, and he came
home generally much fatigued; but Miss Hamilton's presence revived him, when he found
her either with the Queen or the Duchess. There
it was that, not daring to tell her what lay heavy
on his heart, he entertained her with what he
had in his head: telling her miracles of the
cunning of foxes and the mettle of horses;
giving her accounts of broken legs and arms,
dislocated shoulders and other curious and entertaining adventures; after which, his eyes told
her the rest, till such time as sleep interrupted
their conversation; for these tender interpreters
could not help sometimes composing themselves
in the midst of their ogling."

It is not necessary to enter fully into the
history of the Duke's amours, but one curious incident in his life may be noticed here. In the year
1673 he had a passion for Susan, Lady Bellasys,
widow of Sir Henry Bellasys, K.B. (who fell in a

[1] "Diary," Oct. 26.

foolish duel with Tom Porter,[1]), and, although she was a Protestant, he gave her a promise of marriage, after having tried in vain to convert her to the Roman Catholic faith. When her father-in-law, John, Lord Bellasys, who was a Roman Catholic, heard of this, he, fearing that she would convert the Duke, and thus spoil all hope of introducing the Roman Catholic religion into England, went to the King and told him of his brother's matrimonial intentions. Charles thereupon prohibited the marriage.[2]

After James came to the throne, his daughter Mary, Princess of Orange, expressed a desire through Monsieur d'Alberville to know the chief motives of his conversion; and in reply he wrote her a full account of the circumstances that led to it. He tells her that he was bred a strict Church of England man, "And I was so zealous that way, that when the Queen my mother designed to bring up my brother, the Duke of Gloucester, a Catholic, I, preserving still the respect due to her, did my part to keep him steady to his first principles; and, as young people often do, I made it a point of honour to stick to what we had been educated in, without examining whether we were right or wrong."[3]

Anne Hyde, then in the household of the Princess of Orange, was contracted to the Duke of York on November 24th, 1659, and was

[1] Mentioned by Pepys, July 29, Aug. 8, 12, 1667.

[2] "Burnet's Own Time," i. 353. The lady afterwards married a gentleman of fortune named Fortrey, and died in 1713.

[3] James's letter is printed in "Smith's Life, &c., of Pepys," vol. ii. p. 322.

secretly married to him at Worcester House, on
September 3rd, 1660. There is a good story
told by Locke, in his " Memoirs of Lord Shaftesbury," which shows how shrewd that nobleman
was : " Soon after the Restoration the Earl of
Southampton and Sir Anthony Ashley Cooper,
having dined together at the Chancellor's, as
they were returning home Sir Anthony said to
my Lord Southampton, ' Yonder Mrs. Anne
Hyde is certainly married to one of the Brothers.'
The Earl, who was a friend to the Chancellor,
treated this as a chimæra, and asked him how
so wild a fancy could get into his head. ' Assure yourself' (replied he) ' it is so. A concealed respect (however suppressed) showed itself so plainly in the looks, voice, and manner
wherewith her mother carved to her, or offered
her of every dish, that it is impossible but it
must be so.' My Lord Southampton, who
thought it a groundless conceit then, was not
long after convinced, by the Duke of York's
owning her, that Lord Ashley was no bad
guesser." [1]

An infamous conspiracy was formed by Sir
Charles Berkeley and others to induce the Duke
to deny his marriage by accusing his wife of
immoral conduct. Although the Duke in the
end acted honourably by her, he did not dismiss
the miscreants who lied in the basest manner.
There seems reason to believe that a few years
afterwards she did carry on an intrigue with
Henry Sidney, afterwards Earl of Romney, and
Pepys alludes to the rumours respecting this on

[1] *Quoted,* Lister's " Life of Clarendon," ii. 72 (note).

November 17th, 1665, January 9th, 1665-6, and
October 15th, 1666.   Peter Cunningham sums
up the evidence on the point as follows:—
" There cannot, I think, be any doubt of the intrigue of the Duchess of York (Anne Hyde)
with Harry Sidney, afterwards Earl of Romney,
brother of Algernon Sidney and of Waller's
Sacharissa.   See on what testimony it rests.
Hamilton more than hints at it; Burnet is very
pointed about it in his History; Reresby just
mentions and Pepys refers to it in three distinct
entries and on three different authorities." [1]

Pepys tells us that the Duchess sat at her husband's council, and interfered with business,[2] and
the fact that she was the master was generally acknowledged.   On one occasion the King called
his brother " Tom Otter," alluding to the hen-
pecked husband in Ben Jonson's " Epicene, or
the Silent Woman."   Tom Killegrew threw the
sarcasm back upon the King with telling effect,
by saying, " Sir, pray which is the best for a
man to be, a Tom Otter to his wife or to his
mistress ? " [3] it being well known that Charles
was the slave of Lady Castlemaine.

The Duchess possessed great abilities, and
readily adapted herself to her exalted position.
Burnet says of her that she " was a very extraordinary woman.   She had great knowledge,

[1] " The Story of Nell Gwyn," p. 197 (note).
[2] " Diary," Jan. 27, 1667-68.
[3] July 30, 1667.   Mrs. Otter thus addresses her husband
in Act iii. Sc. 1 : " Is this according to the instrument
when I married you, that I would be princess and reign
in my own house, and you would be my subject and obey
me ? "

and a lively sense of things. She understood what belonged to a princess, and took state upon her rather too much."

The next personage of importance at court was Mrs. Palmer, afterwards Countess of Castlemaine and Duchess of Cleveland, who figures so largely in the " Diary." It is greatly to the credit of Lords Clarendon and Southampton that they would have nothing to do with the King's favourite. Burnet tells us that the former would let nothing pass the Great Seal in which she was named, and the latter would never suffer her name to appear in the Treasury books. The King usually held a court at his mistress's lodgings before going to church, and his ministers made their applications there, but Clarendon and Southampton were never to be seen in her rooms.

Clarendon opposed her admission to the post of Lady of the Bedchamber to the Queen, and would not allow his wife to visit her ; in consequence he made an implacable enemy who did not rest until she had compassed his disgrace.

On July 26th, 1662, Pepys heard that when the mistress's name was presented by the King to his wife, the Queen pricked it out of the list. On February 23rd, 1662-63, he heard that the King had given to Lady Castlemaine all the Christmas presents made him by the peers; and that at a court ball she was much richer in jewels than the Queen and Duchess both together. Although our Diarist was a devoted admirer of the lady, he is forced to call this " a most abominable thing."

Lady Castlemaine was a woman of the most abandoned profligacy, and, moreover, of bad manners as well as bad morals. In the Grammont "Memoirs" she is described as "disagreeable from the unpolished state of her manners, her ill-timed pride, her uneven temper and extravagant humours." Pepys knew her only in the distance, and was infatuated with her beauty; at one time he fills his eyes with her, which much pleases him,[1] and at another he "gluts himself with looking at her."[2] The sight of her at any public place was quite sufficient to give him pleasure, whatever the entertainment might be, and his admiration was extended to everything which was in any way connected with the King's mistress.

The greatest beauty at the court of Charles II. was Frances Stuart, who was most assiduously followed by the King. She was the exact opposite of Lady Castlemaine, being as much a lady as her rival was ill-mannered, and as foolish as the other was clever. Her portrait is admirably painted in the Grammont "Memoirs," thus :—" She was childish in her behaviour and laughed at everything, and her taste for frivolous amusements, though unaffected, was only allowable in a girl about twelve or thirteen years old. A child however she was in every other respect, except playing with a doll : blind man's buff was her most favourite amusement : she was building castles of cards, while the deepest play was going on in her apartments, where you saw her surrounded by eager courtiers, who

[1] "Diary," July 23, 1661.   [2] Aug. 23, 1662.

handed her the cards, or young architects, who endeavoured to imitate her."

Her relations with the King were of a very risky character, and scandal made very free with her good fame. Pepys took it for granted after hearing the common report that she was the King's mistress;[1] yet Evelyn told him on April 26th, 1667, that up to the time of her leaving the court to be married there was not a more virtuous woman in the world. A passage in the "Diary" (Nov. 6th, 1663) exhibits very strongly the low state of morality at court. Lord Sandwich told Pepys "how he and Sir H. Bennet, the Duke of Buckingham and his Duchess, was of a committee with somebody else for the getting of Mrs. Stewart for the King, but that she proves a cunning slut, and is advised at Somerset House by the Queen mother, and by her mother, and so all the plot is spoiled and the whole committee broke." By the early part of the year 1667 Mrs. Stewart's position had become quite untenable, and to escape from the King's importunities she accepted the proposal of marriage made to her by the Duke of Richmond. The King threw all the obstacles he could in the way of the marriage, and when the lovers escaped and were united he exhibited the greatest chagrin. Pepys relates a story[2] that Charles one Sunday night took a pair of oars and rowed secretly to Somerset House in order to get sight of the Duchess, who was then living there. The garden door not being open, he is

---

[1] "Diary," Feb. 8, 1662-63; May 18, 1663; April 15, 1666.   [2] May 18, 1668.

said to have clambered over the wall, " which
is a horrid shame ! "

The Duke was afterwards appointed ambassador to Denmark, and died at Elsinore, December 21st, 1672.   After the death of her husband
the Duchess lived at court and attached herself
to the person of the Queen.   In the latter years
of her life she remained in seclusion dividing
her time between cards and cats.   She died in
1702, and by her last will left several favourite
cats to different female friends with legacies for
their support.

> " But thousands died without or this or that,
> Die and endow a college or a cat." [1]

Among the lesser lights of the court was
Elizabeth, Countess of Chesterfield, who figures
so prominently in the Grammont " Memoirs."
The scandal there related did not escape the
open ears of Pepys, who on the 3rd of November, 1662, first hears that the Duke of York is
smitten with the lady; that the Duchess has
complained to the King, and that the Countess
has gone into the country.   The Earl is not
mentioned here, but on January 19th, 1662-3,
the Diarist obtained fuller particulars, and learnt
that Lord Chesterfield had long been jealous of
the Duke.   Pepys calls the Countess " a most
good virtuous woman," and evidently considers
the husband's conduct in carrying off his wife
to his seat in Derbyshire as caused by a fit of
ungrounded jealousy.   The day after Lord
Chesterfield had seen his wife talking with the

[1] Pope's " Moral Essays," Epistle iii.

Duke of York, he went to tell the latter how much he felt wronged, but the Duke answered with calmness, and pretended not to understand the reason of complaint. The story of the *bas verds* that forms so prominent a feature in the Grammont account is not alluded to by the Diarist, but these brilliant coloured stockings introduced by the Countess, seem to have become fashionable subsequently, for on the 15th of February, 1668-9, Pepys bought a pair of green silk stockings, garters, and shoe-strings, and two pairs of jessimy gloves to present to his valentine.

The career of pretty Margaret Brook, who married Sir John Denham on the 25th of May, 1665, was a short one. On the 10th of June, 1666, Pepys hears that she has become the Duke of York's new mistress, and that she declares she will be owned publicly. On November 12th of the same year he hears of her serious illness, an illness that terminated in death.

At this time rumours of poisoning were easily put into circulation, and some supposed that Lady Denham was murdered by her husband. Others whispered that the Duchess of York had poisoned her with powder of diamonds, but when her body was opened after death, as she had desired it should be, no sign of poison was found.[1]

One of the most brilliant of the maids of honour, and, to her credit be it said, one of the few virtuous ladies at court, was Frances Jen-

[1] Lord Orrery to the Duke of Ormond, Jan. 25, 1666-67. (Orrery, " State Papers," fol. 1742, p. 219.)

nings, the eldest sister of Sarah, afterwards
Duchess of Marlborough. The Duke made
advances to her, which she repulsed coolly.
He could not believe in his defeat, and plied
her with love-letters. It was not etiquette for
her to return them to him, so she affected un-
consciousness, and carelessly drawing out her
handkerchief allowed these royal effusions to
fall upon the floor for anyone who chose to pick
up. The King now laid siege to the beauty,
but was equally unsuccessful as his brother had
been. In the Grammont "Memoirs" there is
a full account of the lady's freaks, and Pepys
managed to hear of one of them :—"Mrs. Jennings, one of the Duchess's maids, the other day
dressed herself like an orange wench, and went
up and down, and cried oranges; till falling
down, or by some accident, her fine shoes were
discerned, and she put to a great deal of shame."[1]
This is but a bald account of the adventure so
graphically described by Hamilton, who makes
the object of Miss Jennings's disguise to be a
visit to the famous German doctor and astrologer in Tower Street. Rochester assumed this
character and the name of Alexander Bendo at
the same time, issuing a bill in which he detailed
his cures, and announced his powers of prophecy.
This was on the occasion of one of the wild
young Lord's escapes from court, but we are
not told its date. Hamilton is silent on this
point, but Pepys's corroboration of one part of
the adventure helps to date the other.

Frances Jennings was loved by the dashing

[1] "Diary," Feb. 21, 1664-65.

Dick Talbot, who was accounted the finest figure and the tallest man in the kingdom, but she offended him by her partiality for the lady-killer Jermyn. She was soon disgusted by this empty coxcomb, and in 1665 was married to George Hamilton, brother of the author of the Grammont " Memoirs." After the death of Hamilton, the widow married her first lover Talbot, afterwards created Duke of Tyrconnel. Subsequent to the death of her second husband, she visited London, and hired a stall at the New Exchange in the Strand, where, dressed in a white robe and masked with a white domino, she maintained herself for a time by the sale of small articles of haberdashery. Thus her second and more notorious adventure caused her to be known as the " White Milliner."

This notice of the ladies of the Court of Charles II. may be concluded with a brief mention of the two actresses,—Nell Gwyn and Moll Davis.

Pepys's first mention of the former is under date April 3rd, 1665, where he calls her " pretty witty Nell." He was always delighted to see her, and constantly praises her excellent acting, yet sometimes he finds fault, for instance— " Nell's ill-speaking of a great part made me mad." [1] She disliked acting serious parts, and with reason, for she spoilt them. [2] Pepys mentions on January 11th, 1667-68, that the King had sent several times for Nell, but it was not until some time after that she left the stage finally, and became a recognized mistress of the King.

[1] " Diary," Nov. 11, 1667.   [2] Dec. 26, 1667.

Peter Cunningham tells us, in his " Story of Nell Gwyn," that had the King lived she would have been created Countess of Greenwich. James II. attended to his brother's dying wish : " Do not let poor Nelly starve," and when she was outlawed for debt he paid her debts. Her life was not a long one, and she died of apoplexy in November, 1687, in the thirty-eighth year of her age.

Moll Davis it is well known charmed the King by her singing of the song, " My lodging is on the cold ground," in the character of the shepherdess Celania in Davenant's " Rivals," a play altered from " The Two Noble Kinsmen," and the Duke of Buckingham is said to have encouraged the King's passion for her in order to spite the Countess of Castlemaine. She was also a fine dancer, and greatly pleased Pepys on more than one occasion. On March 7th, 1666-67, he expresses the opinion that her dancing of a jig in boy's clothes was infinitely better than that of Nell Gwyn. About a year after this, when Moll Davis had been "raised" to the position of King's mistress, she danced a jig at court; and the Queen being at this public exhibition of one of her rivals in her own palace, got up and left the theatre.[1]

After the ladies come the male courtiers, but these butterflies of the court do not figure very prominently in the " Diary." Rochester is occasionally mentioned, as is Henry Jermyn rather oftener. Buckingham appears more frequently, but then he set up for a statesman. He was one of the most hateful characters in history,

[1] " Diary," May 31, 1668.

and as one reads in the "Diary" the record of his various actions, the feelings of disgust and loathing that they inspire are near akin to hatred. He gave counsel to the King at which Charles recoiled; he showed himself a coward in his relations with Lord Ossory, and his conduct towards his wife proves that he was not even a gentleman. Grammont calls Buckingham a fool, but he was more of a knave than a fool, for he was too clever for us to be able to despise him. He seems to have exerted the fascination of the serpent over those around him, and the four masterly hands that have drawn his portrait evidently thought it worthy the devotion of their greatest care. Walpole says of these four famous portraits: "Burnet has hewn it out with his rough chisel; Count Hamilton touched it with that slight delicacy that finishes while it seems but to sketch; Dryden caught the living likeness; Pope completed the historical resemblance."[1]

In conclusion, some mention must be made of those who did not take a prominent position at court, but who nevertheless exerted considerable influence in that corrupted circle, such as the Chiffinches, Bab May, and Edward Progers, with all of whom Pepys had constant communication. Thomas Chiffinch was one of the pages of the King's bedchamber, and keeper of his private closet. He died in 1666, and was succeeded in his employments by his brother William, who became a still greater favourite of the King than Thomas, and was the receiver of

[1] "Royal and Noble Authors."

the secret pensions paid by the court of France to the King of England. Progers had been banished from Charles's presence in 1650, by an Act of the Estates of Scotland, " as an evil instrument and bad counseller of the King." Baptist May, Keeper of the Privy Purse, had a still worse rebuff than this, for when he went down in state as the court candidate for Winchelsea, he was rejected by the people, who cried out that they would have " No court pimp to be their burgess." [1]   It would not be fair, however, to throw all the obloquy upon these understrappers, for we have already seen that the bearers of historical names could lend themselves to perform the same duties.

[1] " Diary," Oct. 21, 1666.

CHAPTER X.

PUBLIC CHARACTERS.

"So violent did I find parties in London, that I was assured by several that the Duke of Marlborough was a coward, and Mr. Pope a fool."—VOLTAIRE.

IN dealing with the public characters at the time of the Restoration, the two men who were mainly instrumental in bringing that event about —Monk and Montagu—must needs be given a prominent place.

George Monk, Duke of Albemarle, was a singularly unheroic character. He was slow and heavy, but had a sufficient supply of good sense, and, in spite of many faults, he had the rare good fortune to be generally loved.[1] He was so popular that ballads were continually being made in his praise. Pepys said there were so many

---

[1] "The blockhead Albemarle hath strange luck to be loved, though he be, and every man must know it, the heaviest man in the world, but stout and honest to his country."—"Diary," Oct. 23, 1667.

of them that in after times his fame would sound like that of Guy of Warwick.[1]

Aubrey tells us that Monk learned his trade of soldiering in the Low Countries, whence he fled after having slain a man. Although he frequently went to sea in command of the fleet, he always remained a soldier, and the seamen laughed behind his back when instead of crying "Tack about," he would say "Wheel to the right or left." Pepys tells a story of him to the same effect: "It was, pretty to hear the Duke of Albemarle himself to wish that they would come on our ground, meaning the French, for that he would pay them, so as to make them glad to go back to France again; *which was like a general, but not like an admiral.*"[2]

Monk was fond of low company; both he and his vulgar wife were quite unfit for high—I cannot say refined—society, for there was but little refinement at court. Ann Clarges had been kind to Monk when he was a prisoner in the Tower, and he married her out of gratitude. She had been previously married to Thomas Ratford, of whose death no notice was given at the time of the marriage, so that the legitimacy of Christopher, afterwards second Duke of Albemarle, was seriously questioned. Aubrey relates a story which cannot well be true, but which proves the general feeling of doubt respecting the point. He says that Thomas Clarges came on shipboard to tell Monk that his sister had had a child. Monk cried out, "What is it?" and on hearing the answer, "A boy," he said,

[1] "Diary," March 6, 1667.   [2] April 4, 1667.

" Why, then, she is my wife." Pepys was told a tale by Mr. Cooling which corroborates the opinion expressed on the company kept by the Duke. " Once the Duke of Albemarle, in his drink, taking notice as of a wonder that Nan Hide should ever come to be Duchess of York. ' Nay,' says Troutbeck, ' ne'er wonder at that; for if you will give me another bottle of wine, I will tell you as great, if not a greater miracle.' And what was that, but that our dirty Bess (meaning his Duchess) should come to be Duchess of Albemarle?" [1]

Sir Edward Montagu, Earl of Sandwich, was in every respect the opposite of Monk. He was a courtier and a gentleman, but he did not manage to gain the popularity of his great contemporary, nor to retain such as he did at one time possess. As Pepys's great patron his name naturally occupies a very prominent position in the " Diary," and as such he has already been frequently alluded to in these pages. He appears to have been a very agreeable man, but so easy and careless in business matters that he was continually in want of money. In 1662 Pepys found that he was above £7,000 in debt, and his enemies soon after gave out that his debts amounted to £100,000. At any rate, his finances were so often in an unsatisfactory state that Pepys had a special dislike to lending his money in that quarter. Three years afterwards he had grown very unpopular, and " it was purposed by some hot-heads in the House of Commons, at the same time when they voted a pre-

[1] " Diary," Nov. 4, 1666.

sent to the Duke of York, to have voted £10,000 to the Prince, and *half-a-crown* to my Lord of Sandwich ; but nothing came of it."[1] It was, therefore, well for him when he obtained an honourable exile by being appointed ambassador to the court of Spain, as there he was held in high esteem. His enemies, however, were not satisfied, and they continued to attack him during his absence. Whatever his faults, and they were probably many, Lord Sandwich was by far the most able naval commander of his time, so that the nation had a heavy loss when he was killed in the naval action against the Dutch at Solebay, in May, 1672.

Prince Rupert, as the cousin of the King, naturally held a prominent position in the State, but he did not gain much credit from the undertakings he was thrust into. His fame as a brilliant, though rash, soldier, was gained during the troubles of his uncle's reign, and not from anything he did after the Restoration. He was out of place on board ship, although he is said to have displayed immense bravery and much skill in the sea-fight against the Dutch, from August 11th to 13th, 1673. His interest in science and mechanical art appears to have been real, and to him we owe the invention or introduction into England of mezzotinto engraving, and the introduction of

> . . . " that glassy bubble
> That finds philosophers such trouble,
> Whose least part cracked, the whole does fly,
> And wits are cracked to find out why."

[1] "Diary," Nov. 6, 1665.

The Prince's courage was so patent to all that his friends were rather surprised to find that when he was very ill and like to die, "he had no more mind to it than another man;" so they came to the rather lame conclusion that "courage is not what men take it to be—a contempt of death."[1]

The next great public character was Edward Hyde, Earl of Clarendon, who for the few years before his fall was the greatest man in the kingdom. Public opinion has been much divided as to his merits. In spite of many very evident faults, he certainly exhibited on several occasions a high-minded spirit. He would not consent to do any business with the King's mistresses, and Burnet says that he "kept a register of all the King's promises, and of his own, and did all that lay in his power afterwards to get them performed." His disposition was rather ungracious, and he made many enemies, who attacked him with success when the King was tired of him. Clarendon was very dictatorial with Charles, and sent him such missives as this, "I pray be at Worcester House on Sunday as soon as may be." On one occasion he fixed eight o'clock in the morning, for Lord Broghill to have an audience with the King, who did not think the arrangement quite fair, and wrote, "You give appointments in a morning to others sooner than you take them yourself, but if my Lord Broghill will come at nine, he shall be welcome."

On the institution of the Royal Society, Lord Clarendon was appointed visitor for life, but after his death the position was to be held by

[1] "Diary," Jan. 15, 1664-65.

several high officers, by reason of their offices. Sprat, in his "History of the Royal Society," specially thanks the Lord Chancellor, Attorney-General, and Solicitor-General, for their assistance in the preparation of the charter; a proof, says Sprat, of the falsehood of the reproach that law is an enemy to learning and civil arts.

One day in July, 1664, Lord Sandwich told Pepys that Lord Clarendon was very displeased with him for being forward in the cutting down of trees in Clarendon Park; so the Diarist sought an interview with the Lord Chancellor in order that he might soothe the great man, and he was successful in his endeavour.[1]

Clarendon Park, near Salisbury, was crown-land mortgaged by Charles I. for £20,000, and granted by Charles II. to the Duke of Albemarle subject to this mortgage, and with the right to the timber reserved to the Crown. Lord Clarendon bought the place of Albemarle, and his complaint against the Commissioners of the Navy was, that while they had all the royal forests at command, they chose to spoil the beauty of his property. He further affirmed that he had no intention to contest the King's right, nor to defraud the Crown of timber; but complained that at the very time the Commissioners sent down a person to mark standing timber for felling, there was a large quantity of wood belonging to the Crown lying on the estate unappropriated, which had been "felled divers years" before.[2]

Two of Pepys's patrons—Sir George Down-

[1] "Diary," July 14, 1664.
[2] Lister's "Life of Clarendon," vol. iii. p. 340.

ing and Sir William Coventry—are frequently mentioned in the "Diary;" the first almost always with some expression of dislike, and the other invariably in terms of respect. He sometimes describes his whilom master as "a stingy fellow,"[1] and laughs at his ridiculous pieces of thrift, "and niggardly manner of entertaining his poor neighbours."[2] At another time he calls him "a perfidious rogue" for betraying former friends;[3] still, he could appreciate Downing's business capabilities, and when setting down the fact that the Commissioners of the Treasury had chosen Sir G. Downing for their secretary, he added, "I think, in my conscience, they have done a great thing in it, for he is active and a man of business, and values himself upon having of things do well under his hand; so that I am mightily pleased in their choice."[4] At this time Pepys had forgotten the constant causes of annoyance which Downing had given him, and he could afford to be magnanimous in acknowledging his enemy's good qualities. I have already remarked that Sir William Coventry stands out prominently as the only person who is noticed in the "Diary" in terms of unqualified praise. Other men of the time did not equally admire him, so that it is not easy to come to a just estimation of his character.

Poor Pepys was placed in an awkward predicament on one occasion when he was on a visit to Hampton Court, owing to the enmity between Coventry and Lord Sandwich. He was pleased

[1] "Diary," June 28, 1660.   [2] Feb. 27, 1666-67.
[3] March 12, 1661-62.   [4] May 27, 1667.

when the latter asked him to come privately to his lodgings, but adds, "Lord! to see in what difficulty I stand, that I dare not walk with Sir W. Coventry for fear my Lord or Sir G. Carteret should see me; nor with either of them, for fear Sir W. Coventry should."[1]

When Clarendon fell, in 1667, it was thought likely that Coventry would succeed him as virtual prime minister. His quarrel, however, with the Duke of Buckingham put him out of favour with the King and out of office; so that, although he survived until 1686, he never again took a prominent part in political affairs.

Arthur Annesley, afterwards Earl of Angle sey, is called by Pepys "a grave, serious man,"[2] and "a very notable man,"[3] but he does not appear to have been a very friendly one. Although he was under obligations to Sir Edward Montagu's family, he took the opportunity, when the thanks of Parliament were voted to Montagu, to quash the motion which was made to give him a reward.[4] He was made Treasurer of the Navy in 1667, in succession to Sir George Carteret, and in the following year when he answered the Duke of York's letter, he bid the Duke call for Pepys's books,[5] in hopes that the Clerk of the Acts might get a reprimand. A peace seems afterwards to have subsisted between the two, for in 1672 Lord Anglesey signed himself in a letter to Pepys, "Your affectionate friend and servant."

[1] "Diary," Jan. 28, 1665-66.   [2] Dec. 3, 1664.
[3] July 9, 1667.   [4] June 19, 1660.
                    [5] Sept. 16, 1668.

Sir Thomas Osborne, subsequently Viscount Dunblane, Earl of Danby, Marquis of Carmarthen, and Duke of Leeds, was appointed joint Treasurer of the Navy, with Sir Thomas Littleton, to succeed Lord Anglesey. This appointment was greatly disliked by the Duke of York and the officers of the navy, who looked upon the two men as spies set to watch them. Pepys calls Osborne a creature of the Duke of Buckingham's,[1] and at another time says he is a beggar "having £11 or £12,00 a year, but owes about £10,000."[2] It is clear that the Diarist did not foresee the great figure Osborne was about to make in the world ; a rise somewhat due to his own parts, and much to the favour of the King. When Charles made him Lord High Treasurer, he told him that he ought to take care of himself, for he had but two friends in England. This startled Osborne, until his majesty explained himself by saying that he (the King) was one, and the other was the Treasurer's merits.[3]

Joseph Williamson, who rose from a college tutorship to the office of Secretary of State, has a few words of praise given to him in the "Diary." He was the son of a clergyman, and in early life is said to have acted as secretary to a member of parliament. He graduated at Oxford as a member of Queen's College, and in December, 1661, was appointed Keeper of the State Paper Office. About the same time

---

[1] "Diary," Oct. 29, 1668.   [2] Feb. 14, 1668-69.
[3] Sir John Williamson's "Letters" (Camden Society), vol. i. p. 64.

he was Latin Secretary to the King, an office
the reversion of which had been promised to
John Evelyn.   In 1666 Williamson undertook
the superintendence of the " London Gazette,"
and in 1672 obtained the post of Clerk to the
Privy Council, on the resignation of Sir Richard
Browne, when he was knighted.   The King had
many years before promised to give the place
to Evelyn, but in consideration of the renewal
of the lease of Sayes Court, the latter parted
with it to Williamson.   Honours now came
thick upon the new-made knight.   He was
Plenipotentiary at the Congress of Cologne in
1673 and 1674, and on his return to England
was made Principal Secretary of State, a position
which he held for four years.   He was President
of the Royal Society in 1678, and married
Catherine Stuart, daughter of George, Lord
Aubigny, and widow of Henry O'Brien, Lord
Ibracken, eldest son of the Earl of Thomond,
in 1682.   He died in 1701, and was buried in
the Duke of Richmond and Lennox's vault in
Henry VII.'s Chapel, by right of his wife's
connection with the Duke of Lennox.

The widow's eldest son by her first husband,
Donald O'Brien, was lost in the wreck of the
"Gloucester" in 1682, and he is mentioned in a
letter of Pepys to Hewer, written from Edinburgh on May 8th of that year.   The will of
the father contains the following very remarkable paragraph :—" I conjure my son Donatus
O'Brien, to honour and obey his King in whatever he commands that is not contradictory to
the Holy Scripture and Protestant religion, in
which I conjure him (upon pain of my curse)

not only to continue himself, but to advise his brothers and sisters to do the same; and that he never marry a Papist; and that he take great care if ever God bless him with children (which I trust he will many) to breed them strictly in the Protestant religion. I advise him to cherish the English on his estate, and drive out the Irish, and especially those of them who go under the name of gentlemen." [1]

Before passing on to make a final note on some of the celebrated sailors alluded to in the "Diary," a place must be found for one of the most eccentric women that ever lived—Margaret, Duchess of Newcastle. Pepys writes, "the whole story of this lady is romance, and all she does is romantic." [2] Every one who came in contact with her fooled her to the top of her bent. Evelyn likened her to Zenobia, the mother of the Gracchi, Vittoria Colonna, besides a long line of other celebrities, and when she "took the dust" in the park she was followed and crowded upon by coaches all the way she went, so that nobody could come near her. [3]

Her husband's play, "The Humourous Lovers," was, Pepys says, "the most silly thing that ever came upon a stage," [4] and also "the most ridiculous thing that ever was wrote," [5] yet she and the Duke were "mightily pleased with it, and she at the end made her respects to the players from her box, and did give them thanks."

On the 30th of May, 1667, the Duchess made

---

[1] See that monument of learning and research, Chester's "Westminster Abbey Registers," 1875, p. 194 (note).
[2] "Diary," April 11, 1667.   [3] May 1, 1667.
[4] March 30.   [5] April 11, 1667.

O

a visit to one of the meetings of the Royal Society, when various fine experiments were shown for her entertainment. She was loud in her expressions of admiration as she was led out of the room by several noblemen who were among the company present. There had been great debate among the philosophers as to the advisability of inviting the lady, for many believed that the town would be full of ballads on the event. Her footmen were habited in velvet coats, and she herself appeared in antique dress, so that there is no cause for wonder that people came to see her as if she were the Queen of Sheba. Mrs. Evelyn drew a very lively picture of the Duchess in a letter to Dr. Bohun : "I acknowledge, though I remember her some years since, and have not been a stranger to her fame, I was surprised to find so much extravagancy and vanity in any person not confined within four walls. . . Her mien surpasses the imagination of poets or the descriptions of romance heroine's greatness; her gracious bows, seasonable nods, courteous stretching out of her hands, twinkling of her eyes, and various gestures of approbation, show what may be expected from her discourse, which is airy, empty, whimsical, and rambling as her books, aiming at science difficulties, high notions, terminating commonly in nonsense, oaths, and obscenity." Pepys's summing up of the Duchess's character is shorter, but accords well with Mrs. Evelyn's opinion—he says she was "a mad, conceited, ridiculous woman." [1]

[1] "Diary," March 18, 1668.

In a book written by a man so intimately
connected with the navy as Pepys was, it is not
surprising that mention should occur pretty frequently of sailors and soldiers who commanded
at sea.

In the great victory over the Dutch in 1665,
the Earl of Falmouth, Lord Muskerry, and
Richard Boyle, second son of the Earl of Bur-
lington, were all killed by one shot, as they were
standing on board the "Royal Charles," close
by the Duke of York, into whose face their
blood spurted. The Earl appears very frequently in the "Diary" as Sir Charles Berkeley,
Lord Berkeley, Lord Fitzharding, and Earl of
Falmouth, and he was to have been created a
Marquis had he lived. Charles II. shed a flood
of tears when he heard of his friend's death,
but Pepys tells us that none but the King wished
him alive again.[1]

Lord Clarendon put in a few bitter words the
most thorough condemnation of the man. He
said, "few had observed in him any virtue or
quality which they did not wish their best friends
without." The various allusions to Lord Falmouth in the "Diary" quite bear out this
character, and yet because he was Sir William
Coventry's friend we are told of "his generosity,
good nature, desire of public good, and low
thoughts of his own wisdom; his employing his
interest in the king to do good offices to all
people, without any other fault than the freedom
he do learn in France of thinking himself
obliged to serve his king in his pleasures."[2]

[1] "Diary," June 9, 1665.   [2] August 30, 1668.

A much greater national loss which took place in this engagement was the death of the famous admiral Sir John Lawson. This chief among the "tarpaulins" was well known to Pepys, as he was the vice-admiral under Sir Edward Montagu at the time when Charles II. was brought over by the fleet. He is described as the same plain man as ever after all his successes,[1] yet an enemy called him a false man, and the greatest hypocrite in the world.[2] When Lawson died, Pepys could not but acknowledge that the nation had a loss, although he was not sorry, because the late admiral had never been a friend to him.[3] In the great engagement against the Dutch of the 3rd of June, 1665, Opdam's ship blew up, and a shot from it, or rather a piece of iron, wounded Lawson on the knee, from which he never recovered. The national loss is expressed in one of the " Poems on State Affairs."[4]

> " Destiny allowed
> Him his revenge, to make his death more proud.
> A fatal bullet from his side did range,
> And battered Lawson ; oh, too dear exchange !
> He led our fleet that day too short a space,
> But lost his knee : since died, in glorious race :
> Lawson, whose valour beyond Fate did go,
> And still fights Opdam in the lake below."

In October, 1666, there was a rumour that Sir Jeremy Smith had killed Sir Robert Holmes in a duel, and Pepys was not sorry to hear it, although he soon found that report did not tell

[1] " Diary," Jan. 12, 1662-63.   [2] Nov. 9, 1663.
[3] June 25, 1665.   [4] Vol. i. p. 24.

true.[1] Holmes was very unpopular, and Andrew Marvell called him the "cursed beginner of the two Dutch wars ;" describing him as "first an Irish livery boy, then a highwayman, now Bashaw of the Isle of Wight," who had "got in bonds and by rapine £100,000."[2]

Sir Jeremy Smith was befriended by the Duke of Albemarle, when Holmes delivered articles of accusation against him to the King and Cabinet, and he suffered no ill from the vengeance of his enemy, for in 1669 he was appointed a Commissioner of the Navy in place of Sir William Penn. Pepys was able to find an epithet for him, and although he liked him fairly well, he called him "an impertinent fellow."[3]

This slight notice of some of the sailors of the Restoration period may well be closed by a relation of the remarkable action of certain seamen at the funeral of Sir Christopher Mings. Mings, like Lawson, was of poor extraction, and, like him, grew up a worthy captain. He was wounded in the face and leg in an engagement with the Dutch, and shortly afterwards died of his wounds. Pepys and Sir William Coventry attended the funeral, and on their going away, "about a dozen able, lusty, proper men came to the coach side with tears in their eyes, and one of them that spoke for the rest begun and said to Sir W. Coventry, 'We are here a dozen of us that have long known and loved and served our dead commander, Sir Christopher Mings,

---

[1] "Diary," Oct. 31, 1666.
[2] "Seasonable Argument," 1677.
[3] "Diary," May 10, 1669.

and have now done the last office of laying him
in the ground. We would be glad we had any
other to offer after him, and revenge of him.
All we have is our lives ; if you will please to
get His Royal Highness to give us a fireship
among us all, here is a dozen of us, out of all
which choose you one to be commander, and
the rest of us, whoever he is, will serve him ;
and if possible do that that shall show our
memory of our dead commander and our revenge.'"   When this speech was finished
Coventry was much moved, and Pepys could
scarcely refrain from tears.[1] What became of
these worthy men we are not told.

[1] "Diary," June 13, 1666.

CHAPTER XI.

MANNERS.

"The king's most faithful subjects we,
    In 's service are not dull,
We drink to show our loyalty,
    And make his coffers full.
Would all his subjects drink like us,
    We'd make him richer far,
More powerful and more prosperous
    Than all the Eastern monarchs are."
SHADWELL'S *The Woman Captain.*

NO passages in the "Diary" are more valuable than those from which we can gather some idea of the manners of the time in which Pepys lived. It is chiefly, in fact, on account of the pictures of the mode of life among the men and women of the middle classes portrayed in those passages that the book has attained its immense popularity. History instructs, while gossip charms, so that for hundreds who desire to learn the chronicle of events, thousands long to hear how their ordinary fellow creatures lived, what they ate, what they wore, and what they did.

Pepys liked good living, and he was careful to set down what he ate, so that we are able to judge of his taste. This is what he calls a "pretty dinner"—"a brace of stewed carps, six roasted chickens and a jowl of salmon hot, for the first course; a tanzy and two neats' tongues, and cheese the second."[1] A good calf's head boiled with dumplings he thought an excellent dinner,[2] and he was very proud of a dinner he gave to some friends, which consisted of "fricasee of rabbits and chickens, a leg of mutton boiled, three carps in a dish, a great dish of a side of a lamb, a dish of roasted pigeons, a dish of four lobsters, three tarts, a lamprey pie (a most rare pie), a dish of anchovies, good wine of several sorts and all things mighty noble and to my great content."[3] He was very indignant when Sir W. Hickes gave him and his fellows "the meanest dinner (of beef, shoulder and umbles of venison, which he takes away from the keeper of the forest, and a few pigeons, and all in the meanest manner) that ever I did see, to the basest degree."[4] Pepys liked all kinds of pies, whether they contained fish or swan, but there was one pie in particular that was filled with such a pleasant variety of good things that he never tasted the like in all his life.[5] On two several occasions he records his appreciation of a joint which sounds strange to modern ears—viz., boiled haunch of venison.[6] At special seasons he was in the habit of partaking of the diet appropriate

---

[1] "Diary," March 26, 1662.   [2] Nov. 1, 1663.
[3] April 4, 1665.   [4] Sept. 13, 1665.
[5] Nov. 14, 1661.   [6] Sept. 9, 1662 ; Dec. 28, 1667.

to the festival : thus on Shrove Tuesday he ate fritters,[1] and at Christmas mince pies[2] or plum porridge,[3] plum pudding not having been at that time invented. The meat taken with these sweets was sometimes the orthodox beef, but it was more often something else, as on Christmas day, 1660, when it consisted of shoulder of mutton and chicken.

Breakfast was not formerly made an ordinary meal, but radishes were frequently taken with the morning draught. On May 2nd, 1660, Pepys had his breakfast of radishes in the Purser's cabin of the " Naseby," in accordance with the rule laid down by Muffet in his " Health's Improvement " (1655), that they " procure appetite and help digestion ; " which is still acted upon in Italy.

Ale-houses, mum-houses, and wine-houses abounded in all parts of London, and much money must have been spent in them. The charges seem to have been high, for Pepys relates how on one occasion the officers of the navy met the Commissioners of the Ordnance at the Dolphin Tavern, when the cost of their dinner was 34s. a man.[4] We are not told how much Sir W. Batten, Sir W. Penn, and Pepys had to pay when they ordered their dinner at the Queen's Head at Bow, and took their own meat with them from London.[5]

There is abundant evidence in the " Diary " of the prevalent habits of deep drinking, and

[1] " Diary," Feb. 26, 1660-61.   [2] Dec. 25, 1666.
[3] Dec. 25, 1662.   [4] June 20, 1665.
[5] March 14, 1667.

Pepys himself evidently often took more than was good for him. Men were very generally unfit for much business after their early dinners; thus Pepys tells of his great speech at the bar of the House of Commons that it lasted so long that many of the members went out to dinner, and when they came back they were half drunk.[1] Sir William Penn told an excellent story which exhibits well the habits of the time. Some gentlemen (?) drinking at a tavern blindfolded the drawer, and told him that the one he caught would pay the reckoning. All, however, managed to escape, and when the master of the house came up to see what was the matter, his man caught hold of him, thinking he was one of the gentlemen, and cried out that he must pay the reckoning.[2] Various drinks are mentioned in the " Diary," such as mum (an ale brewed with wheat), buttered ale (a mixture of beer, sugar, cinnamon, and butter), and lamb's wool (a mixture of ale with sugar, nutmeg, and the pulp of roasted apples), among other doctored liquors. Such stuff as this does not indicate a refined taste, and the same may be said when we find that wine was also made up for vitiated palates. On June 10th, 1663, Pepys goes with three friends to the Half Moon Tavern, and buys some sugar on the way to mix with the wine. We read of Muscadel, and various kinds of sack, as Malago sack, raspberry sack, and sack posset, of Florence wine, and of Navarre wine. Rhine

---

[1] " Diary," March 5, 1667-68.
[2] Oct. 9, 1660. This is one of the additions in Mr. Mynors Bright's edition.

wines must have been popular at this time, if we may judge from the numerous Rhenish wine-houses spread about the town. Amongst Pepys's papers was found a memorandum on the dangers England might experience in the event of a war with France. Lord Dartmouth proposed that we might ruin the French by forbidding their wines, " but that he considers, will never be observed with all our heat against France. We see that, rather than not drink their wine, we forget our interest against it, and play all the villanies and perjuries in the world to bring it in, because people will drink it, if it be to be had, at any rate."[1] What Lord Dartmouth thought to be impossible was practically effected by the Methuen treaty in 1703, after the signing of which French wines were driven out of the English market for many years by Spanish wines, and it was long thought patriotic to drink port.

Pepys liked to be in the fashion, and to wear a newly-introduced costume, although he was displeased when Lady Wright talked about the great happiness of "being in the fashion, and in variety of fashions in scorn of others that are not so, as citizens' wives and country gentlewomen."[2] The Diary is full of references to new clothes, and Pepys never seems so happy as when priding himself upon his appearance and describing the beauties of velvet cloaks, silk coats, and gold buttons. In 1663, he found that his expenses had been somewhat too large, and that the increase had chiefly arisen from expenditure on

[1] Smith's " Life, Journals, &c., of Pepys," vol. ii. p. 202.
[2] " Diary," Dec. 3, 1661.

clothes for himself and wife, although, as already remarked, it appears that Mrs. Pepys's share was only £12, against her husband's £55.[1] In fact, our Diarist was at one time rather mean in regard to the money he allowed his wife, although afterwards he was more generous, and even gave £80 for a necklace of pearls which he presented to her.

One of the strangest attempts to fix a fashion was made by Charles the Second, who soon, however, tired of his own scheme. In 1661, John Evelyn advocated a particular kind of costume in a little book entitled "Tyrannus, or the Mode." Whether the King took his idea from this book, or whether it originated in his own mind we cannot tell, but at all events, on the 17th of October, 1666, he declared to the Privy Council his "resolution of setting a fashion for clothes which he will never alter." Pepys describes the costume in which Charles appeared on the 15th of October in the following words:—"A long cassock close to the body, of black cloth and pinked with white silk under it, and a coat over it, and the legs ruffled with black rib and like a pigeon's leg, . . . a very fine and handsome garment." Several of the courtiers offered heavy bets that Charles would not persist in his resolution of never altering this costume, and they were right, for very shortly afterwards it was abandoned. The object aimed at was to abolish the French fashion, which had caused great expense, but in order to thwart his brother of England's purpose, the King of France ordered all his footmen to put on the English

---

[1] "Diary," Oct 31, 1663.

vests.[1] This impertinence on the part of Louis
XIV., which appears to have given Steele a hint
for his story of Brunetta and Phillis in the " Spectator," caused the discontinuance of the so-called
Persian habit at the English Court.

There are occasional allusions in the " Diary "
to female dress. Thus, on October 15th, 1666,
Lady Carteret tells Pepys that the ladies are
about to adopt a new fashion, and "wear short
coats above their ancles," in place of the long
trains, which both the gossips thought "mighty
graceful." At another time Pepys was pleased
to see "the young, pretty ladies dressed like
men, in velvet coats, caps with ribands, and with
laced bands, just like men."[2] Vizards or black
masks appear to have come into general use, or
rather were revived by the ladies about 1663.
By wearing them women were able to sit out
the most licentious play with unblushing face.
We read that Pepys and his wife went to the
Theatre Royal on June 12th of that year:—
"Here I saw my Lord Falconbridge and his Lady,
my Lady Mary Cromwell, who looks as well as
I have known her, and well clad; but when the
House began to fill she put on her vizard, and so
kept it on all the play; which of late is become a
great fashion among the ladies, which hides their
whole face." After the play Pepys and Mrs.
Pepys went off to the Exchange to buy a vizard,
so that the latter might appear in the fashion.

The custom of wearing the hat indoors is
more than once alluded to in the " Diary,"[3] and

---

[1] "Diary," Nov. 22, 1666.   [2] July 27, 1665.
[3] Jan. 21, 1660-61.

on one occasion Pepys was evidently much
elated by the circumstance that he was in a
position to wear his hat—" Here it was mighty
strange to find myself sit here in Committee
with my hat on, while Mr. Sherwin stood bare
as a clerk, with his hat off to his Lord Ashly and
the rest, but I thank God I think myself never
a whit the better man for all that."[1] This practice, which still exists in the House of Commons,
was once universal, and in the statutes of the
Royal Society the right of addressing the meeting with his hat on was reserved to the president, the other members being expected to
uncover on rising to speak. A few years after
the above committee meeting, it became the
fashion of the young "blades" to wear their
hats cocked at the back of their heads.[2] This
obtained the name of the "Monmouth cock,"
after the popular Duke of Monmouth, and according to the "Spectator," it still lingered in the
west of England among the country squires as
late as 1711. "During our progress through the
most western parts of the kingdom, we fancied
ourselves in King Charles the Second's reign,
the people having made little variations in their
dress since that time. The smartest of the
country squires appear still in the Monmouth
cock."[3]

Gloves were then, as now, looked upon as an
appropriate present to a lady, and Pepys often
bought them for this purpose. On October 27th,
1666, he gave away several pairs of *jessimy* or

[1] "Diary," Jan. 17, 1664-65. [2] June 3, 1667.
[3] "Spectator," No. 129.

jessemin gloves, as Autolycus says, "gloves as sweet as damask roses;" and on January 25th, 1668-69, he was vexed when his wife wanted him to buy two or three dozen perfumed gloves for her. Those who did not wear these useful coverings laid themselves open to remark, as we read of Wallington, a little fellow who sang an excellent bass, that he was "a poor fellow, a working goldsmith, that goes without gloves to his hands."[1] The use of muffs by men became common after the Restoration, and continued till Horace Walpole's day, and even later. November, 1662, was a very cold month, and Pepys was glad to wear his wife's last year's muff, and to buy her a new one. The long hair worn by the cavaliers was superseded soon after the Restoration by the use of wigs. Pepys went on the 29th of August, 1663, to his barber's to be trimmed, when he returned a periwig which had been sent for his approval, as he had not quite made up his mind to wear one, and "put it off for a while." Very soon afterwards, however, he ordered one to be made for him;[2] and then he had his hair cut off, which went against his inclination. The new wig cost three pounds, and the old hair was used to make another.[3] This last only cost twenty-one shillings and sixpence to make up, and the peruque-maker promised that the two would last for two years.[4] The Duke of York very soon followed the fashion set by his subordinate, and put on a wig for the first time on February 15th, 1663-4. These magni-

[1] "Diary," Sept. 15, 1667.   [2] Oct. 30, 1663.
[3] Nov. 3, 1663.   [4] Nov. 13, 1663.

ficent ornaments, which look so grand in the portraits, were very apt to get out of order, and on
one occasion Pepys had to send his wig back to
the barber's to be cleansed of its nits.   No wonder he was vexed at having had it sent to him in
such a state.[1] On May 30th, 1668, he came to an
agreement with his barber to keep his wigs in
good order for twenty shillings a year.   It is remarkable that people did not return to the sen-
sible fashion of wearing their own hair after the
plague, when there must have been great dread
of infection from this source.   Pepys bought a
wig at Westminster during the sickness, and was
long afraid to wear it. He adds, "it is a wonder
what will be the fashion after the plague is done,
as to periwigs, for nobody will dare to buy any
hair, for fear of the infection, that it had been
cut off the heads of people dead of the plague."[2]

Before passing on to consider some other customs, a word should be said on the practice of
wearing mourning. When the Duke of Gloucester died, it is related that the King wore
purple, which was used as royal mourning.   At
the same time Mrs. Pepys spent £15 on mourning clothes for herself and husband.[3] We are
told how the whole family went into black on
the death of the elder Mrs. Pepys,[4] and we have
very full and curious particulars of the funeral of
Thomas Pepys.   For this occasion Samuel had
the soles of his shoes blacked, which seems a
rather odd kind of mourning![5]

[1] "Diary," July 18, 1664.   [2] Sept. 3, 1665.
[3] Sept. 17, 1660.   [4] March 27, 1667.
[5] March 18, 1663-64.

The engagement between Philip Carteret and Lady Jemimah Montagu gave the Diarist considerable employment, and from the long account he has written on it we gather that he was very proud of such assistance as he was able to give. Carteret was a shy young man, and needed much instruction, as to how he should take the lady's hand, and what he should do. The whole description is very droll, but too long to quote here. Pepys made the best of the affair, but he evidently thought his *protégé* a very insipid lover. The wedding took place on July 31st, 1665, the bride and bridegroom being in their old clothes, but Pepys was resplendent in a "new coloured suit and coat trimmed with gold buttons, and gold broad lace round his hands, very rich and fine." This is the account of what occurred after supper :—"All of us to prayers as usual, and the young bride and bridegroom too; and so after prayers soberly to bed ; only I got into the bridegroom's chamber while he undressed himself, and there was very merry till he was called to the bride's chamber, and into bed they went. I kissed the bride in bed, and so the curtains drawn with the greatest gravity that could be, and so good night. But the modesty and gravity of this business was so decent that it was to me, indeed, ten times more delightful than if it had been twenty times more merry and jovial."

There are several allusions in the "Diary" to the custom of scrambling for ribbons and garters at weddings, and Pepys expresses himself as not pleased when favours were sent to others after Lord Hinchingbroke's wedding, and he was

P

overlooked.[1] At this time wedding rings were not the plain and inelegant things they are now, but were frequently ornamented with precious stones, and almost invariably had a motto engraved upon them. Pepys's aunt Wight was "mighty proud" of her wedding ring, which cost her twelve pounds, and had been lately set with diamonds.[2]

It is not necessary to remark that there was a considerable laxity of manners during the period with which we are now dealing, as this is pretty well known, but one or two passages in the "Diary" may, perhaps, be alluded to here. On one occasion Mrs. Turner, the wife of a serjeant-at-law, while dressing herself in her room by the fire, took occasion to show Pepys her leg, which she was very proud of, and which he affirms was the finest he had ever seen.[3] At another time, Pepys went to Lady Batten's, when he found her and several friends very merry in her chamber; Lady Penn flung him down upon the bed, and then herself and the others came down one after another upon him. He might well add, "and very merry we were."[4]

This laxity of manners is invariably laid to the demoralizing effect of the Restoration, but it is evident from this portion of the "Diary," which was written before that event, that it was as usual for men to visit ladies in their bedrooms before Charles II. "returned to take possession of his birthright," as it was afterwards. Thus we read that on February 24th, 1659-60, Pepys

---

[1] "Diary," Jan. 17, 1667-68. [2] Dec. 4, 1668.
[3] Jan. 3, 1664-65. [4] April 12, 1665.

took horse at Scotland Yard, and rode to Mr. Pierce, " who rose, and in a quarter of an hour, leaving his wife in bed (with whom Mr. Lucy, methought, was very free as she lay in bed) ; we both mounted and so set forth about seven of the clock." This remark probably offended Lord Braybrooke's modesty, for it appears for the first time in Mr. Mynors Bright's edition.

There are several passages in the " Diary " which are of interest, as showing how our ancestors travelled. Although travelling by coach was a very slow operation, much ground could be got over in a short space of time on horseback. On the 6th of July, 1661, Pepys set out for Brampton about noon, and arrived there at nine o'clock at night; having ridden at the rate of about nine miles an hour, with allowance for stoppages for refreshment.

The first great improvement in coach-building was made soon after the Restoration, when glass-coaches were introduced. The Comte de Grammont did not approve of the coach made for the King, and therefore ordered from Paris an elegant and magnificent calash, which was greatly admired, and cost him two thousand louis.

There were some who did not appreciate the improved carriages, and were alive to the evils that were caused by the change. " Another pretty thing was my Lady Ashly's speaking of the bad qualities of glass-coaches, among others the flying open of the doors upon any great shake ; but another was that my Lady Peterborough being in her glass-coach with the glass up, and seeing a lady pass by in a coach whom she would salute, the glass was so clear that she thought it had been open, and so ran her head through the glass!"[1]

It is a curious instance of the survival of terms in popular language that certain carriages were styled glass-coaches even within living memory.

Although the hours kept by "society" in Charles II.'s reign were considerably earlier than those now adopted, and Pepys often went to bed by daylight,[2] yet people did sit up very late sometimes. On the 9th of May, 1668, the House of Commons sat till five o'clock in the morning to discuss a difference that had arisen between them and the House of Lords. One night Pepys stayed at the office so late that it was nearly two o'clock before he got to bed,[3] and at another time the servant got up at the same hour to do the week's washing.[4] The watchman perambulated the streets with his bell and called out the hours, so that when Pepys was sitting up to fill up the entries in the "Diary," he often heard the cry "Past one of the clock, and a cold, frosty, windy morning,"[5] or some similar information.

It is not easy to settle with any great accuracy the respective values of money at that time and at present, as many things were considerably cheaper, but others were dearer. Bab May said that £300 per annum was an ample income for a country gentlemen; a remark that was repeated by Marvell, and increased by him to £500. The gentry did not like this criticism,

---

[1] "Diary," Sept. 23, 1667.
[2] June 12, 1662; July 1, 1662.   [3] Jan. 30, 1664-65.
[4] March 12, 1659-60.   [5] Jan. 16, 1659-60.

but it shows at least that money had a much greater purchasing power then than now. In the winter of 1666-67 the farmers were very unfortunate, and many were forced to become bankrupts, so that property previously bringing in £1,000[1] suddenly became worth only £500. The wages of a cookmaid were £4 a year, which Pepys thought high,[2] and a coach cost £53,[3] but a beaver hat was charged as high as £4 5s.[4] Twenty-five pounds was paid for a painted portrait, and £30 for a miniature, and £80 for a necklace of pearls. Cherries were sold at two shillings a pound,[5] oranges at six shillings a dozen, and dinners at an ordinary varied from seven shillings to a guinea.

There are so many little items in the "Diary" which are of interest as illustrating old customs, some of which still exist, and others which have died out, that it would be quite impossible to allude here even to a fraction of them. One or two instances, therefore, gathered at random, must be sufficient. Pepys on several occasions mentions the custom of "beating the bounds" in the various parishes on Ascension Day or Holy Thursday, when a boy was in some cases beaten, or, as in Dorsetshire, tossed into a stream, in order to impress very forcibly upon his memory the locality of the parish boundaries. At one time he writes, " This day was kept a holy-day through the

[1] "Diary," Feb. 27, 1666-67. [2] March 26, 1663.
[3] Oct. 24, 1668. [4] June 27, 1661.
[5] "When cherries were first introduced into England they cost as much as 20s. a pound."—Buckle's "Common-place Book," vol. ii. p. 395.

town; and it pleased me to see the little boys walk up and down in procession with their broom-staffs in their hands, as I had myself long ago gone,"[1] and at another, "They talked with Mr. Mills about the meaning of this day, and the good uses of it; and how heretofore, and yet in several places, they do whip a boy at each place they stop at in their procession."[2] Allusion has already been made to the mixed motives that drew Pepys to church, and how he often attended more to the pretty faces in the congregation than to the words of the preacher. He had high authority for his conduct in the demeanour of the court, and he himself tells us how, while Bishop Morley (of Winchester) was preaching on the song of the angels, and reprehending the mistaken jollity of the court, the courtiers "all laugh in the chapel when he reflected on their ill actions and courses."[3]

There is comparatively little in the "Diary" about the Nonconformists, although in the early part of his career Pepys was more favourable to their claims than to those of the conforming clergy. He was once induced to give five shillings to a parson among the fanatics, who said a long grace like a prayer, and was in great want, although he would willingly have done otherwise. His aunt James, "a poor, religious, well-meaning, good soul," told him that the minister's prayers had helped to cure him when he was cut for the stone.[4]

We have a curious peep into a rustic church

---

[1] "Diary," May 23, 1661.　　[2] April 30, 1668.
[3] Dec. 25, 1662.　　[4] May 30, 1663.

which Pepys and his cousin Roger attended on the 4th of August, 1662 : " At our coming in, the country people all rose with so much reverence; and when the parson begins, he begins ' Right worshipful and dearly beloved,' to us.' "

There are several allusions in the " Diary " to various punishments in vogue at the time. In 1663, the parish of St. Olave's was supplied with a new pair of stocks " very handsome," and one Sunday, a poor boy who had been found in a drunken state by the constable, was led off "to handsel them."[1] It was formerly the custom to punish offenders on the spot where their crimes had been committed; thus, on February 18th, 1659-60, two soldiers were hanged in the Strand for their mutiny at Somerset House. The bodies of the criminals were frequently allowed to hang in some conspicuous spot until they rotted away; and on April 11th, 1661, Pepys and "Mrs. Anne ' " rode under the man that hangs upon Shooter's Hill, and a filthy sight it is to see how his flesh is shrunk to his bones." London must have exhibited a ghastly appearance when the heads of traitors were stuck up on the city gates, on Temple Bar, Westminster Hall, and other public places. The heads and the limbs were covered with pitch, and remained in their elevated position for years, until in many cases they were blown down by the wind. Pepys once found the head of a traitor at the top of one of the turrets of Westminster Abbey.[2] Some of Charles I.'s judges received an easier punishment. William Monson, the "degraded" Earl of Castle-

---

[1] " Diary," April 12, 1663.   [2] Oct. 21, 1660.

maine, Sir Henry Mildmay, and Robert Wallop were sentenced to imprisonment for life, and to be drawn on sledges with ropes round their necks from the Tower to Tyburn and back, on the anniversary of the late King's execution. Pepys met the three sledges on Tower Hill on the 27th of January, 1661-62.

If called upon in the character of a judge to sum up the case against the people of England in respect to their manners after the Restoration, I think it would be but fair to say that these were better than those of their rulers. It was not until after the Revolution, when the vices of Charles's court had had time to pollute the children of the men who brought him back, that the lowest depths of immorality were reached.

CHAPTER XII.

AMUSEMENTS.

"The shows of things are better than themselves,
How doth it stir this airy part of us
To hear our poets tell imagin'd fights,
And the strange blows that feigned courage gives."
The Tragedy of Nero.

N dealing with the amusements of Pepys's day, we find how pre-eminent a position the theatre held in popular esteem. The presentation of a new play was looked upon as an event of the greatest moment, and the various appearances of favourite actors were chronicled in the "Diary" with considerable regularity.

Immediately after the Restoration, two companies of actors were organized, who acted at two different houses : one theatre was known as the King's house, and the other as the Duke's house. Sir William Davenant obtained a patent for his company under the name of "The Duke's servants," and as he had succeeded during the

Commonwealth in performing certain dramatic pieces under cover of a musical accompaniment, his theatre was sometimes known as " The Opera." A patent for " The King's servants " was granted to Tom Killigrew, whose house was for distinction's sake called " The Theatre." Pepys has registered as many as 145 plays which he saw acted, some of them several times over, and there is every reason to believe that he saw many more during the period over which the " Diary" extends, that he has omitted to mention.[1] When the theatres were first opened, the old plays were revived until the living dramatists had time to produce new ones, but several of the old masterpieces held their ground for many years. Among the revived dramatists were Marlowe, Shakespeare, Ben Jonson, Beaumont and Fletcher, Ford, Massinger, and Shirley. In the whole of Evelyn's " Diary," Hamlet is the only play of Shakespeare which the author mentions as having seen acted, and his observation upon this is that " now the old plays begin to disgust this refined age, since his Majesty's been so long abroad."[2] Yet, in the one month of December, 1660, Pepys had seen two distinct plays of Shakespeare, and after the date of Evelyn's entry, he saw Henry IV., Hamlet, Twelfth Night, Merry Wives, Romeo and Juliet, Midsummer Night's Dream, Henry VIII.,

[1] These entries are of so much importance in dramatic history, as giving definite dates for the performance of the various plays, that I have thought it well to give a complete list in the Appendix.

[2] Evelyn's " Diary," Nov. 26, 1661.

AMUSEMENTS.

Macbeth, Othello, Taming of a Shrew, and Tempest, which proves that Shakespeare was more generally appreciated than is usually supposed. Here we have eleven plays, which is the largest number of plays by one dramatist, with the exception of Fletcher, whose separate productions and joint ones with Beaumont number as many as twenty-four. Shirley comes next with nine, then Ben Jonson with five, Ford with two, and Massinger with the same number. We have already seen how little Pepys appreciated Shakespeare's genius, but it seems as if he could not enough express his delight in the plays of Ben Jonson. He describes the "Alchymist" as "a most incomparable play,"[1] and the "Silent Woman" as "the best comedy, I think, that ever was wrote;"[2] of "Every Man in His Humour," he writes, "wherein is the greatest propriety of speech that ever I read in my life."

Although some of the actors had gained experience on the stage of Charles I.'s reign, most of them were novices, and it is therefore remarkable to find such an array of talent at both houses.

Most of the old players were attached to the King's company. Hart, Mohun, and Burt were all fine actors, and they had acted female parts before the suppression of the theatre, but Betterton, one of the greatest actors that ever lived, was a host in himself and the mainstay of the Duke's house. Pepys was never tired of lauding his powers, and delighted in seeing him

[1] "Diary," June 22, 1661.   [2] Sept. 19, 1665.

act. His Hamlet was "beyond imagination,"[1] and his Henry V. "incomparable."[2] Mrs. Knipp was one of those actresses of whom little or nothing is known outside the "Diary," but who makes a considerable figure there. Pepys was very partial to this free-and-easy lady, and when we read of his behaviour to her we need not be surprised to find Mr. Knipp alluded to as a "jealous-looking fellow."[3] This is the place to expose a cruel slander against a worthy man, which Pepys has embalmed in his pages and which has not been corrected by the editors. Pepys having occasion to mention Anne and Beck Marshall, the well-known actresses, he sets down that Mrs. Pierce told him how they were the daughters of Stephen Marshall, the great Presbyterian, and then reports Nell Gwyn's often-quoted speech to Beck as to the difference in the education of the two; the latter being "a Presbyter's praying daughter."[4] With such an authority it is not surprising that Lord Braybrooke should reproduce the statement in a note to another passage,[5] but on investigation the whole bubble bursts. Stephen Marshall died on the 19th of November, 1655, and was buried in Westminster Abbey. At the date of his will his wife was dead, and five of his daughters were already married, three of them at least to clergymen. The remaining daughter, Susan, who was unmarried, must have been more than twenty-one years of age at the time of her

[1] "Diary," Aug. 24, 1661.
[2] Aug. 13, 1664.
[3] Dec. 8, 1665.
[4] Oct. 26, 1667.
[5] Feb. 1, 1663-64.

father's death, as she proved his will. These important facts were discovered by Colonel Chester, and set forth in his remarkable volume, " Westminster Abbey Registers." It did not concern the Colonel to discover the parents of Anne and Rebecca, but he proved very conclusively that they were not the children of the Rev. Stephen Marshall. Another blunder is made in the " Memoirs of Count Grammont," where " Roxolana " in Davenant's " Siege of Rhodes," is confused with " Roxana " in Lee's " Rival Queens," and in the notes it is inferred that one of these Mrs. Marshalls was seduced by Aubrey de Vere, last Earl of Oxford, of that name. The " Roxolana " who was deceived by Lord Oxford with a false marriage, was Elizabeth (or Frances) Davenport, who is frequently mentioned by Pepys.

At the revival of the stage after the Restoration, a more lavish expenditure on scenery and dresses became common. Pepys tells us that when Ben Jonson's " Catiline " was acted at the King's House, Charles II. gave the actors £500 for robes which were required.[1] We also learn that "the gallants do begin to be tired with the vanity and pride of the theatre actors, who are indeed grown very proud and rich."[2] But a few years afterwards, when Pepys stepped up to Harris's dressing-room after the play, he observed " much company come to him and the wits, to talk and to assign meetings."[3] When Kynaston was beaten by Sir Charles Sedley for

[1] " Diary," Dec. 11, 1667.   [2] Feb. 23, 1660-61.
[3] April 29, 1668.

imitating him, the manager of the King's theatre was forced to read Kynaston's part in " The Heiress," much to the disadvantage of the *vraisemblance* of the play. Pepys writes, " but it was pleasant to see Beeston come in with others supposing it to be dark, and yet he is forced to read his part by the light of candles, and this I observing to a gentleman that sat by me, he was mightily pleased therewith, and spread it up and down."[1] Pepys had occasional talks with Tom Killigrew on the state of the stage, and heard from him of the scheme for setting up a nursery of young actors in Moorfields, where plays should be acted ; " but four operas it shall have in the year, to act six weeks at a time ; where we shall have the best scenes and machines, the best music and everything as magnificent as in Christendom." For this purpose Killigrew " sent for voices and painters and other persons from Italy,"[2] but all this fine project came to naught, and two years afterwards he explained to Pepys all that he had done for the theatre and what he proposed still to do. He said " that the stage is now by his pains a thousand times better and more glorious than ever heretofore. Now wax-candles and many of them ; then not above 3 lbs. of tallow : now all things civil, no rudeness anywhere ; then, as in a bear-garden : then, two or three fiddlers ; now, nine or ten of the best : then, nothing but rushes upon the ground, and everything else mean ; now, all otherwise : then, the Queen seldom, and the King never would come ; now, not the King

---

[1] "Diary," Feb. 2, 1668-69.   [2] Aug. 2, 1664.

only for state, but all civil people do think they may come as well as any."[1]

The theatres were open in the afternoon, three o'clock being the usual hour for performance, and the plays were therefore acted by daylight during the summer. The roof consisted of skylights made of thin glass, which let the wet into the pit in times of heavy rain. Pepys felt the inconvenience on one occasion, and he wrote: "Before the play was done it fell such a storm of hail, that we in the middle of the pit were fain to rise, and all the house in a disorder."[2] A few years after this the very same inconvenience was experienced. "A disorder in the pit by its raining in from the cupola at top," and this must often have happened.[3]

When plays were acted at court, the performances took place at night, probably because the actors were then free after acting at the theatres. Sometimes even the King had to wait, as we read, "after all staying above an hour for the players, the King and all waiting, which was absurd, saw 'Henry V.' well done by the Duke's people, and in most excellent habits, all new vests, being put on but this night . . . The play continued till twelve at night."[4]

It is here necessary to guard readers of the "Diary" against a mistake very easily fallen into in respect to the various theatres, as the editors have given no explanation to guide them. Davenant's, or the Duke's, company occupied

[1] "Diary," Feb. 12, 1666-67.   [2] June 1, 1664.
[3] May 1, 1668.   [4] Dec. 28, 1666.

the old "Cockpit" in Drury Lane for a short time after the Restoration, until they removed to Lincoln's Inn Fields, in the spring of 1662. Now Pepys frequently mentions the plays acted at the Cockpit, but these were performed at night, and apparently the Cockpit alluded to was the one at Whitehall, not that in Drury Lane. This seems evident by an entry under date Nov. 20, 1660 : " I found my Lord in bed late, he having been with the King, Queen and Princess at the Cockpit all night, where General Monk treated them ; and after supper a play ;" because the Duke of Albemarle lived at the Cockpit in St. James's Park. Peter Cunningham mentions in the " Handbook of London," that he found in the records of the Audit Office a payment of xxx^{li}. per annum, " to the Keeper of our playhouse called the Cockpitt, in St. James's Park," but he gives no further particulars and does not appear to have noticed how far the entries in the " Diary " illustrate this appointment. On December 1st, 1662, the Duke's company acted before the King at the Cockpit, and January 5th, 1662-63, the King's company acted in the same place, but Pepys did not think the latter at all equal to " the Duke's people."

All the entries in the " Diary " relating to the stage require more investigation than they have yet received, as the notes of the editors are quite insufficient. We have seen how the allusions to the " Cockpit " in the years 1660-62, might either refer to the Duke's theatre or to the Court theatre, and the same confusion might easily be made in respect to the Lincoln's Inn

theatre. Pepys says that on November 20th,
1660, he and Mr. Shepley went "to the new
play-house near Lincoln's Inn Fields (which was
formerly Gibbon's tennis-court)." This was the
home of the King's company from 1660 till
1663, when they went to Drury Lane. As already stated, the Duke's company removed to
Portugal Street in 1662, so that for a short
period the two rival theatres were close together
in the neighbourhood of Lincoln's Inn Fields.
Pepys visited all parts of the house, and did not
much care where he sat so that he got in : thus
on November 7, 1667, he was "forced to sit
in the side balcony over against the music-room,
close by my Lady Dorset and a great many
great ones;" and some years before he was
somewhat troubled to be seen by two or three
of his clerks, who were in the half-crown box,
while he was in an eighteenpenny place.[1] The
price of a pit seat was 2s. 6d., and in spite of
the inconvenience of the place in wet weather, it
was frequented by people of fashion; for instance,
the Duke of Buckingham sat there, and was surrounded by Lord Buckhurst, Sir Charles Sedley,
Sir George Etherege, and other poets;[2] and "a
company of fine ladies" was not absent.[3] But
even at that time "citizens, 'prentices and others"
jostled their betters. Pepys writes : "I do not
remember that I saw so many, by half, of the
ordinary 'prentices and mean people in the pit
at 2s. 6d. apiece as now; I going for several
years no higher than the 12d. and then the 18d.

[1] "Diary," Jan. 19, 1660-61.   [2] Feb. 6, 1667-68.
[3] March 31, 1660-61.

Q

places, though I strained hard to go in when I
did."[1] The theatres were generally crowded,
and on special occasions it was difficult to find a
place.   When Etherege's " She Would if She
Could" was first acted, 1,000 persons were turned
away because there was no room in the pit an
hour before the performance commenced.[2] An
ingenious plan for keeping seats which was in
vogue for many subsequent years is mentioned
by Pepys.   On May 2, 1668, he writes : " To
the Duke of York's play house at a little past
twelve, to get a good place in the pit for the
new play, and there setting a poor man to keep
my place, I out and spent an hour at Martin's,
my bookseller's, and so back again, where I find
the house quite full.   But I had my place."

When the theatre built for the King's company in Drury Lane, was opened in 1663,
Pepys found some faults in the construction, one
of these being the narrowness of the passages
in and out of the pit.   He did not approve also
of the placing of the orchestra under the stage,
by which means the basses could not be heard at
all, and the trebles very faintly.[3]

Pepys does not mention Fop's Corner in the
King's theatre, a name which recalls the better-
known Fop's Alley of Her Majesty's Opera
House, but it is alluded to in Dryden's epilogue
spoken at the new house in Drury Lane on
March 26th, 1674 :

"So may Fop Corner full of noise remain,
And drive far off the dull attentive train."

[1] "Diary," Jan. 1, 1667-68.   [2] Feb. 6, 1667-68.
[3] May 8, 1663.

Pepys does, however, tell us how loudly people of fashion talked. One day Sir Charles Sedley had a merry discourse with two ladies, which prevented the Diarist from hearing any of the play. His feelings were divided between pleasure in hearing the wit and annoyance in losing the play.[1] The manners of most of the audience, as exhibited in several little traits, were far from commendable, but it would be difficult to equal the following incident, which is related as if there were nothing particularly unladylike in it : " I sitting behind in a dark place [in the theatre], a lady spit backward upon me by mistake, not seeing me, but after seeing her to be a very pretty lady, I was not troubled at it at all."[2]

One of the institutions of the theatre was Orange Moll, who is frequently mentioned in the "Diary." The orange girls stood with their backs to the stage, and the beaux in the pit broke jests with them. One of these women tried to impose upon Pepys by affirming that she had delivered a dozen oranges to some ladies in a box in accordance to his order, "which was wholly untrue, but yet she swore it to be true." He denied the charge, and would not pay, but for quiet bought four shillings' worth of oranges at 6*d.* apiece.[3] This was the usual price, as we learn from the prologue to Mrs. Behn's "Young King," 1698:—

"Half crown my play, sixpence my orange cost."

The mistress or superior of these women was named, for distinction, Orange Moll.

Pepys makes a passing allusion to the old

[1] "Diary," Feb. 18, 1666-67.   [2] Jan. 28, 1660-61.
[3] May 11, 1668.

practice of placing the notices of performances on posts, but the editors have left the passage without explanation. He writes: " I went to see if any play was acted, and I found none upon the post, it being Passion week."[1] This is well illustrated by an anecdote:—" Master Field, the player, riding up Fleet Street a great pace, a gentleman called him, and asked what play was played that day? He (being angry to be stayed upon so frivolous a demand) answered that he might see what play was to be played upon every *post.* I cry you mercy (said the gentleman) I took you for a *post* you rode so fast."

The other amusements mentioned by Pepys sink into insignificance by the side of the theatre, but a short enumeration of some of them may be given here. The cock-pit, in Shoe Lane, was a well-known place of resort for sporting men, and Pepys went to see some cock-fighting there, but he soon had enough of it, although he was glad to have seen " the strange variety of people."[2] He went on one occasion to the Bear Garden, on the Bankside, " and saw some good sport of the bull's tossing of the dogs : one into the very boxes," but he did not much like the company, and on the whole he thought it "a very rude and nasty pleasure."[3] At another time he went to the same place to see a prize fight, but being ashamed to be seen, he went in a back way (getting among the bulls, and fearing to be too near the bears) and sat with his cloak before his face.[4]

Pepys did not practise athletic sports himself,

---

[1] "Diary," March 24, 1662. [2] Dec. 21, 1663.
[3] Aug. 14, 1666. [4] Sept. 9, 1667.

but he liked to see them practised by others. He was a spectator at a very serious fencing-match where the combatants cut each other rather severely both in the head and legs.[1] The King was a good player at tennis, but Pepys thought it "a loathsome sight" to see his play "extolled without any cause at all."[2] Charles was in the habit of weighing himself before and after a game, and on a certain occasion he lost four and a-half pounds. The best players in England were said to be Prince Rupert, Bab May, Captain Cooke, and Mr. (afterwards Sir Thomas) Chicheley.[3] Pepys liked a game of bowls, because he could play it with the ladies;[4] and he sometimes condescended to have a game at ninepins.[5] Gaming ran high at Court, and we are told that Lady Castlemaine played £1,000 and £1,500 at a cast, winning £15,000 one night, and losing £25,000 on another night.[6] No wonder Bishop Morley denounced this excess in play, and specially commented on the groom-porter's conduct in one of his sermons before the Court.[7]

There are several references in the "Diary" to games of cards, but in most instances the particular game played is not mentioned. Cribbage, handycap (a game like loo), and gleek (played by three persons with forty-four cards), are, however, all specially alluded to.[8]

[1] "Diary," June 1, 1663.
[2] Dec. 28, 1663; Jan. 4, 1663-64.
[3] Sept. 2, 1667.   [4] May 1, 1661.
[5] April 28, 1660.   [6] Feb. 14, 1667-68.
[7] Dec. 25, 1662.
[8] *Cribbage,* Jan. 2, 1659-60, May 15, 1660; *handycap,* Sept. 19, 1660; *gleek,* Jan. 13, Feb. 17, 1661-62.

Pepys played at shuttlecock on January 11th, 1659-60; at shuffle (or shovel) board on July 30th, 1662, and on April 1st, 1665, and at tables or backgammon on September 11th and 16th, 1665. Among the minor amusements must be mentioned the crying of forfeits,[1] blindman's buff,[2] and crambo or tagging of rhymes.[3]

Dancing was in high repute, and Pepys describes the various balls pretty fully. On the 31st of December, 1662, there is some lively dancing at Whitehall. The King (a good dancer) opens the ball with the Duchess of York, and the dancing commences with the Bransle or "brawl," of Shakespeare and Gray. Then follows the swift coranto, and the country dances. When the King stood up, all the ladies, even the Queen herself, rose. A few years later a gallant company again meet at the palace, and the same order of proceeding is followed. First comes the brawl, then the coranto, and last of all a dance from France, which the King calls the "new dance."[4]

Pepys learns the coranto himself in May, 1663, and two years afterwards he disputes with Captain Taylor on the best way of dancing it.[5] At first Pepys's Puritan leanings led him to look rather unfavourably upon dancing, but in the end he became tolerably fond of it. On January 6th, 1667-68, he had a party for which he engaged four fiddlers at a cost of £3, and everything went off very satisfactorily in consequence.

---

[1] "Diary," Feb. 4, 1660-61. [2] Dec. 26, 1664.
[3] May 19, 1660. [4] Nov. 15, 1666.
[5] April 23, 1665.

All that Pepys has to say about amusements is to be found in the " Diary," for his letters contain no information respecting the stage or the balls at Court.   This is only another indication of how much we have lost by the discontinuance of the "Diary," for it is scarcely possible to believe that the man who exhibited so absorbing an interest in the proceedings of the theatre, should suddenly have ceased to visit it.

CHAPTER XIII.

CONCLUSION.

"Let us hear the conclusion of the whole matter."
Ecclesiastes xii. 13.

OW that all the divisions of our subject have been discussed, there is little to add in a concluding chapter. We have seen Pepys in his poverty, when he and his wife struggled to keep up a decent appearance with an empty larder and a fireless grate at home. We have seen the sudden change, when he became rich and increased his expenses with an ever-present sense of the effect of his movements upon the outer world. And, lastly, we have seen how he lived to an honoured old age, and passed out of life as a worthy example of virtue and honour. We have peeped into some of his dearly-loved books, and seen how the "Bibliotheca Pepysiana" helps to illustrate the character of its founder.

Having thus looked at the man as he lived, we passed on to his surroundings. First, we dealt with the town he loved and knew so well, then made the acquaintance of the relations and friends that surrounded him, and lastly, tried to understand the arrangements of the office where he spent so large a portion of his life. This was the inner circle. The frequenters of the Court and the public characters with whom he came into occasional contact or knew only from observation at a distance, formed the outer circle of his life.

Byron, in allusion to the question, " Where is the world ?" asked by Dr. Young at the age of eighty, cried out :—

> " Alas !
> Where is the world of *eight* years past ?   'Twas there—
> I look for it—'tis gone, a globe of glass
> Crack'd, shiver'd, vanish'd, scarcely gazed on, ere
> A silent change dissolves the glittering mass.
> Statesmen, Chiefs, Orators, Queens, Patriots, Kings,
> And Dandies, all are gone on the wind's wings."

Yet we may point to the pages of Pepys's " Diary," and say that there the globe is still whole, and that there men and women of nearly three times eighty years ago live and move before our eyes.

In taking leave of the official, the gossip, the musician, and the man of letters, I can only express the hope that these pages may be found a useful companion to one of the most interesting books in the English language.

APPENDIX.

APPENDIX I.

PORTRAITS OF SAMUEL PEPYS.

AINTINGS BY

1. *Savill* (a painter in Cheapside). 1661. See "Diary," Nov. 23.

Jan. 6, 1661-62: "I sent my lute to the Paynter's, and there I staid with him all the morning to see him paint the neck of my lute in my picture, which I was not pleased with after it was done."

Pepys appears to have sat to this same painter for a miniature or "picture in little," which cost £3. See "Diary," Feb. 20, 1661-62, June 11, 1662.

Jan. 28, 1661-62: "The Paynter, though a very honest man, I found to be very silly as to matter of skill in shadows, for we were long in discourse, till I was almost angry to hear him talk so simply."

2. *John Hales*. 1666.

March 17, 1666: "This day I began to sit, and he will make me, I think, a very fine picture. He promises it shall be as good as my wife's, and I sit to have it full of shadows, and do almost break my neck looking over my shoulder to make the posture for him to work by."

March 30, 1666 : " To Hales's, and there sat till almost quite darke upon working my gowne, which I hired to be drawn in : an Indian gown."

April 11, 1666 : "To Hales's, where there was nothing to be found to be done more to my picture, but the musique, which now pleases me mightily, it being painted true."

This picture was bought by Peter Cunningham, at the sale of the Pepys Cockerell collection in 1848, and it was purchased by the trustees of the National Portrait Gallery in 1866. The eyes look at the spectator, and the face is turned three-quarters to the left. The music is Pepys's own song, " Beauty Retire."

> " There is a similar picture belonging to Mr. Hawes, of Kensington, which Mr. Scharf, the Keeper of the National Portrait Gallery, thinks is either a replica or a good old copy."—REV. MYNORS BRIGHT'S edition of the " Diary," vol. iii. p. 423 (note).

Walpole mentions Hales in his " Anecdotes of Painting," and says that he lived in Southampton Street, Bloomsbury, and died there suddenly in 1679.

3. *Sir Peter Lely.* Pepysian Library, Magdalene College, Cambridge.

4. *Sir Godfrey Kneller.* Andrew Pepys Cockerell, Esq. This picture was lent to the First Special Exhibition of National Portraits, 1866, and was numbered 950.

5. *Sir Godfrey Kneller.* The Royal Society.

6. *Sir Godfrey Kneller.* Hall of Magdalene College, Cambridge.

7. A small portrait attributed to *Kneller*, representing a seated figure ; with a globe in one corner, and a guitar (or lute) and compasses on a table, and a ship in the distance at sea. Mr. Scharf suggests the possibility of this being the portrait by *Savill* described above (No. 1), and this suggestion seems highly probable. Mrs. Frederick Pepys Cockerell.

8. *Anonymous.* 1675.

"The picture is beyond praise ; but causes admiration in all that see it. Its posture so stately and magnificent, and it hits so naturally your proportion and the noble air of your face, that I remain immovable before it hours together," &c. T. Hill to Pepys, Lisbon, July 1, 1675.—SMITH'S " Life of Pepys," vol. i. p. 161.

9. The picture by Verrio at Christ's Hospital, of James II. on his throne receiving the mathematical pupils of the school, contains a portrait of Pepys. The original drawing for the picture by Verrio is in the possession of Andrew Pepys Cockerell, Esq.

ENGRAVINGS BY

1. Robert White. Kneller, painter. Portrait in a carved oval frame, bearing inscription SAM. PEPYS. CAR. ET. JAC. ANGL. REGIB. A. SECRETIS. ADMIRALIÆ. Motto under the frame, "Mens cujusque is est quisque." Large book-plate.

2. Robèrt White. Kneller, painter. Portrait in an oval medallion on a scroll of paper. Motto over his head, " Mens cujusque is est quisque ;" underneath the same inscription as on No. 1. Small book-plate.

These two engravings are described by Granger.

3. J. Bragg. Kneller, painter. Frontispiece to vol. i. of the first edition of the " Diary," 1825 (4to.). "From the original in the possession of S. P. Cockerell." Picture described as No. 7, now in the possession of Mrs. Frederick Pepys Cockerell.

4. J. Bragg. Kneller, painter. Frontispiece to vol. i. of the second edition of the "Diary," 1828 ; much worn in the third edition, 1848. "From the original picture in the possession of S. P. Cockerell." Picture described as No. 4, now in the possession of Andrew Pepys Cockerell, Esq.

5. W. C. Edwards. Kneller, painter. Frontispiece to vol. i. of the fourth edition of the "Diary," 1854. From the same original as the preceding article.

6. Charles Wass. Walker, painter. In Smith's "Life, Journals, and Correspondence of Pepys," vol. i. 1841, said to be in the collection of the Royal Society, but this is a mistake.

PHOTOGRAPHS.

1. From the portrait by Kneller (No. 4), series of photographs published by the South Kensington Museum under the superintendence of the Council of the Arundel Society.
2. From Edwards's engraving of Kneller's Portrait, "Diary," ed. Mynors Bright, vol. i. 1875.
3. From Hales's Portrait (No. 2), "Diary," ed. Mynors Bright, vol. iii. 1876.

BUST.

The following extracts from the "Diary" refer to a bust which was made for Pepys:—

Feb. 10, 1668-69: "So to the plaisterer's at Charing Cross that casts heads and bodies in plaister: and there I had my whole face done; but I was vexed first to be forced to daub all my face over with pomatum: but it was pretty to feel how soft and easily it is done on the face, and by and by, by degrees how hard it becomes, that you cannot break it, and sits so close, that you cannot pull it off, and yet so easy, that it is as soft as a pillow so safe is everything where many parts of the body do bear alike. Thus was the mould made; but when it came off there was little pleasure in it, as it looks in the mould, nor any resemblance whatever there will be in the figure when I come to see it cast off."

Feb. 15, 1668-69: "To the plaisterer's, and there saw the figure of my face taken from the mould: and it is most admirably like, and I will have another made, before I take it away."

APPENDIX II.

THE SCHEMES OF ALEXANDER MAR-
CHANT, SIEUR DE ST. MICHEL
(MRS. PEPYS'S FATHER.)

HE unpractical schemes of Mons. St. Michel are alluded to on pages 7-8 of this book, but the editors of the "Diary" have taken no pains to obtain any information respecting him, and his name even does not appear in the "Diary." Lord Braybrooke suggests, without any justification for the suggestion, that Mrs. Pepys's mother had married again (see "Diary," March 29th, 1667).

Pepys was wrong in the date of the patent, which is numbered 138, and Sir Edward Ford's name does not appear in it. Sir John Colladon, a Fellow of the Royal College of Physicians, was naturalized by Charles II., and appointed one of the Physicians to the Queen.

St. Michel's name evidently puzzled the man who drafted the patent. The following is a copy of the original patent :—

"CHARLES THE SECOND, by the grace of God, &c., to all to whom these p̃sents shall come, greeting

"WHEREAS we are informed that John Colladon, Doctor in Phisicke, and Alexander Marchant, of St. Michall, have, with much paines and charge, found "A WAY TO p̃VENT AND CURE THE SMOAKEING OF CHIMNEYS, EITHER BY STOPPING THE TUNNELL

R

TOWARDS THE TOP, AND ALTERING THE FORMER
COURSE OF THE SMOAKE, OR BY SETTING TUN-
NELLS WITH CHECKE WITHIN THE CHIMNEYES;
wch Invencon soe found out as aforesaid was never
publickly exercised or made vse of in anie of our
kingdomes or dominions: And whereas the said John
Colladon and Alexander Marchant have humbly besought vs for their better incouragem^t to exercise and
put in practice the said Invencon, that wee would be
gratiously pleased to graunt vnto them, the said Joh.
Colladon and Alexander Marchant, our Lr̃es Patents
of Priviledge for the sole vse and benifitt thereof, for
the time and terme of fowerteene yeares, according to
the statute in that case made and provided.

"NOWE KNOWE YE, therefore, that we, of our
princely inclinacon, being willing to incourage and
promote works of this nature, and to give all due and
fitting incouragem^t to the inventers of such arts as
may be of publicke vse and benifitt, of our especiall
grace, certeine knowledge, and meere mocon, and vpon
the humble peticon of the said John Colladon and
Alexander Marchant, have given and graunted, and
by these p̃sents, for vs, our heyres and successors,
doe give and graunt vnto the said John Colladon and
Alexander Marchant, their executors, administrators,
and assignes, speciall licence, full power, priviledge, and
authoritie, that they and every of them, by themselves,
their or anie of their deputie or deputies, servants,
workmen, or assignes, at all times and from time to
time hereafter, dureing the terme of yeares hereafter in
these p̃sents expressed, shall and lawfully may vse,
exercise, imploy, and enioy the said newe Invencon in
and throughout all our realmes and dominions, and
every or anie of them, in such manner as to them or
anie or either of them, in their or anie of their discrecons
shall seeme meet, and shall and may have and enioy
the sole benifitt and advantage comeing or ariseing by
reason thereof, dureing the terme of yeares hereby
graunted; and to the end, the said John Colladon and

Alexander Marchant, their executors, administrators,
and assignes, and every of them, may the better enioy the
full and whole benifitt and the sole vse and exercise of
the Invenĉon aforesaid, wee doe by these psents, for
vs, our heyres and successors, require and streightly
comaund all and every person and persons, bodyes
politicke and corporate, of whatsoever qualitie or degree,
name or addiĉon, they be, that neither they nor anie
of them, dureing the terme of yeares hereby graunted,
either directly or indirectly, doe or shall vse or put in
practice the said Invenĉon, soe by the said John Colladon
and Alexander Marchant attained vnto or invented as
aforesaid, nor doe or shall counterfeit, imitate, or
resemble the same, nor doe or shall make anie addition therevnto, or substracĉon from the same, whereby
to ꝑtend themselves the inventors or devisors thereof,
without the licence, consent, or agreement of the said
John Colladon and Alexander Marchant, their executors, administrators, or assignes, in writeing vnder their
hands and seales, first had and obteined in that behalfe, vpon such paines and penalties as can or may be
inflicted vpon such offendors for their contempt of this
our cōmaund in that behalfe, and further to be answerable to the said John Colladon and Alexander Marchant, their executors, and administrators, and assignes,
according to lawe and justice, for their damages
thereby susteined; to have and to hold all the said
licences, powers, privileges, and authorities hereby
graunted as aforesaid vnto them, the said John Colladon and Alexander Marchant, for & dureing the terme
of fowerteene yeares from the makeing of these psentꝭ
next ensueing, and fully to be compleate and ended,
according to the statute in such case made and provided. And further, wee doe by these ꝑsents, for vs,
our heyres and successors, give and graunt vnto the
said John Colladon and Alexander Marchant, their
executors, administrators, and assignes, full power
and authoritie that they and every of them, their,
every or anie of theyr deputies, servantꝭ, and agents,

or anie of them, haveing first obteined a warrant in this behalfe from the Lord Cheife Justice of the Courte of King's Bench for the time being, may, with the assistance of a constable or anie other lawfull officer, at convenient times in the day, dureing the terme aforesaid, and in lawfull manner, enter into and make search in anie houses or other places where there shall be iust cause of suspicõn, for discovering and findeing out all such persons as shall, within the terme of fowerteene yeares aforesaid, imitate or cause to be imitated, or shall vse or put in practize the said Invencõn, by the said John Colladon and Alexander Marchant invented and found out as aforesaid, that soe such offenders may be proceeded ag^t, and punished according to theyr demeritts, and theyr invencõns and works tending to the ends aforesaid then and there found, to be seized upon, broken in peeces, and defaced, and the materialls thereof left in the hands and custodie of some constable or officer, to be disposed in such manner and forme as wee, our heyres and successors, shall from time to time direct and appoint. And further, wee doe by these p̃sens, for vs, our heyres and successors, will, authorize, and require all and singuler justices of the peace, mayors, sheriffes, bayliffes, constables, headboroughes, and all other officers and ministers whatsoever, of vs, our heyres and successors, for the time being, that they and every of them respectively, be from time to time dureing the said terme hereby graunted, in theyr respective places, favouring aydeing, helping, and assisting vnto the said John Colladon and Alexander Marchant, theyr executors, administrators, and assigns, and to theyr and every of their deputy and deputies, servantẽ and agents, in and by all things in and about the accomplishment of our will and pleasure herein declared, and in the exercise and execucõn of the powers and privileges herein and hereby graunted, or mencõned to be graunted, as aforesaid. And moreover, wee will and comaund by these p̃sents, for vs, our heyres and suc-

cessors, that our said officers and ministers, or anie of
them, doe not molest, trouble, or interrupt the said
John Colladon and Alexander Marchant, or either of
them, theyr or either of theyr executors, administrators, or assignes, or theyr or either of theyr deputie or
deputies, servants, or agents, or anie of them, in or
about the use or exercise of the said Invencõn, or in
any matter or thing concerneing the same. Provided
alwayes, that if at anie tyme dureing the said terme of
fowerteene yeares, it shall be made appeare vnto vs,
our heyres or successors, that this our graunt is contrary to lawe, or p̃iudiciall or inconvenient, and not of
publicke vse or benifitt, then vpon significacõn and
declaracon thereof to be made by vs, our heyres or
successors, these our Lr̃es Patents shall forthwith
cease, determine, and be vtterly voyde to all intents
and purposes, and the same not to be vsed, exercised,
or imployed, anie thing herein-before mencõned to the
contrary notwithstanding. Provided further, that in
case it shall be found or made appeare that the said
Invencõn is not a newe Invencõn of the said John
Colladen and Alexander Marchant, as to the publicke
vse and exercise thereof within this our kingdome of
England, then at all tymes from thenceforth these
p̃sents shall cease, determine, and be voyde, anie
thing in these p̃sents before conteined to the contrary
notwithstanding. Provided alsoe, that these our Lr̃es
Patents, or anie thing herein conteined, shall not extend, or be construed to extend, to give priviledge to the
said John Colladon and Alexander Marchant, or either
of them, their or either of theyr executors, administrators, or assignes, or anie of them, to vse, or imitate any
invencõn or worke found out or invented by anie
other person or persons, and publickly exercised within
these our said relmes, or anie the dominions or terri-
tories thcrevnto belonging vnto whom wee have
alreadie graunted our like Lr̃es Patents of Priviledge
for the sole vse, exercise, and benifitt thereof ; it being
our will and pleasure that the said John Colladon and

Alexander Merchant, their executors, administrators,
and assignes, and all and singuler other person and
persons to whom we have alreadie graunted our like
Lr̃es Patentꝭ of Priviledge as aforesaid, shall distinctly
vse and practize their severall Invencõns by them invented and found out, according to the true intent and
meaneing of the said severall and respective Lr̃es
Patents, and of these ꝑsents. And lastly, wee doe by
these ꝑsents, for vs, our heyres and successors, graunt
vnto the said John Colladon and Alexander Merchant,
their executors, administrators, and assignes, that
these our Lr̃es Patents, or the inrollmᵗ thereof, shall
be in and by all things good, valid, sufficient, and
effectuall in the lawe, according to the true intent &
meaneing thereof, and shall be taken, construed, and
adiudged most favourable and benificiall for the best
benifitt and advantage of the said John Colladon and
Alexander Marchant, theyr executors, administrators,
and assignes, aswell in all courts of record as elsewhere, notwithstanding the not full and certeine de-
scribeing the manner and quality of the said Invencõn,
or of the matialls thereof, or of the true and certeine
vse and benifitt thereof, and notwithstanding anie
other defecte, incerteintyes, or imperfeccõns in these
ꝑsents conteined, or anie act, statute, ordinance, provision, proclamacõn, or restreint to the contrary
thereof, in anie wise notwithstanding.
   "In witnes, &c. Witnes the King at Westm̃, the
            "Second day of May.
       "℞ br̃e de privat. sigill.," &c.

   In 1665 St. Michel was again anxious for a patent.
The following is a copy of a petition preserved among
the State Papers in the Record Office :—
       "To the Kings most Excellᵗ Maᵗⁱᵉ.
       "The humble peticĩon of Major Allexandʳ Mar-
chant aᛚs de Sᵗ. Michell upon the River Couanon neare
the Towne of Bauge in Anjou in France Esqᵉ. Sheweth—

"That yo pet^r hath invented the two following publick conveniences, first, for a generall forme how to keepe alwayes cleare water in ponds to wash horses, sweete & with as little Mudd in the bottome as the Owner thereof shall wish, if hee follow the direct modell of yor M^{te} pet^r so being no Mudd Stincks (as now it is) a horse may safely bee washed in it & drinke there. Fire with it may be extinguished if accidents should happen, the stirring then being not noysome wch now is so much, that in Somer time may cause an increase of the plague. All which Evills may bee prevented with as little charge to the owner as in the old fashion, so great inconveniences are (by the filthiness of these waters) contracted to horses with losses both to rich & poore especially those of the Army although Farriers for their gains, Ostlers to save themselves a Labour of going to the River doth mainteyne stincking water good to heale horses, but are convinced by the Argum^t: That the King having nowhere (as his M^{ty} may) the most stinking ponds to wash his M^{te} horses (if that were good) that through the Three Kingdomes by Rivers side & other sweete water where horses doe goe to Drink, no such corrupt ponds are erected to enter them in it, coming out of the cleare water.

"All these things considered of y^r M^{tie} y^r pet^r beseecheth yor Royall pleasure for a patent for this publick goode for 14 years that hee may manifest it. And that y^r M^{tie} bee pleased to have incerted in the said patent that nobody whatsoever may not for the space of the said 14 yeares use the said invention without your pet^r Lycense under his hand & Seal or the hand & Seale of his Deputyes in any part of yor M^{te} Dominions, wherein many ponds for cattle being so full of Mudd that there remaineth no room for water, without often great charges or Labour ill spent, Fish ponds also may bee so ordered. And that your pet^r may find no obsticle in receiving what hee shall contract for, with the severall partyes who shall make use of his said Modell.

"Your pet[r] further sheweth as to his second publick Convenience That hee hath also invented, That by Moulding (or by rubbing bricks ready made in a Mould of ruffe Stone) to any proportion of externall ornam for building as that being sooner ready then them that wich are carved & with great wast, Labour, time & cost spent.

"Your M[ties] pet[r]: humbly desires yo[r] Royall Graunt also for it, And that it may bee inserted in the recited patent, that nobody may make none, nor cause none to bee made by y[r] pet[rs] Invention of what proporcon or Figure whatsoever to bee moulded or rubbed, but by Lycence of yo[r] pet[r]: in the space of the said 14 yeares the patent also bearing what forfeiture yo[r] Ma[te] may thinke just, & as also for the former demand that the discoverers of Transgressing, yo[r] Ma[te] patent ag[t]: this publick good may find some encouragem[t].

"And yo[r] pet[r] shall pray," &c.

The petition was referred to the Attorney-General.

"Att y[e] Court at Whitehall, June 2, 1665.

"His Ma[ty] is graciously pleased to referre this Peticon to M[r]. Attorney Genrall to consider of this petition[ers] suit & y[e] nature of y[e] invencon, & to certify his M[ty] what his Opinion is upon it. And then his M[ty] will be glad to signify his further Pleasure for y[e] encouragem[t] of a publicke Good.
                              "ARLINGTON."

The Attorney-General reported as follows:—

"May it please yo[r] most Excellent Maj[ty].

"In obedience to yo[r] Maj[ties] referrence I have considered of this peticon, & conferred with the pet[r] thereopon, And in case the perticulers therein mencoed to bee invented by him bee new Invencons

(as for any thing yett appeareing to mee they are) Yo^r
Maj^{ty}, if soe graciously pleased, may grant the peticon^r
the sole use & benefitt thereof for fourteene yeares
according to the statute in that behalfe made.

" And such Grants usually have a provisor therein
which render the same void in case the thing granted
bee not a new Invention within the meaneing of that
statute.

"Which I humbly submitt to yor Maj^{ties} further
pleasure.

"G. PALMER."

The result was a warrant for a patent.

" S^t. Michel's Invenc̃on.
"Whereas Major Alexander Merch^t al̃s S^t.
Michaell has by his long travailes, study, paines, &
charges found out an invenc̃on or way for to keep y^e
water that is in ponds wherein people wash their
horses & in other ponds wholsome sweet & with
little or noe mudd in ye botome as also a way for y^e
moulding, grinding or rubbing of bricks in any forme
or shape w^tsoever fit for the internall & externall
ornam^t of any buildings within any of these Our
Dominions. And whereas the s^d. Alex. Marchant al̃s
S^t. Michael hath humbly besought us y^t Wee would bee
graciously pleased to grant unto him Our Lr̃es Patents
of licence & priviledge for ye sole use & benefit of his
severall Invenc̃ons for ye terme of 14 yeares according
to ye statute in such case made & provided. Our &c :
containing our Grant, licence or priviledge unto ye s^d
Alexander Merchant al̃s S^t. Michael of ye sole use &
benefit of his s^d sr̃all invenc̃ons within these Our
Realmes & Dominions for ye terme of 14 yeares according to ye statute in y^t behalfe made with such powers
clauses & provisoes as are usually incerted in grants
of like nature.

"Snd. &c. ye 7th of July, 1665.

To Our Attorney Genr̃all.   ARLINGTON."

Not contented with curing smoky chimneys, purifying water, and moulding bricks, St. Michel proposed in 1667 to raise submerged ships, and to prevent others from being submerged.

"Propositions dedicated to the King by Alex. Marchant, Sieur de St. Michel sur Couanon les Bauges, in Anjou, Captain and Major of English troops in Italy and Flanders, offering to show that he can draw up all submerged ships ; can prevent others from being submerged ; has discovered King Solomon's gold and silver mines, much vaster than those discovered by Columbus, and now much fuller than they were in that King's time. He wishes to satisfy His Majesty on his first proposition, lest the other should be deemed unworthy an audience."—*Calendar of State Papers, Domestic,* 1667, pp. 252-3.

What a curious comment upon this statement of the discovery of gold and silver mines is to be found in the following extract from the "Diary" :—

March 29, 1667 : "4*s.* a week which his (Balty St. Michel's) father receives of the French Church is all the subsistence his father and mother have, and about 20*l.* a year maintains them."

APPENDIX III.

PEPYS'S MANUSCRIPTS AT OXFORD.

HAPTER V. p. 82.—Pepys's manuscripts in the Rawlinson Collection at the Bodleian Library, Oxford, are very fully described in the "Oxford Catalogue of Manuscripts," and the Rev. W. D. Macray's Index to the same. Besides the letters from various persons which are noted further on in the list of Pepys's correspondents, are a large number of copies of letters from Pepys himself. The other papers are described as (1) Naval and Official, (2) Personal and Miscellaneous. In the first class are various notes on the state of the navy at different periods, questions respecting shipbuilding, memorials, minutes, and reports. In the second class are accounts of expenses, bonds, inventories, lists of books, &c.; and in both classes are papers of considerable interest for the purpose of elucidating the particulars of Pepys's life. Besides the above there are papers relating to other members of the family.

APPENDIX IV.

MUSICAL INSTRUMENTS.

HAPTER V. p. 98.—The following notice of old musical instruments will help to illustrate some of Pepys's allusions:—
"The lute about three hundred years ago was almost as popular as is at the present day the pianoforte. Originally it had eight thin catgut strings arranged in four pairs, each being tuned in unison; so that its open strings produced four tones; but in the course of time, more strings were added. Until the sixteenth century twelve was the largest number, or rather, six pairs. Eleven appear for some centuries to have been the most usual number of strings: these produced six tones, since they were arranged in five pairs and a single string. The latter, called the *chanterelle*, was the highest. According to Thomas Mace, the English lute in common use during the seventeenth century had twenty-four strings, arranged in twelve pairs, of which six pairs ran over the finger-board and the other six by the side of it. This lute was therefore, more properly speaking, a theorbo. The neck of the lute, and also of the theorbo, had frets consisting of catgut strings tightly fastened round it at the proper distances required for ensuring a chromatic succession of intervals. . . . The lute was made of various sizes according to the purpose for which it was intended in performance. The treble

lute was of the smallest dimensions, and the bass lute of the largest. The theorbo, or double-necked lute, which appears to have come into use during the sixteenth century, had, in addition to the strings situated over the finger-board, a number of others running at the left side of the finger-board, which could not be shortened by the fingers, and which produced the bass tones. The largest kinds of theorbo were the *archlute* and the *chitarrone.*

" The most popular instruments played with a bow at that time [1659] were the treble-viol, the tenor-viol and the bass-viol. It was usual for viol players to have 'a chest of viols,' a case containing four or more viols of different sizes. Thus Thomas Mace, in his directions for the use of the viol,' Musick's Monument,' 1676, remarks : 'Your best provision and most complete, will be a good chest of viols six in number, viz., two basses, two tenors, and two trebles, all truly and proportionably suited.' The violist, to be properly furnished with his requirements, had therefore to supply himself with a larger stock of instruments than the violinist of the present day.

" That there was, in the time of Shakespeare, a musical instrument called *recorder* is undoubtedly known to most readers from the stage-direction in ' Hamlet ' : ' Re-enter players with recorders.' But not many are likely to have ever seen a recorder, as it has now become very scarce."—ENGEL'S *Musical Instruments* (S. K. M. Art Handbooks), pp. 114-119.

APPENDIX V.

PEPYS'S CORRESPONDENTS.

HAPTER VII.—The following is a list of those friends and acquaintances whose letters to Pepys are still extant. The greater proportion of the letters are at Oxford, but some printed in the " Diary " are at Cambridge.

[The date is that of the letter. B. affixed shows that the MS. is in the Bodleian Library; S. that the letter is printed in Smith's "Life, &c., of Pepys;" and P. that it is printed in the Correspondence attached to the " Diary."]

Ackworth, William, Storekeeper in Woolwich Dock-yard, 1664. B.

Agar, Thomas, 1679-87. B.

Ailesbury, Robert Bruce, Earl of, 1684. B.

Alberville, Marquis d' [otherwise White], 1687. B.

Alcock, Thomas, Master Caulker at Portsmouth, 1682-6. B.

Allais, Denise d', 1680. B.

Andrewes, Sir Matthew, 1686-87. B.

Andrews, Thomas, Contractor for the Victualling of Tangier, 1664. B.

Anglesey, Arthur Annesley, 1st Earl of, 1672. B., S.

Atkins, Samuel. B.

Aylmer, Lieut. George, 1677-78. B.

Baesh, Sir Edward, 1689. B., S. (spelt Beash).

Bagwell, William, Carpenter of H.M.S. " The Prince," 1668, 1681. B.

Banks, C., 1678. B.
Banks, Sir John, 1672-9. B.
Barlow, Thomas, Clerk of the Acts, 1660-1. B.
Barrow, Philip, Storekeeper at Chatham, 1663. B.
Barry, James, 1678. B.
Bastinck, Francis, 1674, 1679. B.
Batelier, Joseph, Clerk in the Navy Office, 1681-83. B.
Battine, Edward, Clerk of the Survey at Portsmouth, 1687. B.
Beach, Sir Richard, 1677-88. B.
Beane, R., 1682. B.
Beaumont, Basil, Midshipman in the "Phœnix," 1687. B.
Bedford, Thomas, Deputy-Registrar of the Admiralty, 1687. B.
Belasyse, John, Lord, 1675. B.
Berkeley, John, 3rd Lord, of Stratton, 1678. B., P.
Bernard, Sir John, 1677. B.
Berry, Sir John, 1674-87. B.
Berry, Captain Thomas, 1673. B.
Bertie, Peregrine, 1688. B.
Betts, Isaac, Master Shipwright at Portsmouth Dockyard. B.
Bibaud, Henry, 1686-7. B.
Bickerstaffe, Sir Charles, 1685-88. B.-
Bland, Mrs. Sa., 1664. B.
Blathwayt, William, Secretary to James II., afterwards Clerk of the Council and Secretary at War, 1687. B.
Bodham, W., of Woolwich Ropeyard, 1665-71. B.
Bolland, Captain Richard, 1676-7. B.
Booth, Sir William, Captain of H.M.S. " Adventure," and Commissioner of the Navy, 1679-88. B.
Bounty, Captain John, 1680. B.
Bourk, William, Purser, 1687. B.
Bowles, George, 1681. B.
Bowles, Phineas, 1680-9. B.
Brisbane, John, 1679. B.
Brooke, Sir Robert, 1667. B.
Brouncker, William, Lord, 1667. B., P.

Browne, Captain John, afterwards a Cutler, 1682.   B.
Browne, John, Alderman and Mayor of Harwich,
     1689.   B.
Bulkeley, Lord, 1687.   B.
Bulteel, P., 1687.   B.
Bunce, Stephen, 1676.   B.
Burchett, Josiah, 1687-8.   B., P., S.
Burton, Dr. Hezekiah, 1677.   B., P.
Butler, Sir Nicholas, 1688.   B.
Canham, Ambrose, 1684.   B.
Carteret, Sir Philip, 1686-7.   B., S.
Chamberlayne, C., 1687.   B.
Chardin, Sir John, 1687.   B.
Charlett, Dr. A., 1700-2.   P.
Chetwood, K., 1687.   B.
Chicheley, Sir John, 1673.   B., S.
Child, John, 1680.   B.
Child, Sir Josiah, 1673.   B.
Churchill, Captain George, 1688.   B.
Clarendon, Henry, 2nd Earl of, 1700-1.   P.
Clutterbuck, Sir Thomas, 1671.   B., S.
Colinge, Richard.   B.
Compton, Dr. Henry, Bishop of London, 1691.   P.
Cooke, Thomas, 1687.   B.
Copleston, Sir John, 1679.   B.
Corie, Thomas, 1675.   B.
Cotton, Captain Andrew, 1687.   B.
Coventry, Sir William, 1664-76.   B.   1665, 1673.   P.
Cowse, William, 1688.   B.
Cramporne, Thomas, 1674.   B.
Creed, John, 1667-87.   B.
Custis, Edmund, 1675.   B.
Cuttance, Sir Roger, 1667.   B.
Dartmouth, George Legge, Lord, 1683-4. B., P. 1684-
     89. S.
Deane, Sir Anthony, 1666-89.   B.   1689.   S.
Delaune, Dr. W., 1702.   P.
Denise, Claude, Secretary to the Consistory of the
     Savoy, 1679-81.   B.

Dering, Sir Edward, 1687-8. B.
Des Glereaux, Paul Thevenin Sieur, 1680. B.
Des Moulins, Mdlle. Marie Lecoq, 1680-1. B.
Done, Andrew, 1679. B.
Donluis, Felix, 1680-88. B.
Dore, James, 1689. B.
D'Oyly, Edmund, 1679. B.
Dryden, John, 1699. S.
Duck, Mrs. Ann, 1682. B.
Dummer, Edmund, 1679. B., S.
Dunlope, Charles. B., S.
Dyre, Captain William, 1679-81. B.
Elkins, Richard, 1667. B.
Ellis, John, Scrivener, 1678. B.
Erlisman, Captain John, 1681. B.
Ernle, Sir John, 1671. B.
Evelyn, John, 1666-89. B. 1667, 1700. P. 1687-9. S.
Evelyn, Mrs. Mary, 1687. B., S.
Fairfax, George, 1677. B.
Falkener, John, Woolwich Ropeyard, 1664. B.
Feilding, Captain Henry, 1682. B.
Ferrer, Mrs. Jane, 1668. B.
Fist, Anthony, 1671. B.
Fitzpatrick, Colonel John, 1687. B.
Flawes, William, Captain of H.M.S. " Falcon," 1679. B.
Fletcher, Mathias, Carver to the Navy at Deptford, 1689. B.
Ford, Lieut. Samuel, 1678-88. B.
Fowler, Mrs. Anne, Widow of Capt. Fowler, 1687-8.
Fowler, Thomas, Captain of H.M.S. " Swallow," 1683-87. B.
Fox, Simon, 1675. B.
Francklin, Samuel, 1682. B.
Frederick, Sir John, 1677. B.
Frowde, Philip, Master of the Post Office, 1688. B.
Furzer, Daniel, Assistant Shipwright at Chatham Dockyard, 1685. B.
Gale, Roger, 1702-3. P.

s

Gale, Thomas, D.D., 1680-90. B. 1680-8. S. 1688-9, 1700. P.

Galeniere, Mons. de, 1702-3. P.

Gauden, Sir Denis, 1671-1682. B.

Gauden, Jonathan, 1689. B.

Gelson, John, 1683. B.

George, Lieut. John, 1679. B.

Gibbon, John, 1675. B., S.

Gibbon, Mary, Wife of Capt. Thomas Gibbon, 1681. B.

Gibbon, Captain Thomas, 1681. B.

Gibson, Dr. Edmond, afterwards Bishop of London, 1696. P.

Gibson, Richard, Victualling Agent to the Navy, 1670-88. B. 1688. P.

Gifford, Captain William, 1688. B.

Gordon, Sir Robert, 1687. B.

Gough, Richard, 1683. B.

Gray, J., son of Lord Gray, of Stamford, 1680. B.

Gregory, Edward, Commissioner of Chatham Dockyard, 1670-89. B.

Guilford, Sir Francis North, Lord, 1677-82. B.

Guillym, S., 1688. B.

Guy, Henry, 1680-1. B.

Gwynn, Francis, 1688. B., S.

Haddock, Sir Richard, 1681. B.

Hall, Thomas, 1681. B.

Hamilton, Thomas, 1679. B.

Hancock, Giles, 1682. B.

Harbord, William, M.P., 1679. B.

Hardesnell, J., 1681. B.

Harman, William, Captain of H.M.S. " Bristol," 1675. B.

Harris, Alexander, Messenger to the Admiralty, 1679. B.

Hawer, Nathaniel, 1688-9. B. 1688-9. S.

Hayes, Sir James, Commissioner of the Treasury in Ireland, 1666-73. B.

Hayter, Thomas, Clerk of the Acts, and Secretary to the Admiralty, 1673-9. B.

Hebdon, Sir John, 1666, 1681. B.
Herne, Sir Nathaniel, 1674. B.
Hewer, William, 1675-88. B. 1682, 1688. P. 1675-88. S.
Heywood, Captain Peter, 1679. B.
Hickes, Dr. George, 1700-2. P.
Hill, Joseph, B.D., 1676-88. B. 1681-9. S.
Hill, Thomas, 1673-5. B., S.
Hodges, William, Merchant at Cadiz, 1684-88. B.
Holmes, Henry, 1688. B.
Holmes, Sir John, 1677-9. B.
Holmes, Lady M., 1687. B.
Holmes, Sir Robert, 1688. B.
Homewood, Edward, Chatham, 1686-7. B.
Hopson, Sir Thomas, 1688. B.
Hosier, Francis, 1666. B.
Houblon, James, 1674-89. B. 1677-86. S.
Houblon, Mrs., 1683. B., S.
Houblon, Wynne, 1688. B., S.
How, Edward, Carpenter of H.M.S. "Oxford," 1686. B.
How, Lieut. John, 1675. B.
Howard, Mrs. E., Housekeeper to the Duke of York, 1671. B.
Howard, Sir Robert, 1679. B.
Howe, William, Judge at Barbadoes, 1681-88.
Hughes, Thomas. B., S.
Hunter, S., Clerk to the Trinity House, 1680-87. B.
Jackson, John, brother-in-law of Pepys, 1676. B.
Jackson, John, nephew of Pepys, 1687. B. 1699-1700. P.
Jackson, Samuel, 1688. B., S.
James II., 1688. B., P. 1679-81. P.
Jaques, Captain William, 1678. B.
Jeffreys, George, Lord Chancellor, 1687. B., P.
Jenifer, Captain James, 1667, 1679. B.
Jenkins, Sir Leoline, 1676-85. B. 1678-9. P.
Jenner, Sir Thomas, Baron of the Court of Exchequer 1687. B.

Jodrell, Paul, Clerk of the House of Commons, 1684-5. B.

Jordan, Sir Joseph, 1667. B.

Joyne, John, Watchmaker at Paris, 1680-1. B.

Kember, James. B.

Kennedy, Sir James, Consul in Holland, 1687-8. B.

Killigrew, Admiral Henry, 1679-88. B.

King, Gregory, 1692-3. P.

Kirke, Colonel Piercy, of Tangier, 1683. B.

Kneller, Sir Godfrey, 1690. B., S. 1701-2. P.

Langley, Captain Thomas, Mayor of Harwich, 1667-87. B.

Lanyon, John, Contractor for the Victualling of Tangier, 1664-6. B.

La Pointe, — de, 1683. B.

Latour, Raphael de la Bordasse, Seigneur de, 1680. B.

Lee, Robert, Master Shipwright at Chatham Dockyard, 1685. B.

Legendre-Tunier, T., 1669. B.

L'Estrange, Sir Roger, 1681. B.

Lewsley, Thomas, of Chatham, 1664. B.

Lhostein, Captain Augustus, 1674. B.

Littleton, Edward, 1689. B.

Lloyd, Captain David, 1688. B.

Loke, George, of Brampton, 1681. B.

Lorrain, Jacques, 1680. B.

Lorrain, Paul, son of Jacques, 1681. B. 1700. P.

Loton, Rev. John, of Chatham, 1670-88. B. 1688. S.

Lovelace, Thomas, 1680. B.

Lowther, Sir John, Commissioner of the Admiralty, 1689. B.

Luzancy, Hippolitus de, Vicar of Harwich, 1689. B., P.

Lynch, Thomas, Purser, 1680-1. B.

McDonnell, Captain, afterwards Sir Randal, 1687. B.

Martin, Samuel, Consul at Algiers, 1667-76. B.

Maryon, Joseph, of Clare Hall, Cambridge, 1681. B. 1680-1. S.

Matthews, John, of Huntingdon, 1681-7.

Maulyverer, John, of Magdalene College, Cambridge, 1679. B., P.

Mayden, Thomas, Merchant, 1676. B.

Middleton, Martha, Countess of, 1682. B.

Middleton, Colonel Thomas, 1665-7. B.

Miller, Thomas, of Brampton, 1683. B.

Milles, Daniel, D.D., 1681-2. B. 1687. S.

Mills, Rev. Alexander, of Sandwich, 1687. B., S.

Montagu, Rev. John, 1674. B., S.

Moore, Henry, 1667-9. B.

Moore, Sir Jonas, 1678. B., S.

Morales, — de, Portuguese Captain, 1680. B.

Mordaunt, Lady Elizabeth, 1680-2. B.

Moreau, Claude, Porter in Paris, 1680-3. B.

Morelli, Cesare, 1674-87. B. 1681. P. 1674. S.

Morland, Sir Samuel, 1677-88. B. 1686-8. P. 1687. S.

Munden, Sir Richard, 1679-80. B.

Murcott, Anne, 1687. B.

Narborough, Sir John, 1679. B.

Nelson, Robert, 1702-3. P.

Nevett, Richard, Purser, 1681. B.

Newlin, Robert, of Seville, 1684. B.

Newton, Sir Isaac, 1693. P.

Nicolls, Captain Matthias, 1681-2. B.

Norfolk, Jane Howard, Duchess of, 1681. P. 1687. B., S.

Norfolk, Thomas Howard, 7th Duke of, 1673. B., S.

Norman, James, 1667. B.

Norwood, Colonel Henry, 1679-81. B. 1679. S.

Orford, Edward Russell, afterwards 1st Earl of, 1689. B., S.

Papillon, Thomas, Merchant, 1673. B.

Parker, Abraham, Muster-master in the Navy, 1673-4. B.

Parry, Francis, Envoy to Portugal, 1679. B.

Peachell, John, D.D., 1680-8. B., P. 1680-8. S.

Pearse, Elizabeth, Laundress to the Queen of James II., 1682. B.

Pearse, James, Surgeon-General to the Fleet, 1666-80.
B.
Pearse, James, Jun., 1677-86. B. 1679. S.
Pedley, Sir Nicholas, of Huntingdon, 1682. B.
Peletyer, Antoine, of Paris, 1669-80. B.
Pellissary, Madame Bibaud, of Paris, 1680, 1687. B.
Penn, Sir William, 1664. B.
Pepys, Charles, Master Joiner at Chatham Dockyard,
1689. B., S.
Pepys, John, Sen., 1664. B.
Pepys, John, from H.M.S. "Sapphire," 1687. B.
Pepys, Richard, 1688. B., S.
Pepys, Roger, M.P., 1674. B.
Pepys, Thomas, 1681. B.
Pepys, Mrs. Ursula, 1680-87. B. 1683. P. 1680. S.
Perriman, J., of Rotherhithe, 1668. B.
Peterborough, Penelope Mordaunt, Countess of, 1680.
B.
Pett, Mrs. Ann, widow of Christopher Pett, 1670. B.
Pett, Christopher, 1666. B.
Pett, Sir Peter, 1664-1684. B. 1684. S.
Pett, Peter, 1682. B.
Pett, Sir Phineas, 1672-89. B. 1686-88. S.
Pett, Samuel, 1679. B.
Petty, Sir William, 1683-87. B. 1683. S.
Philipson, John, of Newcastle, 1682. B.
Poole, Sir William, Captain of H.M.S. "St. David,"
1675-9. B.
Povey, Thomas, 1672-86. B. 1672. P. 1680. S.
Prestman, John, 1679. B.
Priaulx, Thomas, of Seville, 1684. B.
Prowd, Captain John, 1676. B., S.
Puckle, James, 1679-80. B.
Raines, Sir Richard, Judge of the Court of Admiralty,
1686-88. B.
Rand, William, Governor of the Sea-Chest, 1672. B.
Reay, Lord, 1699-1700. P.
Reresby, Gars, 1683-4. B.
Rich, Peter, 1680. B.

Richmond, Charles Lennox, Duke of, 1671-2. B., S.
Robins, Judith, 1687. B.
Robinson, Sir Robert, 1667-79. B.
Rochester, Laurence Hyde, Earl of, 1677. B.
Rolfe, John, Alderman of Harwich, 1689. B.
Rooke, Sir George, 1679. B.
Rooke, Colonel W., 1679. B.
Rooth, Sir Richard, 1674-87. B.
Ross, Thomas, 1674. B., S.
Row, Richard, 1675. B.
Roydon, Charles, Captain of H.M.S. " Guernsey,'
    1677-8. B.
Rushworth, Mrs. Hannah, 1676-7. B.
Russell, Charles, 1683. B., S.
Ruvigny, Henri, Marquis de, 1679, 1681-2. B.
Rycaut, Paul, 1686. B.
Sackville, Captain Edward, 1679. B.
St. John, Dr. John, Judge in the East Indies, 1688. B.
St. John, Lady, 1687. B.
St. Michel, Balthasar, 1670-89. B. 1672. P. 1673-4,
    1689. S.
St. Michel, Mrs. Esther, 1681-2. B., S.
St. Michel, Samuel, 1689. B., S.
Salisbury, Hugh, 1670. B.
Sandford, S., Alderman of Harwich, 1683, 1686, 1689.
    B.
Sandwich, Edward Montagu, 1st Earl of, 1665. B., P.
Sandwich, Edward, Lord Hinchinbroke, 2nd Earl of,
    1667. B., S.
Sansom, John, 1675. B.
Savile, Henry, 1672-9. B. 1672. P.
Scott, Robert, Bookseller, 1681-8. B. 1688. P. 1681.
    S.
Seaman, Dr. Robert, Alderman of Harwich. 1688-9.
    B.
Shadwell, Edward, 1688. B.
Shales, Captain John, 1688. B.
Sheres, Sir Henry, 1675-87. B. 1683. S.
Sheridan, Thomas, 1680. B., S.

Sherwin, Judith, 1680. B.
Shish, Jonas, Shipwright at Sheerness and Deptford,
    1664. B.
Silvester, Edward, 1671. B.
Skelton, Bevil, 1686. B.
Skinner, Daniel, 1676-7. B.
Skinner, Ephraim, 1674. B.
Skinner, Mrs. Frances, 1699. B., S.
Skinner, O'Brien, 1679-82. B.
Skinner, Peter, 1686-89. B. 1689. S.
Slingar, Roger, 1684. B., S.
Slingsby, Sir Henry, 1687. B., P.
Smith, Sir Jeremiah, 1667. B.
Smith, Dr. Thomas, 1702. P.
Sotherne, James, 1680. B.
Southwell, Edward, 1682. B.
Southwell, Sir Robert, 1671-88. B. 1681-8. S.
Spencer, William, Bursar of Peter House, Cambridge,
    1686. B.
Spragg, Captain Thomas, 1688-9. B.
Spragge, Sir Edward, 1672. B.
Stock, Abraham, of Dover, 1677-88. 1688. S.
Stockdale, Robert, 1674. B.
Stokes, W., Mayor of Dover, 1678. B.
Strickland, Sir Roger, 1688. B.
Sussex, Anne Fitzroy Lennard, Countess of, 1688.
    B., S.
Taylor, Captain John, of Chatham Dockyard, 1667.
    B.
Taylor, Captain Silas, 1672. B.
Teddiman, Thomas, 1681. B., S.
Thynne, Henry Fred, 1687. B.
Tilghman, Abraham, Clerk to the Commissioners at
    Deptford, 1687. B., P., S.
Tippetts, Sir John, Commissioner of the Navy at
    Portsmouth, 1664-85. B.
Torrington, Arthur Herbert, Earl of, 1679. B.
Tosier, Captain John, 1679. B.
Trenchepain, Francois, 1679-80. B.

Trevanion, Ri, 1680. B.
Trevor, Sir John, 1687. B.
Tuke, Lady (M.), 1687. B., S.
Turner, Dr. John, 1682-87. B. 1680-88. S.
Turner, Mrs. Mary, 1682. B.
Turner, Tim, 1680. B., S.
Tyler, Richard, 1667. B.
Tyrrell, Captain John, 1687. B.
Tyrrell, Sir Timothy, 1679-80. B.
Vernon, John, 1681. B.
Villiers, Sir Edward, 1681. B.
Vincent, Nathaniel, D.D., 1682-8. B. 1682-8. S.
Vittells, Captain Richard, Master Superintendent at
    Chatham, 1687-8. B.
Walbanke, John, 1681. B.
Wallis, John, D.D., 1688. B., S. 1699-1702. P.
Waltham, Thomas, 1667. B.
Warner, John, 1685. B., S.
Warren, Sir William, 1664-88. B.
Wells, Jeremiah, Rector of West Hanningfield, Essex,
    1670-9. B.
Wescombe, Sir Martin, Consul at Cadiz, 1686. B.
Wheler, George, 1681. B.
Williamson, Sir Joseph, 1689. B., S.
Wivell, E., 1674-87. B.
Wood, Dr. Robert, 1682. B., S.
Woolley, William, 1684. B.
Wren, Matthew, 1669-70. B., P.
Wrenn, Captain Ralph, 1687. B.
Wright, Edward, 1680. B. 1696. P.
Wyborne, Sir John, Deputy Governor of Bombay,
    1680-8. B. 1686-8. S.
Wyborne, Lady (K.), 1683-8. B. 1686-7. S.
Wylde, Captain Charles, 1683. B., S.
Yeabsley, Thomas, Contractor for the Victualling of
    Tangier, 1664-5. B.

APPENDIX VI.

LISTS

Of the Secretaries of the Admiralty, and Principal Officers of the Navy; viz., Treasurers, Comptrollers, Surveyors, Clerks of the Acts, and Commissioners of the Navy at Chatham; to the beginning of the 18th century. (Compiled by Colonel Pasley, C.B., R.E.)

FROM the middle of the 16th to the end of the 17th century, Chatham was by far the most important of the English naval stations, and the Commissioner resident there had from the first a seat and vote at the Board in London— a privilege which was not extended to his colleague at Portsmouth until a much later date. The rise of the latter port dates from the alliance with the Dutch, and war with France which followed the accession of William and Mary, and which made it necessary to establish a first-class naval yard at a less distance from the French coast than Chatham. The same cause led to the construction of a dry dock at Plymouth. See "Edmund Dummer," in the list of Surveyors of the Navy.

The figures in the first column represent the year of appointment, when that can be ascertained. The prefix "circ." implies that the person named in the second column is known to have held the office at the time stated, although the date of first appointment is not known. In some cases the only date that can be found is that of an order to the

Attorney-General to prepare letters patent; sometimes that of the patent itself; sometimes of a warrant to execute the office, notwithstanding that the patent is not yet passed; and occasionally that of a letter from some person at Court informing his correspondent that the King or Queen has signed such and such a patent. It has been thought better, therefore, to state only the *year* of appointment, as the insertion in lists of this kind of the month and day tends to give them a delusive appearance of accuracy.

The scantiness of MS. records before the Revolution arises from the practice which existed of retiring Officers taking away with them their office books and papers, which they regarded as their own property. This was put a stop to in the Dockyards by a Navy Board Order of the 18th August, 1692. Unless otherwise stated, the manuscripts in the following lists are in the British Museum.

SECRETARIES OF THE ADMIRALTY,

From the first placing of the Office of Lord High Admiral in Commission to the commencement of the 18th century.

NOTE.—An asterisk (*) *before* the name of a titled office-holder signifies that the title (knighthood or other) was conferred upon him during his tenure of that office.

Date of Appointment.	Name.	Authority.	Lord High Admiral.
1628	Edward Nicholas.	Cal. St^te Papers (Domestic Series).	In Commission.

Nicholas had been Secretary to Lord Zouch, Warden of the Cinque Ports, and afterwards to the Duke of Buckingham, Lord High Admiral. On the assassination of the latter, in 1628, the office of Lord High Admiral was for the first time entrusted to a body of commissioners instead of to an individual, and Nicholas was appointed Secretary of the Admiralty. When the Earl of Northumberland was appointed Lord High Admiral, ten years later, Nicholas ceased to hold any office immediately connected with the Navy, but retained the post of Clerk of the Council. He

Date of Appointment.	Name.	Authority.	Lord High Admiral.
	was afterwards knighted, and became Secretary of State to Charles I., and (after the Restoration) to Charles II.		
1638	Thomas Smith.	Cal. St. Pap.	Earl of Northumberland.
1643	—— ?		Earl of Warwick.
1645	—— ?		A Committee of both Houses of Parliament.
1648	—— ?		Earl of Warwick again.

I have not met with any record of the names of the Secretaries during the period from 1643 to 1649.

1649	Robert Coytmor.	Cal. St. Pap.	A Committee of the Council of State.
1652	Robert Blackborne.	Cal. St. Pap.	Commissioners appointed by Act of Parliament.

Blackborne had previously held the office of Secretary to the "Navy Committee," a Committee of the House of Commons. The precise relations existing between the numerous committees and commissions at this period are not very clear.

1653	Robert Blackborne.	Cal. St. Pap.	Commissioners appointed by Act of the Convention.
1654	Robert Blackborne.	Addit. MS. 18,986, fo. 150 (Letter to Blackborne from Commissr. Pett).	Do. by Patent of the Protector Oliver.

Date of Appointment.	Name.	Authority.	Lord High Admiral.
1658	Robert Black-borne.	Admiralty Orders and Instructions, 1656 to 1658 (Admiralty Library MS.).	Do. by Patent of the Protector Richard.
1659	Robert Black-borne.	Addit. MS. 9,302, fo. 183 (List of Officers and Salaries of the Admiralty and Navy before the Restoration).	Commissioners appointed by the Rump.

Blackborne continued to hold the office of Secretary until the appointment of the Duke of York as Lord High Admiral in July, 1660. He is frequently mentioned by Pepys.

1660	*Sir William Coventry.	From "Mr.	Duke of York.
1667	Matthew Wren.	Hewer's account	Duke of York.
1672	Sir John Werden.	of the Secretaries of the Admiralty	Duke of York.
1673	Samuel Pepys.	from King Charles II.'s restoration to King	King Charles II., with a Commission.
1679	Thomas Hayter.	James II.'s withdrawing, December, 1688."	In Commission
1680	John Brisband.		In Commission
1684	Samuel Pepys.	(MS. in Pepysian Collection, "Naval Minutes.")	King Charles II. (assisted by the Duke of York).
1685	Samuel Pepys.		King James II.
1688	Samuel Pepys.		Prince of Orange.
1689	Phineas Bowles.		In Commission.
1690	James Sotherne.	Luttrell, ii. p. 10.	In Commission.

Date of Appointment.	Name.	Authority.	Lord High Admiral.
1694	William Bridg-man.	Luttrell, iii. p. 341.	In Commission.
1695	William Bridg-man and Josiah Bur-chett, joint Secretaries.	Haydn's "Book of Dignities."	In Commission.

The *date* of the joint appointment is taken from Haydn, but the *fact* is proved by Admiralty letters in the Chatham Dockyard Records, which about this time bear the signature sometimes of Bridgman and sometimes of Burchett as Secretary.

1698	Josiah Bur-chett, alone.	Luttrell, iv. 396.	In Commission.
1702	Josiah Bur-chett.		Earl of Pembroke.
1702	Josiah Bur-chett, George Clark, joint.	Luttrell, v. 176.	Prince George of Denmark.
1705	Josiah Bur-chett, alone.	Luttrell, v. 605.	Prince George of Denmark.
1708	Josiah Bur-chett.		Earl of Pembroke.
1709	Josiah Bur-chett.		In Commission.

NOTE.—Mr. Burchett continued to hold this office until 1742, when he retired. ("British Chronologist," 29th Oct., 1742.)

TREASURERS OF THE NAVY,

To the commencement of the 18th century.

Date of Appointment.	Name.	Authority.
circ. 1546	Robert Legg.	Harleian MS. 249.

The first paper in this volume of the Harleian Collection is a " Confession taken of 23 of the crediblest forfathers at Deptford-Strande the 29th day of October (anno R. R. Hen. VIII. 38vo.) consernynge the taking of the Gallye Blancherd, in the presens of Sir Thomas Cleire, Lieuftennaunt, Robert Legg Esq. Treasourer, Will. Brocke, Comptroller, Benjamin Gonson, Surveour, and Rich Brocke, Capitaigne of the Kynges Majesties Gallye Subtill." I have not found any record of the date of Legg's appointment.

1549	Benjamin Gonson.	Addit[l]. MSS. vol. 9295, fo. 56.
1577	Benjamin Gonson and *Sir John Hawkins, joint.	Addit[l]. MSS. vol. 9295, fo. 56.
1578	Sir John Hawkins, alone.	Cal. St. Papers.
1595	Vacant.	Cal. St. Papers.

On Sir John Hawkins's death in 1595, Roger Langford, his deputy, was appointed to do the duty of Treasurer, with the title of "Paymaster of Marine Causes," pending the appointment of a new Treasurer, which did not take place till 1598.

1598	*Sir Fulke Greville.[1]	Cal. St. Pap.
1604	Sir Robert Mansell.	Cal. St. Pap., and Phineas Pett's Autobiography.
1618	Sir William Russell.	Cal. St. Pap.

---

[1] Afterwards Lord Brooke.

Date of Appointment.	Name.	Authority.
1627	*Sir Sackville Crowe, Bart.	Cal. St. Pap.

Sir Sackville Crowe was one of the Special Commissioners appointed in 1618 by James I. to inquire into abuses in the navy. In 1627 Sir W. Russell was superseded in his favour, but three years later he was charged with misappropriation, or embezzlement, and was compelled to resign, when Russell was reinstated.

1630	Sir William Russell, again.	Cal. St. Pap.
1639	Sir William Russell, and *Sir Henry Vane, joint.	Cal. St. Pap.
1642	Sir Henry Vane, alone.	Forster,"Statesmen of the Commonwealth."
1651	Richard Hutchinson.	Cal. St. Pap.

Hutchinson had been Deputy Treasurer to Sir H. Vane, whom he succeeded as Treasurer in 1651. He continued to hold that office until the Restoration. He is several times mentioned in Pepys's "Diary."

1660	Sir George Carteret.	Pepys, &c.

Sir George Carteret had been Comptroller of the Navy before the Civil War.

1667	Earl of Anglesey.	Duke of York's Memoirs, p. 235.
1668	Sir Thomas Osborne, Bart., Sir Thomas Littleton, Bart., joint.	Duke of York's Memoirs, p. 236.
1671	Sir Thomas Osborne, alone.	Duke of York's Memoirs, p 236.

The patent of Sir Thomas Osborne (afterwards Duke of Leeds) to be sole Treasurer is printed in the Duke of York's "Memoirs of the English Affairs," pp. 235-238. It recites and revokes the appointments of 1667 and 1668.

T

Date of Appointment.	Name.	Authority.
1673	Edward Seymour.	Collins's " Peerage of England" (Sir E. Brydges' edition), vol. i. p. 195.

Afterwards Sir Edward Seymour, Bart. The Duke of Somerset and the Marquis of Hertford are descended from him.

| 1681 | Viscount Falkland. | Luttrell, vol. i. p. 76. |

Lord Falkland died in 1694. (Luttrell, iii. 317.)

| 1689 | Edward Russell. | Collins's " Peerage," vol. i. p. 283. |

A distinguished naval commander. Afterwards Earl of Orford, which title became extinct at his death.

| 1699 | Sir Thomas Littleton, Bart. | Luttrell, v. 521. |

Died in 1710. (Luttrell, vi. 530.)

| 1710 | Robert Walpole. | Luttrell, vi. 534. |

Afterwards Prime Minister and Earl of Orford.

COMPTROLLERS OF THE NAVY,

To the commencement of the 18th century.

Date of Appointment.	Name.	Authority.
circ. 1514	John Hopton.	Cal. of Letters, &c., Henry VIII.

Hopton certainly held the office of Comptroller in 1514, but I have been unable to ascertain the date of his appointment. He died about 1524.

Date of Appointment.	Name.	Authority.
circ. 1542	John Osburne.	Byng MSS. vol. x.[1] Admiralty Library (Pepys's Naval Collections).
circ. 1546	William Brock.	Harleian MS. 249, No. 1.
1562	William Holstock.	Cal. St. Pap.
circ. 1585	William Holstock and William Borough, joint.	Lansdowne MS. 43, No. 33.

At this period (1585) W. Borough was Clerk *and* Comptroller of the Ships, but as Holstock certainly retained the office of Comptroller till 1589, I presume they must have held it jointly.

circ. 1590	William Borough, alone.	Cal. St. Pap.

After 1589 Holstock's name appears no more at the foot of certificates or other papers connected with the navy recorded in the Calendars of State Papers, and it is probable that he died or retired then, leaving Borough sole Comptroller. The latter died about the end of 1598. (Cal. St. Pap.)

1598	Sir Henry Palmer.	Cal. St. Pap.
1611	Sir Guilford Slingsby.	Cal. St. Pap.
1631	Sir Henry Palmer, junior.	Cal. St. Pap.
1639	Sir Hen. Palmer, jun., and Capt. George Carteret,[2] joint.	Cal. St. Pap.

[1] This volume contains a transcript of part of Pepys's Naval Collections in the Library of Magdalene College, Cambridge. It comprises some extracts from Lord Clarendon's copy of the Council Books of King Henry VIII. from 1541 to 1543, one of which records a letter being written to Mr. Stanhopp and John Osburne, "Comptroller of the King's H.'s Ships." I cannot find the date of his first appointment.

[2] Afterwards Sir George Carteret, Treasurer of the Navy.

Date of Appointment.	Name.	Authority.
1642	In abeyance.	Addit. MSS. vol. 9311, fo. 188.

In 1642 the Parliament abolished the offices of Comptroller, Surveyor, and Clerk of the Acts, and constituted instead of them a Board of equal Commissioners.   The Treasurer remained, but was no longer a member of the Navy Board.

1660	*Sir Robert Slingsby.	Cal. St. Pap. ; Pepys's Diary.

The Navy Board in its old form was re-established at the Restoration.

1661	Sir John Minnes.	Pepys's Diary.
1671	Sir Thomas Allen.	Duke of York's Instructions (MS. Admiralty Library).

Died in 1685.   (Luttrell, i. p. 358.)

1685	Sir Richard Haddock.	Addit. MS. 9322.
1686	In abeyance.	Pepys's Memoir.

The principal officers (except the Treasurer) were suspended, and the office placed temporarily under the charge of a body of equal Commissioners, as described in Pepys's " Memoir."

1688	Sir Richard Haddock, restored.	Pepys's Memoir.

Special Commission revoked, and former officers restored.

1715	Sir Charles Wager.	Byng MSS. vol. 13 (Admiralty Library)

SURVEYORS OF THE NAVY,

To the commencement of the 18th century.

Date of Appointment.	Name.	Authority.
circ. 1546	Benjamin Gonson.	Harleian MS. 249. (*See* Robert Legg, Treasurer.)

Gonson was appointed Treasurer of the Navy in 1549.

1549	*Sir William Winter.	Addit. MS. 5752, fo. 6ᵇ.

Letters Patent of Philip and Mary, dated 2nd Nov. 1557, recite a patent of Edward VI. appointing William Wynter to be "Surveyor of our Ships," and go on to appoint him "Master of our Ordnance of our Ships," in addition to the Surveyorship. He continued to hold the joint offices for many years—certainly till 1589, perhaps later. The date of his death is uncertain.

1598	*Sir John Trevor.	Cal. St. Pap.
1611	*Sir Richard Bingley.	Phineas Pett's Autobiography.
1616	*Sir Thomas Aylesbury.	Cal. St. Pap.
1632	Kenrick Edisbury.	Cal. St. Pap.

This is the "Old Edgborough," whose ghost was supposed to haunt the Hill House at Chatham. (Pepys's Diary, 8th April, 1661.) He died in 1638.

1638	William Batten.	Cal. St. Pap.
	Afterwards Sir William.	(See 1660 below.)
1642	In abeyance.	Addit. MSS. vol. 9311 fo. 188.

A body of Commissioners appointed by Parliament instead of the principal officers.

Date of Appointment.	Name.	Authority.
1660	Sir William Batten, restored. Died in 1667.	Cal. St. Pap., and Pepys's Diary.
1667	Colonel Thomas Middleton.	Pepys's Diary, 10th Dec. 1667.

See Middleton in List of Commissioners at Chatham, 1672.

1672	*Sir John Tippetts.	Duke of York's Instructions (MS. in Admiralty Library).
1686	In abeyance.	Pepys's Memoir.
1688	Sir John Tippetts, restored.	Pepys's Memoir.
1692	Edmund Dummer.	Luttrell, ii. 522.

In the British Museum (King's MS. 40) there is an interesting account by Dummer of a tour made by him in the Mediterranean on board H.M.S. "Woolwich" in 1682-84. The volume contains many plans and drawings. In the reign of William III., Dummer contrived a simple and ingenious method of pumping water from dry docks below the level of low tide, which enabled Portsmouth for the first time to possess a dry dock capable of taking in a first-rate man-of-war, previously regarded as impracticable, owing to the small rise of tide there as compared with that at Woolwich, Deptford, Chatham, and Plymouth. He also designed and constructed the first docks at Plymouth. (See Harl. MS. 4318; Lansdowne MS. 847; King's MSS. 40, 43.)

1699	Daniel Furzer.	Luttrell, iv. 556.
1715	Jacob Acworth.	Byng Collection, vol. xiii. (MS. in Admiralty Library).

CLERKS OF THE SHIPS, OF THE NAVY, OR OF THE ACTS,

To the commencement of the 18th century.

Date of Appointment.	Name.	Authority.
circ. 1482	Thomas Roger, or Rogiers.	Pepys's "Miscellanies" (MS.) and Harleian MS. 433.

The office of "Clerk of the King's Ships," or of the Navy, afterwards "Clerk of the Acts of the Navy," is in all probability a very ancient one; but the first holder of the office whose name I have met with is Thomas Roger or Rogiers, who seems to have held it in the reigns of Edward IV., Edward V., and Richard III. In the third volume of Pepys's MS. "Miscellanies," p. 87, is an entry of an order dated 18th May, 22nd Edward IV. (1482), to the Treasurer and Chamberlain of the Exchequer to examine and clear the account of "our well beloved Thomas Roger Esq. Clerk of our Ships." Harleian MS. 433 (supposed to have belonged to Lord Burghley) is a register of grants, &c., passing the Privy Seal, &c., during the reigns of Edward V. and Richard III., with some entries of other reigns. No. 1690 is the appointment of "Thomas Rogiers to be Clerc of all maner shippes to the King belonging." It has no date, but is very probably a reappointment by Richard III. on his assumption of the throne.

Temp. Henry VII.	William Comersale.	"Letters and Papers, Henry VIII.," vol. i. p. 48.
Temp. Henry VII. 1509	Robert Brigandyne, or Brikenden.	

"Privy Seal 28 July 1509 for Robert Brikenden to be Keeper or Clerk of the King's Ships in

Date of
Appoint-   Name.   Authority.
ment.

the Realm of England, with 12*d.* a day for himself, and 6*d.* a day for his Clerk, in the same
manner as William Comersale,—out of the customs of Exeter and Dartmouth."

> "Letters and Papers,
> Henry VIII.," vol.
> iii. pt. 2, p. 1263.

"Grant 21 April 1523:—Rob. Briganden, of
Smalhed, Kent, alias of Portesmouth. Release, as
Clerk of the King's Ships to Henry VII. and
Henry VIII., and purveyor of Stuffs and timber
for the same."

From these two documents it appears that
Brigandyne's appointment as Clerk of the Ships
in 1509 was a reappointment on the accession of
Henry VIII., and that he had held the same office
under Henry VII. after Comersale, who may very
probably have succeeded Rogiers.

Brigandyne's name appears very frequently in
connection with naval matters down to October,
1525, after which there is no mention of him in
the Calendar of letters and papers.

1526   Thomas Jermyn, or   "Letters and Papers,
           Germyn.   Henry VIII.," vol.
                            iv. pt. 1, p. 954.

Patent 1526, April 3rd. Thomas Jermyn, Yeo-
man of the Guard and Crown, to be Keeper or
Clerk of the Navy, and Keeper of the Dock at
Portsmouth, with 12*d.* a day, and 6*d.* a day for a
Clerk, out of the issues of the Ports of Exeter and
Dartmouth.

From this date to 1530 there are numerous
entries connected with Jermyn's accounts as Clerk
of the Ships.

circ. 1540   Sir Thomas Spert.   Pepys's "Miscellanies,"
                               vol. vii. (MS. at
                               Magdalene College).

This volume of the "Miscellanies" includes a
collection of payments made to the navy between

Date of
Appoint-   Name.   Authority.
ment.

1537 and 1541. Amongst these are regular half-
yearly payments at the rate of £33 6s. 8d. to "Sir
Thomas Spert, Clerke of the King's Ships."

circ. 1563   George Winter.   Addit. MSS. vol. 5752.

This volume contains an order of Queen Elizabeth, dated 16th July, 1563, to Lord Clinton, Lord
High Admiral, to deliver certain stores to George
Winter, "Clerk of our Ships." I have been unable to find the date of his appointment to this
office, which he continued to hold till his death in
1581. His epitaph in Dyrham Church, Glouces-
tershire, is printed in Bigland's Collection. He
was brother to Sir William Winter, Surveyor of
the Navy and Master of Sea Ordnance.

circ. 1585   William Borough.   Lansdowne MS. 43,
                                   No. 33.

In February of this year Borough was Clerk *and*
Comptroller: see his letter of this date (Feb. 1584,
meaning no doubt 1585 as years are counted now)
to Lord Burghley (Lansd. MSS. 43, 33) beginning,
"To the righte honnorable the L. Burghley Lord
Highe Treasourer of Englande—your suppliant
William Borough Clarke and Comptroller of her
Matie Shippes," &c. The paper is endorsed, "A
dewtifull declaration, February An°. 1584. By
William Borough Clarke and Comptroller of her
Matie Navie." It is an original letter, the body
written in a very neat hand of the period, and
signed by Borough himself in a different, but also
very neat, hand. As William Holstock was certainly Comptroller at this time, and had been so
for more than twenty years, it is probable that he
and Borough held that office jointly, whilst Borough also performed the functions of Clerk of
the Ships. (*See* List of Comptrollers.) As Winter
died in 1581, and Borough had certainly been
Clerk for some time before the date of his letter,

Date of Appointment.	Name.	Authority.

it is probable that he immediately succeeded
Winter.

circ. 1600   *Sir Peter Buck.   Phineas Pett's Auto-
biography.

As Borough died in 1598 (Cal. St. Pap.), it is probable he was succeeded about that time by Peter
Buck; but the first occasion on which I find the name
of the latter mentioned as Clerk of the Ships is in
the year 1600, by Phineas Pett. Sir Henry Palmer
certainly succeeded Borough in the Comptroller-
ship in 1598 (Cal. St. Pap.). Buck died in 1625.
He had been for some years Clerk of the Cheque
at Chatham before his appointment to the Board.
He is mentioned by Pepys as one of his predecessors ("Diary," 14 Dec. 1660), who was not a
little proud of his office having once been held by
a knight. Lord Braybrooke, in his note to this
entry, says that Buck was Secretary to Algernon
Percy, Earl of Northumberland; but Buck was
Clerk of the Navy at least two years before the
Earl was born, and died when the latter was only
twenty-three years of age.

1625	Dennis Fleming.	Cal. St. Pap.
1638	Dennis Fleming and Thomas Barlow, joint.	Cal. St. Pap.
1642	In abeyance.	Addit. MSS. vol. 9311, fo. 188.

A body of Commissioners appointed by Parliament instead of the principal officers.

1660   Samuel Pepys.

Lord Braybrooke, in his note to the entry of the
27th June, 1660, quotes Pepys's patent, in which
Fleming and Barlow's joint patent is recited and
revoked, and Pepys was appointed Clerk of the
Acts at a salary of £33 6s. 8d. per annum. But
this amount was only the ancient "fee out of the
Exchequer" which had been attached to the office

Date of Appointment.	Name.	Authority.

for more than a century. Pepys's salary had been previously fixed at £350 a year. Lord Braybrooke says, in a note to 9th Feb. 1664-65, that "Barlow had previously been Secretary to Algernon, Earl of Northumberland, when High Admiral;" but he was appointed Clerk of the Acts two months before the Earl became Lord High Admiral. Barlow had, however, been in his service at an earlier date, and had been appointed by the Earl Muster-Master of the Fleet under his command in 1636. (Cal. St. Pap.)

1674	Thomas Hayter and John Pepys, joint.	Addit. MSS. vol. 9307.

When Pepys was promoted to be Secretary of the Admiralty, he was succeeded in the office of Clerk of the Acts by his clerk and his brother jointly.

1677	Thomas Hayter and James Sotherne, joint.	Orders and Warrants, 1676-78 (MS. in Admiralty Library).

Sotherne was appointed "one of the Clerkes of ye Acts of our Navy Royall," in the place of John Pepys "lately deceased :" 12th March, 1676-77.

1679	James Sotherne, alone.	

Hayter was promoted to be Secretary of the Admiralty when Pepys was thrown into prison.

1686	In abeyance.	Pepys's Memoir.

Special temporary Commission appointed, and the principal officers suspended.

1688	James Sotherne, restored.	Pepys's Memoir.

Special Commission revoked.

circ. 1690	Charles Sergison.	

Sotherne was made Secretary of the Admiralty in January, 1690, and it is probable that Sergison immediately succeeded him. The Letter-books of

Date of Appointment.	Name.	Authority.

the Navy Board at Chatham show that he held the
office in 1691, and held it until 1719.

1719	Tempest Holmes.	Byng Collection, vol. xiii. (MS. in Admiralty Library).

COMMISSIONERS OF THE NAVY AP-
POINTED TO RESIDE AT CHATHAM,

*From the first establishment of that office in 1630 to the com-
mencement of the 18th century.*

Date of Appointment.	Name.	Authority.
1630	Phineas Pett.	Phineas Pett's Autobiography (Addit. MS. 9298).

This interesting MS., in Pett's own handwriting, contains full details of the life of the
celebrated builder of the " Royal Sovereign," or
"Sovereign of the Seas," from his birth in 1570
until 1637, when it breaks off abruptly. It is
endorsed, in a much later handwriting : "The life
of Com'. Pett's father, whose place he did enjoy."
A few leaves are wanting, but their contents are
supplied by a complete transcript in the Harleian
MS. 6279, in which, however (as well as in another
transcript in the Pepysian Library), the ortho-
graphy is somewhat modernized, and the handwriting is that of the latter part of the 17th century.   Extracts from a copy of the Harleian transcript are printed in " Archæologia," vol. xii.
Pett died in 1647, at Chatham. Having sub-

Date of Appointment.	Name.	Authority.

mitted to the Parliament in 1642, he retained his office until his death in 1647.[1]

| 1647 | Peter Pett. | Addit. MSS. vol. 9306 (Navy Board Letter-book), shows that in Nov. 1648, Peter Pett held this office. |

I have not met with Peter Pett's original appointment, but I have no doubt that he immediately succeeded his father Phineas, on the death of the latter in 1647. He was continued in the same office after the Restoration. In 1667, in consequence of the Dutch attack on Chatham, he was superseded, sent to the Tower, and threatened with impeachment. The threat was not carried out, but he was never restored to office.

| 1667 | Vacant. | |

No new appointment was made for nearly two years after Pett's removal.

| 1669 | *Sir John Cox. | Pepys' Diary: Narborough's Diary. |

Cox was master of the Duke of York's flagship, "Royal Charles," in the victory over the Dutch Admiral Opdam, 3rd June, 1665. Was captain of the "Sovereign" in the three days' battle with the Dutch fleet in June, 1666. Master Attendant at Deptford in 1667. Resident Commissioner at Chatham, March, 1669. Appointed, 15th Jan. 1672, Flag-Captain to the Duke of York in the "Prince," without vacating his office at Chatham. Knighted by King Charles II., on board the "Prince," at the Nore, on the 27th April. Killed at the Battle of Sole Bay, on the 28th May in the same year.

[1] Chatham Parish Register, quoted in "Archæologia," vol. xii. p. 284.

Date of Appoint-ment.	Name.	Authority.

(See " Diary " of Captain John Narborough (afterwards Sir John), whilst serving as First Lieutenant on board the " Prince." It is amongst the Pepysian MSS. at Magdalene College, and there is a transcript in the Admiralty Library.)

1672   Colonel Thomas Mid-   Duke of York's Instruc-
dleton.   tions (MS. in Admi-
ralty Library).

Colonel Middleton was one of the Commissioners of the Admiralty appointed by the Rump in January, 1660. Engaged in the West India trade after the Restoration (see Duke of York's " Memoirs," p. 9). Appointed Commissioner at Portsmouth in 1664, and Surveyor of the Navy in 1667. Removed to Chatham as Resident Commissioner in June, 1672. Died in December of the same year.

1672   *Sir Richard Beach.   Duke of York's Instructions (MS. in Admi-
ralty Library).

Captain of H.M.S. the " Crown " in February, 1663. Served at sea till 1672, in which year he captured an Algerine man-of-war. Appointed Resident Commissioner at Chatham in Dec. 1672, and transferred to Portsmouth in the same capacity in 1679. Removed to the Board in London as Comptroller of Victualling Accounts in 1690. Died in May, 1692.

1679   *Sir John Godwin.   Addit. MS. 9312.

Served in the navy as a lieutenant, and subsequently in the Victualling Department. Appointed Commissioner at Chatham in Dec. 1679; removed to the Board in London, March, 1686; died in 1689.

1686   Sir Phineas Pett.   Pepys's Memoirs.

Son of Peter Pett, shipbuilder, of Ratcliffe, and grand-nephew of Phineas Pett, the first Commis-

Date of Appointment.	Name.	Authority.

sioner at Chatham. Appointed Master Shipwright at Portsmouth in June, 1660, and transferred to Chatham in the same capacity in the following month. Dismissed for misbehaviour in office on the 25th Sept., 1668, but restored three months afterwards on making submission and surrendering his patent. Promoted to the Board in London as Comptroller of Victualling Accounts on the 5th August, 1680, and knighted by the King on the same day. Transferred to Chatham as Commissioner in 1686. Dismissed on account of his political opinions on the accession of William and Mary.[1]

1689   *Sir Edward Gregory.   Admiralty Orders, 1688-9 (MS. in the Public Record Office).

Served as a purser in the navy in 1662-3. Succeeded his father as Clerk of the Cheque in Chatham Yard in Feb. 1665, which office he resigned after holding it nearly twenty years. Appointed Commissioner at Chatham on the 20th April, 1689. Knighted by William III. in Jan. 1691. Retired on a pension of £300 a year in June, 1703. Died in 1713.

1703   Captain George St.   Chatham Records.
            Lo.

---

[1] *Note respecting Sir Phineas Pett.*—There were so many shipbuilders of the name of Phineas Pett, that it is often difficult to trace the history of any one of them. In February, 1660, Phineas Pett, son of John Pett, and grandson of Commissioner Phineas Pett, being then Assistant-Master Shipwright at Chatham, petitioned to be promoted, and was appointed Master Shipwright at Chatham in the same month. But it would appear that the appointment was revoked, or never carried into effect, for in the following July we find Phineas Pett, "of Ratcliffe," who had been appointed Master Shipwright at Portsmouth in June, transferred to Chatham in the same capacity. And in September Phineas Pett, Assistant-Master Shipwright at Chatham, was suspended from office on the accusation of having, *when a child*, spoken contemptuously of the King ! For this offence he was dismissed in the following month.

Name.

Authority.

Attained the rank of captain in 1682. When in command of the "Portsmouth," in 1689, was captured with his ship, and taken into Brest severely wounded. In 1693 he published a tract, entitled, "England's Safety or a bridle to the French King." In the same year he was appointed a member of the Navy Board. Transferred to Plymouth as Commissioner in 1695, and from thence to Chatham in 1703. Superseded on the accession of George I., in 1714, by the omission of his name from the new patent for the Navy Board.

APPENDIX VII.

PLAYS WHICH PEPYS SAW ACTED.

HAPTER XII.—Pepys was not very careful in setting down the titles of the plays he saw, and in many instances he quotes the second titles alone. This caution must be remembered by those consulting the following list :—

Adventures of Five Hours (Tuke), "Duke's," Jan. 8, 17, 1662-63; Jan. 27, 1668-69; "Court at Whitehall," Feb. 15, 1668-69.

Aglaura (Suckling), "King's," Jan. 10, 1667-68.

Albumazar (Tomkis), "Duke's," Feb. 22, 1667-68.

Alchymist (Ben Jonson), "Theatre," June 22, Aug. 14, 1661; "King's," April 17, 1669.

All's Lost by Lust (W. Rowley), "Red Bull," March 23, 1661.

Antipodes (R. Brome), "Theatre," Aug. 26, 1661.

Argalus and Parthenia (Glapthorne), "Theatre," Oct. 28, 1661.

Bartholomew Fair (Ben Jonson), "Theatre," June 8, Sept. 7, 1661; "King's," Aug. 2, 1664; "Court at Whitehall," Feb. 22, 1668-69.

Beggar's Bush (Beaumont and Fletcher), "Lincoln's Inn Fields" (King's Company), Nov. 20, 1660; "Theatre," Oct. 8, 1661; "King's," April 24, 1668.

Black Prince (Lord Orrery), "King's," Oct. 19, 23, 1667; April 1, 1668.

Bondman (Massinger), "Whitefriars," March 1, 1660-
61 ; "Salisbury Court," March 26, 1661 ; "Opera,"
Nov. 4, 26, 1661 ; April 2, 1662.
Brenoralt (Suckling), "Theatre," July 23, 1661 ;
"King's," Aug. 12, Oct. 19, 1667. (*See* "Discon-
tented Colonel.")
Cardinal (Shirley), "Cockpit" (Whitehall), Oct. 2,
1662 ; "King's," Aug. 24, 1667 ; April 27, 1668.
Catiline (Ben Jonson), "King's," Dec. 11, 1667.
Catiline's Conspiracy (Stephen Gosson), "King's,"
Dec. 19, 1668.
Chances (Beaumont and Fletcher), "Theatre," April 27,
Oct. 9, 1661; "King's," Feb. 5, 1666-67.
Change of Crowns (Edward Howard), "King's," April
15, 1667.
City Match (Mayne), "King's," Sept. 28, 1668.
Claracilla (Thomas Killigrew), "Theatre," July 4,
1661 ; "Cockpit" (Whitehall), Jan. 5, 1662-63 ;
"King's," March 9, 1668-69.
Coffee House (St. Serfe), "Duke's," Oct. 5, 15,
1667.
Committee (Sir Robert Howard), "Royal Theatre,"
June 12, 1663 ; "King's," Aug. 13, Oct. 29, 1667 ;
May 15, 1668.
Country Captain (Duke of Newcastle), "Theatre,"
Oct. 27, Nov. 26, 1661; "King's," Aug. 14, 1667;
May 14, 1668.
Coxcomb (Beaumont and Fletcher), "King's," March
17, 1668-69.
Cupid's Revenge (Beaumont and Fletcher), "Duke's,"
Aug. 17, 1668.
Custom of the Country (Beaumont and Fletcher),
"King's," Aug. 1, 1667.
Cutter of Coleman Street (Cowley), "Opera," Dec.
16, 1661. (*See* "Guardian.")
Discontented Colonel (Suckling), "King's," March 5,
1667-68. (*See* "Brenoralt.")
Duchess of Malfy (Webster), "Duke's," Sept. 30, 1662 ;
Nov. 25, 1668.

Duke of Lerma (Sir Robert Howard), "King's," Feb. 20, 1667-68.
Elder Brother (Fletcher), "Theatre," Sept. 6, 1661.
English Monsieur (Hon. James Howard), "King's," Dec. 8, 1666; April 7, 1668.
English Princess, or Richard III. (J. Caryl), "Duke's," March 7, 1667.
Evening Love (Dryden), "King's," June 19, 1668.
Faithful Shepherdess (Fletcher), "Royal Theatre," June 13, 1663; "King's," Oct. 14, 1668; Feb. 26, 1668-69.
Father's Own Son, "Theatre," Sept. 28, Nov. 13, 1661.
Faustus, Dr. (Marlow), "Red Bull," May 26, 1662.
Feign Innocence, or Sir Martin Marr-all (Duke of Newcastle, corrected by Dryden), "Duke's," Aug. 16, 20, 1667. (*See* "Sir Martin Marr-all.")
Flora's Vagaries (Rhodes), "King's," Aug. 8, 1664; Oct. 5, 1667; Feb. 18, 1667-68.
French Dancing Master, "Theatre," May 21, 1662.
General (Shirley), "King's," April 24, 1669.
Generous Portugals, "King's," April 23, 1669.
German Princess (Holden), "Duke's," April 15, 1664.
Ghosts (Holden), "Duke's," April 17, 1665.
Goblins (Suckling), "King's," May 22, 1667.
Grateful Servant (Shirley), "Duke's," Feb. 20, 1668-69.
Greene's Tu Quoque (Cooke), "Duke's," Sept. 12, 16, 1667.
Guardian (Cowley), "Duke's," Aug. 5, 1668. (*See* "Cutter of Coleman Street.")
Guzman (Lord Orrery), "Duke's," April 16, 1669.
Hamlet (Shakespeare), "Opera," Aug. 24, 1661; "Theatre," Nov. 27, 1661; "Duke's," May 28, 1663; Aug. 31, 1668.
Heiress (Duke of Newcastle?), "King's," Feb. 2, 1668-69.
Henry IV. (Shakespeare), "Theatre," Dec. 31, 1660-61; June 4, 1661; "King's," Nov. 2, 1667; Jan. 7, 1667-68; Sept. 18, 1668.

Henry V. (Lord Orrery), "Duke's," Aug, 13, 1664; July 6, 1668; "Court at Whitehall," Dec. 28, 1666.

Henry VIII. (Shakespeare or Davenant), "Duke's," Dec. 10, 22, 1663; Jan. 1, 1663-64; Dec. 30, 1668-69.

Heraclius (Corneille), "Duke's," March 8, 1663-64; Feb. 4, 1666-67; Sept. 5, 1667.

Horace (Corneille, translated by Catherine Phillips), "King's," Jan. 19, 1668-69.

Humorous Lieutenant (Beaumont and Fletcher), "Cockpit" (Whitehall), April 20, 1661.

Hyde Park (Shirley), "King's," July 11, 1668.

Impertinents (Shadwell), "Duke's," May 2, 4; June 24, 1668; April 14, 1669. (*See* "Sullen Lovers.")

Indian Emperor (Dryden), "King's," Aug. 22, 1667; Nov. 11, 1667; March 28, April 21, 1668.

Indian Queen (Howard and Dryden), "King's," Jan. 31, 1663-64; June 27, 1668.

Island Princess (Beaumont and Fletcher), "King's," Jan. 7, Feb. 9, 1668-69.

Jovial Crew (R. Brome), "Theatre," July 25, Aug 27, Nov. 1, 1661; "King's," Jan. 11, 1668-69.

King and no King (Beaumont and Fletcher), "Theatre," March 14, 1660-61; Sept. 26, 1661.

Knight of the Burning Pestle (Beaumont and Fletcher), "Theatre," May 7, 1662.

Labyrinth (Corneille), "King's," May 2, 1664.

Ladies a la-Mode (Dryden? Translated from the French), "King's," Sept. 15, 1668.

Lady's Trial (Ford), "Duke's," March 3, 1668-69.

Law against Lovers (Davenant), "Opera," Feb. 18, 1661-62.

Liar (Corneille), "King's," Nov. 28, 1667.

Little Thief (Fletcher), "White Friars," April 2, 1661; "Theatre," May 19, 1662.

Love and Honour (Davenant), "Opera," Oct. 21, 1661.

Love at first Sight (Killigrew), "Theatre," Nov. 29, 1661.

Love Despised (Beaumont and Fletcher), "Duke's," Aug. 17, 1668.

Love in a Maze (Shirley), "Theatre," May 22, 1662 ;
June 10, 1663; "King's," May 1, 1667 ; Feb. 7,
1667-68 ; April 28, 1668.
Love in a Tub (Etherege), "Court at Whitehall,"
Oct. 29, 1666 ; " Duke's," April 29, 1668.
Love's Cruelty (Shirley), " King's," Dec. 30, 1667.
Love's Mistress (T. Heywood), " Theatre," March 11,
1660-61.
Love's Quarrel, " Salisbury Court," April 6, 1661 ;
" King's," May 15, 1665 ; Aug. 15, 1668.
Love's Tricks or the School of Compliment (Shirley),
"Duke's," Aug 5, 1667.
Macbeth (Shakespeare), " Duke's," Nov. 5, 1664; Dec.
28, 1666; Jan. 8, 1666-67 ; Oct. 16, Nov. 7, 1667 ;
Aug. 12, Dec. 21, 1668 ; Jan. 15, 1668-69.
Mad Couple (Hon. James Howard), " King's," Sept.
20, Dec. 28, 1667 ; July 29, 1668.
Mad Lover (Beaumont and Fletcher), "White Friars,"
Feb. 9, 1660-61 ; "Opera," Dec. 2, 1661 ; " Duke's,"
Feb. 18, 1668-69.
Maid of the Mill (Fletcher and Rowley), "Opera,"
April 1, 1662 ; "Duke's," Sept. 10, 1668.
Maid's Tragedy (Beaumont and Fletcher), " Theatre,"
May 16, 1661 ; "King's," Dec. 7, 1666; Feb. 18,
1666-67; April 15, May 9, 1668.
Maiden Queen (Dryden), "King's," March 2, 1666-67;
May 24, Aug. 23, 1667 ; Jan. 24, 1667-68; Jan. 1,
13, 1668-69.
Man is the Master (Davenant, translated from Scarron),
" Duke's," March 26, May 7, 1668.
Merry Devil of Edmonton, "Theatre," Aug. 10,
1661.
Merry Wives of Windsor (Shakespeare), " Theatre,"
Dec. 5, 1660; Sept. 25, 1661 ; " King's," Aug. 15,
1667.
Midsummer Night's Dream (Shakespeare), " King's,"
Sept. 29, 1662.
Mistaken Beauty (Corneille), "King's," Nov. 28, 1667.
Mock Astrologer, "King's," March 8, 1668-69.

Monsieur Ragou (J. Lacey), "King's," July 31, 1668.

Moor of Venice (Shakespeare), "Cockpit" (Whitehall), Oct. 11, 1660; "King's," Feb. 6. 1668-69.

Mulberry Garden (Sedley), "King's," May 18, June 29, 1668.

Mustapha (Lord Orrery), "Duke's," April 3, 1665; Jan. 5, 1666-67; Sept. 4, 1667; Feb. 11, 1667-68.

Northern Castle, "King's," Sept. 14, 1667.

Othello (Shakespeare), "Cockpit" (Whitehall), Oct. 11, 1660; "King's," Feb. 6, 1668-69.

Parson's Wedding (T. Killigrew), "King's," Oct. 11, 1664.

Philaster (Beaumont and Fletcher), "Theatre," Nov. 18, 1661; "King's," May 30, 1668.

Queen Elizabeth's Troubles (T. Heywood), "Duke's," Aug. 17, 1667.

Queen of Arragon (W. Habington), "Duke's," Oct. 19, 1668.

Queen's Masque (T. Heywood), "Salisbury Court," March 2, 25, 1660-61. (*See* "Love's Mistress.")

Rival Ladies (Dryden), "King's," Aug. 4, 1664.

Rivals (Davenant, from "Two Noble Kinsmen"), "Duke's," Sept. 9, Dec. 1664.

Rolla [Query, same as "Rollo"], "King's," April 17, 1667.

Rollo, Duke of Normandy (J. Fletcher), "Theatre," March 28, 1661; "King's," Sept. 17, 1668.

Roman Virgin (Betterton's alteration of Webster's "Appius and Virginia"), "Duke's," May 12, 1669.

Romeo and Juliet (Shakespeare), "Opera," March 1, 1661-62.

Royal Shepherdess (alteration by Shadwell of Fountain's "Rewards of Virtue"), "Duke's," Feb. 26, 1668-9.

Rule a Wife and have a Wife (J. Fletcher), "Whitefriars," April 1, 1661; "Theatre," Feb. 5, 1661-62.

School of Compliments (Shirley), "Duke's," Jan. 7, 1667-68.

Scornful Lady (Beaumont and Fletcher), "Cockpit"

(Whitehall), Nov. 17, 1662 ; "King's," Dec. 27, 1666; Sept. 16, 1667 ; June 3, 1668.

Sea Voyage (Beaumont and Fletcher), "King's," May 16, 1668.

She Would if She Could (Etherege), "Duke's," Feb. 6, 1667-68 ; Feb. 1, 1668-69.

Siege of Rhodes, Part 2 (Davenant), "Opera," Nov. 15, 1661 ; May 20, 1662 ; "Duke's," Dec. 27, 1662, May 21, 1667.

Silent Woman (Ben Jonson), "Theatre," May 25, 1661 ; King's," June 1, 1664 ; April 16, 1667 ; Sept. 19, 1668.

Sir Martin Marr-all (Duke of Newcastle, corrected by Dryden), "Duke's," Aug. 16, 20, Sept. 28, Oct. 14, 1667 ; Jan. 1, 1667-68 ; April 25, May 22, 1668.

Slighted Maid (Sir R. Stapylton), "Duke's," Feb. 23, 1662-63 ; May 29, 1663.

Spanish Curate (Beaumont and Fletcher), "White-friars," March 16, 1660-61 ; July 28, 1668·; "King's," May 17, 1669.

Spanish Gipsy (Middleton and Rowley), "King's," March 7, 1667-68.

Storm (Fletcher), "King's," Sept. 25, 1667; March 25, 1668.

Sullen Lovers or the Impertinents (T. Shadwell), "Duke's," May 2, 4, June 24, 1668 ; April 14, 1669. (*See* "Impertinents.")

Surprisal (Sir Robert Howard), "King's," April 8, Aug. 27, 1667 ; Dec. 26, 1667 ; April 17, May 1, 1668.

Tamer tamed (Fletcher), "Cockpit," Oct. 30, 1660 ; "Theatre," July 31, 1661.

Taming of a Shrew (alteration from Shakespeare), "King's," April 9, Nov. 1, 1667.

Tempest (Shakespeare), "Duke's," Nov. 7, 13, Dec. 12, 1667 ; Jan. 6, Feb. 3, 1667-68 ; April 30, May 11, 1668.

'Tis a pity she's a Whore (Ford), "Salisbury Court," Sept. 9, 1661.

Traitor (Shirley), "New Playhouse," Nov. 22, 1660;
"Theatre," Oct. 10, 1661; "King's," Jan. 13, 1664-
65; Sept. 2, 1667.

Tryphon (Lord Orrery), "Duke's," Dec. 8, 9, 1668.

Twelfth Night (Shakespeare), "Opera," Sept. 11, 1661;
"Duke's," Jan. 6, 1662-63; Jan. 20, 1668-69.

Unfortunate Lovers (Davenant), "Duke's," March 7,
1663-64; April 8, Dec. 3, 1668.

Ungrateful Lovers [Query, same play as previous one],
"Duke's," Sept. 11, 1667.

Usurper (E. Howard), "King's," Jan. 2, 1663-64;
Dec. 2, 1668.

Valiant Cid (translation from Corneille), "Cockpit"
(Whitehall), Dec. 1, 1662.

Victoria Corombona (Webster), "Theatre," Oct. 2,
1661.

Villain (T. Porter), "Duke's," Oct 20, Dec. 26, 1662;
Jan. 1, 1662-63; Oct. 24, 1667.

Virgin Martyr (Massinger), "Theatre," Feb. 16, 1660-
61; "King's," Feb. 27, 1667-68; May 6, 1668.

Volpone (Ben Jonson), "King's," Jan. 14, 1664-65.

Wild Gallant (Dryden), "Court at Whitehall," Feb.
23, 1662-63.

Wild-goose Chase (Beaumont and Fletcher), "King's,"
Jan. 11, 1667-68.

Wit in a Constable (Glapthorne), "Opera," May 23,
1662.

Wit Without Money (Fletcher), "Cockpit," Oct. 16,
1660; "King's," April 22, 1663.

Wits (Davenant), "Opera," Aug. 15, 17, 23, 1661;
"Duke's," April 18, 20, 1667; Jan. 18, 1668-69.

Women pleased (Beaumont and Fletcher), "Duke's,"
Dec. 26, 1668.

Worse and Worse (G. Digby, Earl of Bristol),
"Duke's," July 20, 1664.

INDEX.

The titles of Chapters are printed in italics.

PAGE

[1] The charge was not so frivolous after all, for the writer of an article
on the " Diary " in the " Edinburgh Review " for July, 1880, points out

that although Pepys denied publicly that he ever possessed a crucifix, he positively states in the "Diary" that he had one. See July 20, August 2, and November 3, 1666. I ought to have noted this, as the facts are given in the Index to the " Diary."

CHISWICK PRESS: C. WHITTINGHAM AND CO. TOOKS COURT, CHANCERY LANE.

For EU product safety concerns, contact us at Calle de José Abascal, 56–1°,
28003 Madrid, Spain or eugpsr@cambridge.org.

www.ingramcontent.com/pod-product-compliance
Ingram Content Group UK Ltd.
Pitfield, Milton Keynes, MK11 3LW, UK
UKHW010350140625
459647UK00010B/965